D1158128

THE OIL HUNTERS

The Oil Hunters

Exploration and Espionage in the
Middle East 1880–1939

Roger Howard

hambledon
continuum

Hambledon Continuum is an imprint of Continuum Books
Continuum UK, The Tower Building, 11 York Road, London SE1 7NX
Continuum US, 80 Maiden Lane, Suite 704, New York, NY 10038

www.continuumbooks.com

First published 2008

British Library Cataloguing-in-Publication Data
A catalogue record for this book is available from the British Library.

ISBN 978 1 84725 232 6

Typeset by Pindar New Zealand (Egan Reid), Auckland, New Zealand
Printed and bound by MPG Books Ltd, Cornwall, Great Britain

Contents

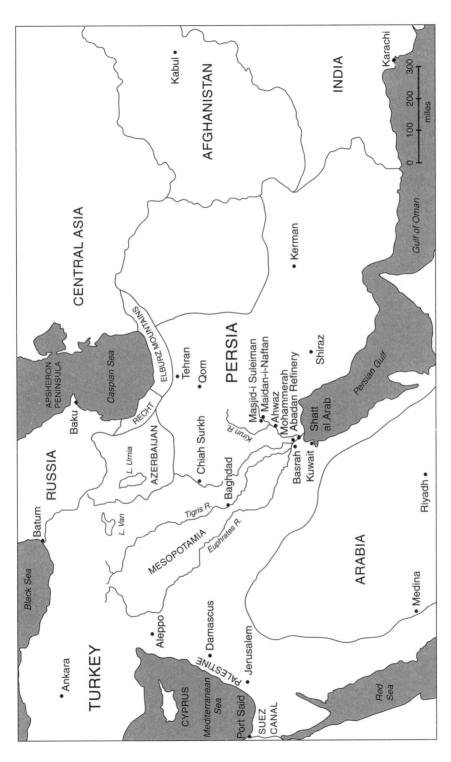

Opening up the Middle East. Oil in Persia, 1901.

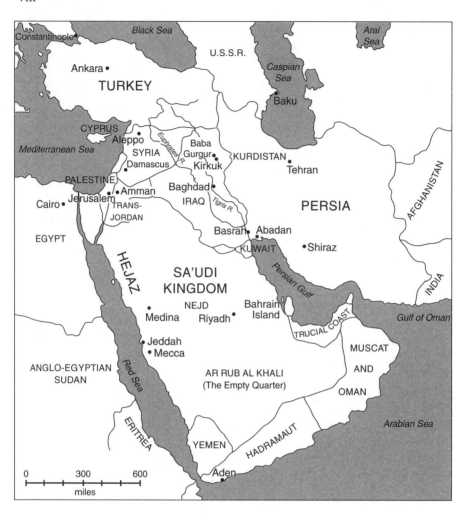

The Middle East 1928.

Introduction

In recent decades, the oil of the Middle East has continued to cast a very long shadow over the rest of the world. In the mid-1970s an embargo by regional producers created a massive worldwide economic recession and even today, as new sources of supply in Africa, Russia and elsewhere come on tap, the level of Saudi output still has a vastly important bearing on the market price of crude oil. Wars have been fought for control over these strategic assets, such as Saddam Hussein's attack on Kuwait in 1990 and the subsequent US-led military campaign to push him back out, while other conflicts, such as the American invasion of Iraq in 2003, are often said to have been motivated by an acquisitive desire for regional oil reserves.[1] And elsewhere, in places as far afield as London's most expensive residential districts and some of Pakistan's most remote and backward towns, all the signs of the Middle East's massive oil wealth are plain to see, as petrodollars buy up supremely expensive homes and businesses or else fund religious schools where a virulent form of Wahhabi extremism is sometimes taught.

But at the turn of the twentieth century almost no one thought that the Middle East harboured such superb natural assets. The region as a whole had strategic value really only because its coasts overlooked the transit routes to the jewel in the crown of Britain's imperial empire – India. When in November 1903 Viscount Curzon sailed into the Persian Gulf with a flotilla of eight British warships and proclaimed it as a 'British lake', he did so in his capacity as Viceroy of India, the land whose fate and fortune mattered to him above almost all else. But culturally fascinating though it undoubtedly was, the Middle East was otherwise widely considered to be little more than a destitute and economically backward irrelevance.

True, the region had long been awash with all manner of rumours and legends of oil, rumours that had gradually seeped into Western Europe. Such stories doubtless gave the prospect of finding oil there a rather romantic appeal, one that occasionally seized the imagination of a maverick investor or individual of particular daring. The Greek historian Herodotus had once described the existence of 'oil-pits' in Mesopotamia, while an anonymous Arab was supposed to have scooped idly in the sand one day and found that his finger had become sticky with a black liquid that it could easily be set alight. Similar stories had also long been told about other areas of the Middle East, notably Egypt. For it had long been common knowledge that oil was present at the foot of Jebel Zeit, a mountain on the west coast of the Gulf of Suez that the ancients had called Mons Petroleus, while there were also deposits of oil-saturated sandstone at Abu Zenima and Abu Durba on the Sinai peninsula. And in Cairo torches had for thousands of years been lit with the substance, and it was said that, at one terrible moment in the late eleventh century, the equivalent of more than a thousands barrels of petroleum distillate had suddenly caught fire, creating a massive and deadly fireball.

The question was not, however, whether there was any oil in the region. No one doubted that any more than they doubted that there was some oil to be unearthed in almost any other part of the world. The question was whether it was to be found in commercial quantities – whether, in other words, there were any underground reserves that were sufficiently accessible to justify the enormous costs of finding and then exploiting them. And on this note virtually every expert thought the same: there was absolutely no geological evidence, went the received wisdom promulgated by these experts, that the Middle East boasted such large petroleum deposits and any oil hunter would do much better to spend his time, effort and resources on other, much more promising places elsewhere in the world.

But by the 1880s a mere handful of adventurous spirits were just starting to question this received wisdom and turn their eyes to the Middle East as a possible source of oil supply. This was partly because Persia, in particular, lay so close to the region where oil had only just been discovered in what seemed to be vast, unfathomable quantities – Baku in Russia. The Baku oil boom had begun to take off late, only in the course of the 1870s. For in 1874 Russia produced a meagre 600,000 barrels of oil, but within a decade that figure had skyrocketed to a staggering 10.8 million, nearly all of which came from a remote place where hundreds of refineries produced a filthy, black smoke that earned it the unenviable title of 'The Black Town'. But Baku lay just a very short distance from Persia and had at one time even fallen within its borders. So if oil could be found there in such vast quantities then surely, it must have seemed to some, it could also lie elsewhere in the region. After all, every geologist knew that petroleum lay in vast underground rock formations that generally covered huge areas, quite big enough to sprawl from Baku all the way into central Persia.

At the same time the region as a whole was starting to look far more alluring than ever, because the opening of the Suez Canal had immediately heralded new opportunities in a region that had always looked tantalizingly close to Western Europe on a map, but which was really dauntingly hard to reach. Until the Canal opened a traveller could reach the Arabian Sea only after weeks of arduous sailing, as ships journeyed southwards to the far tip of Africa, moved through the treacherously rough seas of the Cape of Good Hope and then made their way back up the African coast. But in 1869, after seven years of backbreaking work, the creation of the French engineering genius Ferdinand de Lesseps was finally born, allowing ships to sail straight from the Mediterranean into the Gulf of Suez and then the Red Sea in a matter of days.

Suddenly the entire Middle East seemed to be beckoning. When in 1865 an intrepid Englishman called Lieutenant-Colonel Lewis Pelly had heroically crossed the few hundred miles of desert that separated Riyadh from the Persian Gulf, he was only the fifth European known to have ever visited a place whose precise location, even by this time, Western geographers could not even pinpoint. With the opening of the Canal, however, a start could at least be made.

By 1880 much of the Middle East also seemed to be standing just a short step from a far-reaching political transformation, one that promised to make life far easier for any foreign investors who wanted to stake their claim. For more than three centuries the region had formed part of the vast Ottoman Empire and been ruled from Constantinople[2] by a succession of sultans and their advisers. But in the course of the second half of the nineteenth century it had become increasingly clear that this empire was rapidly crumbling to the forces of nationalism. In 1876 the sultan had been forced to sign an armistice at San Stefano on such humiliating terms that the British government insisted on its immediate revision. Another conference was subsequently held – one that the sultan was not even invited to attend – and the empire was then stripped of nearly half of its territories and almost a quarter of its population.

While nearly all of these losses were in Europe, the sultan's grip over his Middle Eastern territories also looked more vulnerable than at any previous moment. For by this time the empire's territories in the Middle East were, despite its European losses, still enormous. The sultan ruled Palestine and the huge swathe of surrounding territory as far eastwards as the border with Persia, a kingdom that the Ottoman armies had never quite been able to capture. He also held sway over the eastern and western coastlines of the Arabian peninsula, as well as over the holy cities of Mecca and Medina, while elsewhere he had managed cleverly to exploit fierce tribal divisions to his own advantage. But how much longer would it be before these areas also broke free?

Any collapse in Ottoman authority promised to open up enormous new commercial opportunities throughout their vast former territories. It was well known that, even for the most determined visitor, the task of obtaining a travel permit from the Ottoman authorities, whose tardiness, obstinacy and petty bureaucracy were legendary, presented a daunting task. But an oil hunter, or any other businessman, faced an even greater challenge because he was readily seen not as an opportunity but as an exploitative threat to their own natural resources. Even this was just the beginning. Getting permission to travel to Ottoman controlled territories in the Middle East was easy compared with the real political challenge of formally obtaining a concession to explore for oil, or for any other substance, and then exploit it.

But by 1876 Ottoman authority in the Middle East was already being steadily eroded by a stronger British presence. Anxious to ward off the threat of attacks by pirates, who had used some of the islands as their bases and hideaways, the British had secured control over whole stretches of the Persian Gulf. Nominally at least, much of this area had belonged to the Ottomans, but they found themselves unable to do more than watch helplessly as British gunboats arrived from Bombay and then laid down terms to local rulers, most of whom were pleased to rid themselves of both a pirate menace and of centuries of Ottoman overlordship.

These rulers now agreed to forfeit some of their freedoms in return for British naval protection, and this arrangement allowed the British to carve out a sphere of influence that was administered from the town of Bushire, on Persia's southern coast, and which extended over the island principalities of Bahrain, Kuwait, Dubai and Muscat. The key figures in this local power network were a number of British colonial servants who were known simply as 'Political Agents'.

But more than any other single event, it was the British invasion and occupation of Egypt in 1882 that seemed to mark the demise of the Ottoman Empire in the region and give rise to the birth pangs of a new Middle East. After days of heavy rioting in which British and French subjects had been killed and their property burnt and looted, London had despatched a 20,000 strong army under the inspired leadership of General Sir Garnet Wolseley to crush the rebellion and impose order. Within weeks the rebels had been defeated and the British expeditionary force had reached Cairo, beginning an occupation that was supposed to be only a temporary affair but which in fact went on for considerably longer.[3]

Suddenly Egypt seemed rife with commercial opportunity. With the rebels defeated and the Royal Navy patrolling the shores, it was a safer place to explore and invest in than at any previous time. And any British businessman who was bold enough to make such a move would go with the full backing and protection of his government, which recognized how much this new land might have to offer.

Some contemporaries must also have wondered if the decline of the Ottoman Empire was a symptom of a wider malaise that was affecting the entire Muslim world. For by the end of the nineteenth century it was clear that the West had started to pull significantly ahead in almost every way – in scientific expertise, military prowess, financial power and political and administrative organization. Exactly when this sense of relative decline crept in is of course very difficult to determine, and it is possible that its origins go back at least a century, when Napoleon had led his army into Egypt and inflicted a massive defeat on the defenders, or perhaps long before. But what is clear is that by 1880, not only was the entire Middle East a cultural and economic backwater, but also that some of its rulers were highly conscious of their dire predicament and anxious to push their kingdoms out of an antiquated past and into the modern age. Always fearful that their rivals elsewhere in the Middle East might suddenly forge ahead, and sometimes deeply conscious of their standing on the international stage, no leader worth his salt could afford to stand back and watch his kingdom sink into a state of relative decline. Even travelling overseas to meet other leaders or turn up at international conferences was becoming a much more expensive affair than ever before. Such events were by this time starting to put a serious strain on the financial sinews of cash-strapped Middle Eastern rulers, who were amazed to discover how diminutive were their own currencies when compared to those of the highly prosperous Western world.

These fears played right into the hands of any budding Western entrepreneur who was searching for new markets and opportunities. Rulers who had always been insular, even xenophobic, in their outlook were by this time just starting at least to consider a suggestion that had always been out of the question – that foreign ideas, inventions and personalities, even if they were Western infidels, should play a part in the domestic affairs of their kingdom. This was clearly not an ideal scenario and, for a ruler whose authority was traditionally unchallenged, it was an option that carried risks. But by the 1880s some leaders, notably the shah of Persia, were starting to recognize that it may be the only way forward if their kingdoms were not to be fated to perpetual irrelevance or subjugation.

The European oil hunters would have known that they might perhaps need to be quick off the mark if they were going to seize these opportunities before anyone else did. Their chief competitors in this regard were undoubtedly the Russians and Americans, who by the 1880s had come to dominate the world's oil production. Above all others, however, the Europeans would have particularly feared the long reach of just one company that outsized all others – the Standard Oil Trust. Operating vast wells in Pennsylvania, New York, Ohio, Kansas and elsewhere, Standard Oil had by this time become a vast conglomerate that controlled nearly all of the American domestic market. But it also kept abreast of developments farther afield, and its agents, always keeping an eye open for foreign opportunities and maintaining close tabs on its competitors, were said to be scattered all over the Middle East. At a moment's notice, it must have seemed, this mighty force might swoop on and seize any overseas source of oil, perhaps using its massive financial resources to outbid any offer its competitors could make, or to outstrip any exploration operation that they could undertake.

After all, Standard and its European competitors knew just how much money they could make from tapping into the world's huge demand for a new commodity: kerosene. This was distilled from oil and then used as fuel for household and industrial lamps that lit people's homes and kept them warm. The Canadian-born geologist Dr Abraham Gesner and, on the other side of the Atlantic, a Scottish scientist, Dr James Young, had discovered how to produce this substance in the middle of the nineteenth century, but demand boomed a few years later when a new lamp was developed that considerably reduced the amount of smoke emitted, and the overpowering smell that had made earlier models so unpopular. By the 1880s a number of other uses for oil were also fast being pioneered. Several other scientists had been building on Gesner's discoveries and had developed a process to turn oil into lubricants that could keep railways, steamships and industrial machinery all working smoothly.

But if the stakes for finding any large new source of oil were high, then the Middle East must have seemed particularly alluring. This was because it was relatively close to Western Europe, whose sprawling, industrialized cities were generating so much demand for oil, and clearly very much closer than the fields of Borneo and Sumatra that were helping to keep Europe supplied. So Middle Eastern oil, were it ever found, could be moved to major markets at a fraction of the time and cost than any Far Eastern output.

There was, however, a rather obvious downside. First of all, no investor would want to get involved in a search for petroleum unless clear geological signs of its presence were found. That was just the beginning, because nothing could subsequently be done unless the local authorities granted a concession to dig underground, and haggling for such an agreement could take almost as many years as a proper exploratory drilling operation. And even if oil was then unearthed in commercial quantities, it would still have to be moved overland to the nearest harbour, from where it could with relative ease be shipped first to refineries, where the crude oil was processed, and then to its ultimate markets. But the entire Middle East was so backward that there were barely any roads there, let alone a sophisticated, integrated transport system that had by now made the Baku oilfields so formidably efficient. So transporting oil overland from its original source would involve the very arduous and expensive construction of overland pipelines, as well as of the transport infrastructure that drilling teams would always need if they were ever to undertake even the most basic exploratory operations.

In other words, the obstacles would have been formidable and daunting enough even if the Middle East had been known to harbour serious quantities of oil. But when such evidence was altogether lacking, then only a truly exceptional individual would have wanted to bear such risks and play the game.

However, it was of just such exceptional stuff that the oil hunters were made.

The Intrepid Frenchman

Late one morning in September 1889, a young Frenchman was making his final preparations before heading off on what promised to be a truly epic journey. He was planning to be away for some considerable time, just under two years in total, but knew that, given the inevitable delays and miscalculations, he might be gone for much longer. And as the train pulled away from the station at Marseilles and farewells were waved, he would also have been painfully aware that he might equally be leaving his homeland forever.

His destination was a land that only a relative handful of his European con- temporaries had ever visited, although, conjuring romantic images of desert sands, long-buried empires and, of course, magic carpets, it was one that many doubtless dreamed of. For while so much closer to home than where France, Great Britain and other powers had built their empires, Persia had remained remote from, and indeed almost entirely untouched by, Western hands. Maps of the region were full of blank spaces that were simply marked 'high hills' or 'unexplored', and some areas, ran an old Persian saying, were 'barely known even to God himself'. There were many places that no Europeans were known ever to have visited, and where the local people would regard them as a clear threat to their independence and make their overwhelming hostility plain to see.

For Jacques de Morgan, even getting as far as the true starting-point of his journey, the capital Tehran, was no easy feat. To begin with, there was a long train journey to Constantinople, the capital of the vast Ottoman Empire, where he would board a steamship that would take him across the Black Sea to the major port of Batum. He would then move eastwards across the Russian Caucasus, stopping off for a couple of days in Tiflis before reaching the coastal city of Baku, where he would take another boat to transport him southwards and harbour on the Persian coast, a short distance from the town of Recht.[1]

De Morgan had heard several people say that, to begin with, his initial impression of Persia would be favourable. In and around Recht, as one traveller had described it, was a 'wealth of wood and water' where there were 'lanes, hedgerows and gardens which speak to him of other lands'.[2] And for a mile or so outside the town they would also be moving on horseback along some well-worn tracks that offered a comfortable ride. But he knew that it would not be long before everything would start to change. Soon they would have to travel sharply uphill, ascending high into the Elburz Mountains along some very rough paths. After that they would enter into dense forests and then, as they climbed higher, the pines would start to thin out and then disappear as olive trees started to take their place. As they went higher still, only bushes and shrubs could thrive. Then, at a height of 7,000 feet, they would reach the mountain station of Menjil and tread warily over an arched bridge that spanned a narrow gorge and river. This particular place was notorious in the winter, and every year a good many travellers and their pack animals fell to their deaths, dashed to pieces on the rocks far below where their rotting carcasses, and skeletons, remained. But eventually de Morgan's own party would reach the town of Kazvin, where conditions would get much easier. For around Kavzin was a flat plain through which a relatively flat road – almost the only one in the whole kingdom – had been built, and this would take them directly to the capital. If all went well, then all this travelling would take three whole weeks, after which he would have finally reached his proper starting-post.

Then his journey would begin in earnest, and de Morgan knew that thereafter, and throughout his 27 months in Persia, he would always have to face all manner of dangers and obstacles. From the writings and descriptions given by other Western travellers, he knew that the climate and landscape, though highly varied, would often prove harsh and unforgiving. Yet it would not be long before he would have to cross the Elburz range once again, since he intended to start off his journey by moving north of the capital, reaching Demavend and Amol and then heading eastwards towards the town of Asterabad. And, as winter began to set in, he knew that in a few weeks' time the going would get tougher still.

His next move would be to move westwards, making a second visit to Recht before moving northwards to the Russian border. After that he would travel southwards from the city of Tabriz to explore the regions that lay close to Persia's border with neighbouring, Turkish-controlled Mesopotamia. But in these harsh places even the local people, born and bred in such parts, were known to find the summer temperatures of the plains almost unbearable. They were also well familiar with the ferocity of the region's infamous windstorms, which blew up suddenly, particularly in the early spring, and could then bury everything within their range under an avalanche of sand and dust: a whole army was once said to have been consumed by such a storm, as well as innumerable convoys – or caravans as they were known – of private travellers. Other unfortunate itinerants, and even one Persian king, were claimed by the lethal quicksands that were difficult, sometimes impossible, to see even from very close range.

The intrepid de Morgan faced a whole host of other dangers. At lower altitudes, he and his party would always have to be on the lookout for a wide variety of snakes and scorpions, all of which thrived in the summer heat and, in the dense woods and forests that would lie in their way, for predatory wolves, bears and wild boar. Other travellers were claimed by the various fevers and diseases that could be highly contagious in the hot weather, and died deaths that were sometimes slow, lingering and painful or, in other cases, terrifyingly rapid, almost instant. But the biggest single source of danger did not come from wild animals or from the local climate. It came from people. Whether they were in groups or even escorted by members of the shah's armed forces, anyone who strayed beyond the relative sanctuary of Persia's cities, towns and village could make easy prey for armed bandits, or for the wild and fiercely independent tribes whose random and sudden outbursts of ferocious violence the government authorities in Tehran had always struggled to control.

With such danger to contend with, the mere discomfort of the journey was doubtless a very small matter indeed. De Morgan well knew that he would hardly ever be able to enjoy the relative luxury of sleeping within solid confines. True, the main routes that ran across the kingdom in various directions were dotted with *chapar-khaneh*, the post houses where for a modest fee a traveller would be able to stop and sleep, nearly always on the bare mud floor. But elsewhere de Morgan would have to rely on his tent and the thick blankets that he bought along the way, lighting campfires to keep warm and living off the land.

The Frenchman was not one to give up easily, however. At just 32, he felt he not only had the fitness but also the enthusiasm to give his career a hard push forward by making the most of this superb chance to explore such a relatively unknown region. Just a few weeks before, the French Minister of Culture had approached de Morgan personally and offered him government sponsorship to undertake the trip, seeing him as an experienced mining engineer with several years of working in the Russian Caucasus, and therefore the ideal man for the job. Quite apart from his own sense of personal adventure, to make such a journey on behalf of his country was a huge privilege, one that, like any patriotic Frenchman, de Morgan immediately leapt at with barely a second thought.

His patrons in the French government had briefed de Morgan in very general terms, asking him to undertake a survey of almost every aspect of Persia. He made the most of his professional training as a geographer and geologist by sketching detailed maps of all the regions he visited, but he was also expected to make detailed descriptions of the people he encountered, their language and the dialects they spoke, their work, appearance, customs and ways. He would record the land's flora and fauna, assess the state of the roads and look at its astonishing archaeological treasures, such as the ruins of Susa in the west, where King Darius the Great had built his fabled palace nearly 2,500 years before. In short, he was tasked with providing as full a picture as he could of the land under survey.

There was, however, one particular aspect of Persia that interested the Paris authorities far more than any other, even if they did not formally admit as much. Above all, they wanted to know what signs the intrepid young Frenchman would discover of a particular substance that earlier visitors had noticed in the region and commented on. That substance was oil.

For years many travellers had felt sure that oil was brimming under the surface of Persia. It was well known that there were occasional, sometimes frequent, seepages of oil into the Gulf seas and, every so often, on the mainland. Western visitors often noticed, and were occasionally somewhat overwhelmed, by its distinctive smell as they made their way through the kingdom, and commented on how local people, especially in the south-western provinces of the kingdom, were highly adept at making the most of oil, utilizing it to make boats, bond bricks, set jewellery and produce flaming missiles. In 1812, as he rode from the coastal town of Bushire to Shiraz, the British diplomat James Morier noted 'a most sulphereous smell, at the foot ... of a stream of mineral water', and as he and his small convoy moved on, he saw 'a little further on, on the left of the road, two springs of naphtha.[3] The oil swims on the surface of the water, and the peasantry take it off with a branch of date tree and collect it into small holes around the spring ready for their immediate use. They daub the camels all over with it in the spring, which preserves their coats, and prevent a disease in the skin, which is common to them.'[4]

In recent years, such stories had prompted some other European governments to take a closer look. In 1848, a British member of the Persian–Turkish Frontier Commission spotted signs of oil in the vicinity of Masjid-i Suleiman, little more than a village in a remote south-western region of Persia that no one in London had ever heard of, and everyone struggled to find on the map. A few years later various scientific expeditions also ventured some favourable reports on the prospects of finding Middle Eastern oil. In 1871 a German research party travelled to Mesopotamia to undertake some independent assessments, while in the years that followed several other reports were formally commissioned by individual governments or by various private research organizations. Most of these came back with findings that were broadly positive, if vague.

Now, in September 1889, it was the turn of the French government to try and find out more about what Persia had to offer, and Jacques de Morgan was just the man to undertake such an important and challenging task. Accompanied by a servant, Pierre Vaslin, in whom he had immense personal trust and who was keen not to miss out on such a venture, and with Toby, his beloved Irish setter that was always at his side, de Morgan felt ready to begin his journey.

Before leaving, the young Frenchman had studied carefully the reports written by earlier oil explorers in the region to get clues about Persia's geological formations, and to find some suggestions about what to take and how to conduct himself in such an unfamiliar land. From these writings – and from conversations with French diplomats and businessmen familiar with the kingdom – de Morgan laid down a number of golden rules. He would, he decided, keep well away from local women, knowing that any outsider, let alone an infidel Westerner, who probed too closely into the veiled, secluded world of Persian womanhood would immediately provoke a savage retribution. This, he felt, was 'a golden rule' of Western travel through any Islamic country, even if he felt that it was not one that all of his predecessors had always acknowledged or respected.[5]

As soon as he left the elite circles of Tehran society, where his journey would begin in earnest, he decided that he would wherever possible try to steer well clear of the local people, who he was told would often be untrustworthy, and more keen to disappear with his kit and valuables than to assist him in any way. It was essential, he heard, not to pitch camp too close to any of the rural villages, since the local population would mob them, partly out of the curiosity they felt about foreigners, but also because they were keen to steal whatever they could. And he would try to keep the details of his movements as secret as possible, fearing that word of his future whereabouts could easily be overheard and then spread with such prodigious speed that robbers, bandits or rivals would be ready and waiting for him.

For the purposes of surviving this journey, de Morgan also knew from other travellers that several items in his baggage would be particularly vital. Not only could he at some point expect to use the rifles that, along with hundreds of rounds, he had packed carefully away, but would doubtless also make great use of personal gifts in winning the favour of those he met and whose cooperation he would depend upon. Such personal gifts, known as *baksheesh* in local culture, would be indispensable.

Almost everything else, other than fairly basic necessities, de Morgan planned to buy either in Tehran or else along the way. Soon after arriving in the Persian capital, he purchased several mules and horses, hired several domestic servants and managed to find a good interpreter, one who was familiar not just with French and Persian but also with most of the highly varied dialects and tribal tongues – notably Kurdish and Azeri – that they would at some point be hearing. In total this caravan would be made up of a party of twelve, a number that was small enough to melt into the background and pass by largely unnoticed, but also big enough to deter many of the robbers and bandits who, along some stretches, would be watching them closely.

After being briefed and entertained by the French envoy in Tehran, M. Paulze d'Ivoy, they were ready to move, and on 23 November, just over two months after leaving Marseilles, headed northwards towards the Caspian Sea to begin in earnest their exploration of the kingdom of Persia. As de Morgan's journey got under way, the French officials in both Tehran and Paris would have begun waiting anxiously for any news of his progress. It seemed quite possible that the small party might suffer the fate of some earlier, unlucky, travellers and simply disappear without trace. If they did eventually return, after two years of arduous trekking, perhaps they would be barely recognizable from the men who were now setting out. Maybe they would even be driven to madness by stress or by the sheer adversity of what they had endured. Or would they return in triumph, bearing a wealth of information about the Persian kingdom, and perhaps vital clues to the whereabouts of oil?

For the French, much could depend on Jacques de Morgan. To find oil in large, commercial quantities would be a hugely lucrative scoop, one that would give France a clear lead, in prestige as well as in raw economic terms, over its European rivals. After all, for the previous 40 years or so, oil had been used to produce the kerosene (heating oil) that was much needed to keep the rapidly increasing populations of both Europe and North America warm, and to keep their lights glowing. Scientists the world over were also competing to find new and more efficient uses for the substance, uses that could win them and their sponsors huge profits and instant fame.

But where could new sources of supply be found? Over the preceding few years, the Paris authorities and their counterparts in other Western capitals had started to wonder what Persia might have to offer. To some extent their interest had been aroused by the experiences of the remarkable Anglo-German magnate Julius de Reuter. De Reuter had had a remarkably successful career as the founder of the eponymous agency, and as a guiding spirit behind the construction of international telegraphic communications that immediately proved to be of huge importance. In the 1860s the British government worked hard to arrange a direct overland telegraph line that ran from London to India, and this line, part of which crossed Persia, was now constructed with the help of several companies, including the Indo-European Telegraph Company. The Persian king, the shah, and his officials had proved surprisingly cooperative, and this now prompted a lot of Western businessmen to take a lively interest in building up links with Persia, not least because they knew that they would have the support of the British government, which regarded the region as essential to the security of its empire. De Reuter, who had been closely involved with the telegraphic project, now stepped into the arena and in 1872, with the British government's support, succeeded in obtaining a royal concession that gave him control over whole swathes of the Persian economy. Perhaps not surprisingly, the concession provoked domestic uproar in Persia and was cancelled shortly afterwards.

But though nothing else had come of it, de Reuter had shown that, with influence and determination, Westerners could make serious headway inside Persia. Such a prospect became all the more tempting in 1887, when a British representative in Tehran persuaded the shah to open the Karun river – which flowed through the province of Khuzestan in the far south-west – to international shipping. British engineers helped their Persian counterparts to widen and deepen the river, thereby allowing ships an easy highway from the Persian Gulf into some of the kingdom's richest and most inaccessible regions, creating new commercial prospects for both Persians and outsiders, whilst also whetting foreign appetites.

De Morgan would have been well aware of the strength of international interest in the region as he and his handful colleagues made their arduous journey with their mules and horses through the exhilarating heights of the Elburz Mountains, a vast range that stretched for hundreds of miles from east to west before descending to meet the shores of the Caspian. During this leg of the journey de Morgan did not entertain particularly high hopes of finding any traces of oil, since nearly all of the other travellers who had made their way through the kingdom had noticed it in the western provinces. It was only the following summer, when he reached villages and towns such as Piranshahr, Rayat and Mahabad, and continued with his journey further south, that he got ready to begin a proper investigation.

Predominant in these regions were Kurdish tribes whose languages, dress, customs and traditions differed markedly from those of the Persians. Nearly all of them were autonomous, owing no real allegiance to the shah at all, and all were heavily armed. Their sporadic and unpredictable outbursts of violence often left the armies of the central government reeling and made travel in these parts – for anyone – extremely dangerous. In the valley of Ho-round, near Bouroudjird, a large-scale tribal rebellion had recently broken out, and law and order had only been restored after the local governor had used brutal tactics, ordering the mutilation of fifteen leading tribal leaders, along with the shooting on sight of a number of others.

Foreign travellers often made tempting targets, partly because the tribesmen feared and resented any sign of alien incursion, partly too because they could sometimes be ransomed as a valuable commodity. Only shortly before de Morgan and his party arrived in the small town of Poucht-i-Kouh, a Swiss trader, working under the protection of the French government, had been attacked and killed by a local tribesman, perhaps feeling threatened by the appearance of outsiders. The young Frenchman was not one to be easily deterred, however, and although his fellow travellers and their animals were all suffering badly from exhaustion, they pushed ahead along their arduous path. At the village of Rou-i-Delaver they came under heavy attack from local people, who perhaps saw them as a hostile force as well as a possible source of riches, but after returning fire with their rifles they managed to save their skins. And in the notoriously wild area that lay between Bane and Sakkiz, the Kurdish tribes soon showed their renowned ferocity, making several bids to kill de Morgan and his men. It was near here that one of the scouts opened fire and shot dead a Kurdish tribesman; the enraged locals demanded immediate revenge and forced the unwelcome visitors to seek sanctuary in nearby forests.

But through hard experience, the Frenchman was becoming highly skilled at bluffing his way through difficult situations and getting the hospitality that he hoped to find, or at least avoiding the outright hostility that he so feared. Brandishing letters of introduction written by officials at the shah's court and by local governors, he was able to persuade some of the tribal leaders that he was an ally, not a threat, and that he was also a visitor of considerable importance: anyone who harmed him, he intimated, would feel the wrath of the Tehran government. On numerous occasions these letters got him by: near the village of Tchobankere, for example, his servants got lost and disappeared with nearly all their baggage just as winter temperatures were falling to –17 degrees. To avoid dying of cold, de Morgan was forced to find shelter among some nearby Kurdish villagers, huddling round their campfire and saving his life by doing so.

It was only in February 1891 – after fifteen months of hard journeying – that de Morgan finally reached the remote area that lay between Hamadan and the border with Mesopotamia. It was in this place that his sponsors back in Paris had expressed a real interest, because it was from here that numerous stories of oil seepages had emerged.

De Morgan quickly got to work to find out just how much truth these stories held, for he was soon taken to a remote village where Kurdish villagers had for centuries lifted crude oil straight out of the ground. Here such practice was just a simple fact of life, and the villagers were wholly oblivious of the significance of finding and using oil in this way. Employing techniques that had barely changed for hundreds, perhaps even thousands, of years, a team of a dozen or so men used long ropes to lower large buckets into two wells, each of which was about nine metres deep. If the buckets were positioned in just the right way, and were only used once every few days, then around 250 litres of oil, pungent and dark green, could be lifted straight out. This extract was then moved by cart along the difficult, arduous tracks that led to the nearest town, Kermanshah, where it was sold for only a modest fee to local traders. Seeing such practices first-hand made de Morgan more determined than ever to find what lay under the geological surface of this intriguing region. He now had the full support of Essam-el-Moulk, the governor of Kermanshah, who gave him tribal escorts and a reliable source of food and new clothing. But his task would still not be easy, especially as it was now midwinter and everything was covered in thick snow.

Undeterred by the harsh conditions, de Morgan started his geological investigations. His chosen venue lay along a river that the local tribes called Tcham-i-Tchiasorkh. This was very close to the village of Kend-i-Chirin, about 12 miles distant from the small town of Qasr-i-Chirin. De Morgan had already noticed that between Hamadan and Sahna the geology was very complicated and the rock formations very unusual. But did they conceal anything of real interest? With a small pickaxe, he was able to unearth the stones and rocks he needed and – with the geological instruments he had carried with him ever since leaving Marseilles – was able to look at them closely. Surface work was vital in determining the age of a rock and any secrets of what lay beneath, indicated by the direction and angle at which a stratum of rock undulated under the surface, and the general shape of the geological structure. And by drawing up a map that covered a much wider region, de Morgan might perhaps have been able to make a reasonable guess about the interior nature of the underground rock structures, the sequence of strata and the depth at which any oil bearing layers might lie.

After two weeks' work he felt ready to move on. But although he had by now been gone for fifteen months, he still had much ground to cover before being able to return to Tehran. Dezful and Ahwaz lay to the south and then Mohammerah,[6] close to the Persian Gulf, where he could be taken on horseback to the capital. But even this last leg of the journey would have moments at least as testing as those already endured. For in between was the lawless province of Lorestan, where the tribes had a particularly fearsome reputation. And as de Morgan's party made its way in the mountains near Lake Gehar, they were frequently attacked by the wild Haddjivend tribe, and were once again forced to return fire. To make things worse they again managed to lose their way. Without any experienced guides to help them, de Morgan recorded how 'we were lost in a maze of wooded ravines and impassable mountains, always following the tracks that wild bears had made, and had to make frequent stops to try and find our way'.[7] But by now they were expert in living off the land, fishing in the region's fast-flowing rivers and using their marksmanship to down wild game.

Just under two years after he set out, the young French explorer and his companions finally made it back to Tehran. They arrived there, as they had expected to, heavily bearded, unkempt and half-starved. The oil hunters had, after all, covered around 20,000 kilometres, and most of the animals they had set off with had collapsed and died en route, while they themselves were suffering from severe exhaustion. Of the survivors perhaps the most fighting fit was Toby, the Irish setter that had barely strayed from his master's side ever since they left Marseilles.

But quite apart from fulfilling their own sense of personal adventure, had such remarkable exertions really been worthwhile? Above all, had they managed to find what the Paris government so badly wanted: clear signs that oil lay under the surface of Persia in sizeable quantities? At his Tehran quarters, de Morgan needed time to recover from his journey, relishing such luxuries as washing thoroughly, eating fully and sleeping properly. As he did so the French government officials awaited anxiously to hear the full story of what he had encountered, and what he had discovered.

But before long, de Morgan was able to lay his conclusions before his masters: they were startling. Though there was much, he emphasized, that he simply could not be certain about, and which only deep drilling would confirm, he was quite sure that one corner of Kurdistan lay on top of a vast petroliferous zone that perhaps even extended in one direction as far the city of Kirkuk, in neighbouring Mesopotamia, and in the other to the Persian district of Pusht-i-Kuh. The deposits that he had found and looked at closely near Kend-i-Chirin, he felt, formed the very middle of this zone, and the river at Tcham-i-Tchiasorkh was the tip of this underground iceberg, exposing the crest of a formation that undulated, at different depths, beneath the surface. Persia, in other words, was the oil world's equivalent of a vast gold mine.

Even before he had arrived back in Paris on 1 December 1891, de Morgan was busy writing up detailed reports of his findings. As he got to work, he argued that Persia was 'unquestionably petroliferous territory' and made careful descriptions of oil prospects in the vicinity of Qasr-i-Chirin in Persian Kurdistan. When it had such deposits of oil to draw on, he claimed, a Persian oil trade would have great prospects. Such an industry, he wrote, 'would be a source of considerable revenue for the Tehran government', not just because its oil could be exported but also because it would be indispensable to local industries and provide the kingdom with its own source of heating and lighting fuel.[8] Persian oil consumption may have been small but it was, after all, rising steadily and by this time oil imports into the kingdom's main port, at Bushire, had risen threefold to nearly £8,000 in the space of just three years.[9]

De Morgan's upbeat findings soon found their way into print. A few months after arriving back home, he wrote a geological article in the academic journal *Annales des Mines* that discussed the possibility of finding oil in Kurdistan, but his more detailed reports appeared later and were published, one by one, in five separate volumes. In particular it was his second volume – in which more detailed descriptions of oil prospects appeared – that aroused most interest. Published in 1895, it was immediately read in a number of highly influential circles.

In Constantinople, de Morgan's articles prompted the Ottoman administrators who ruled much of the Middle East to orchestrate a change of policy in case any large oil discoveries were made. In 1888 and 1898, on the suggestion of Hagop Pasha, the director of the Privy Purse in the Ottoman Empire, Sultan Abdul Hamid issued special decrees, or *firmans*, that would henceforth place the revenues of any newly discovered oil deposits under the sole control of Constantinople, blocking the path of any local administrators who might try to claim them.

There was someone else who had also heard much about what de Morgan had to say, and who was not slow to grasp its significance. For while recuperating in Tehran at the end of his two-year journey, de Morgan had made the acquaintance not only of numerous Persian officials but of a remarkable Englishman, Sir Henry Drummond Wolff. Acting as the official representative of the British government,

Drummond Wolff made it his business to know exactly what was going on in a kingdom with which he had become so well acquainted and was so keen to establish strong ties.

Confident, outgoing, determined and deeply patriotic, Drummond Wolff had spent several years in Tehran, working hard to win the favour of Nasser al-Din, the late father of the present shah. He had several impressive political and diplomatic victories of which to boast. For not only had he persuaded the shah to open the Karun River to international traffic but had also helped the de Reuter family get some compensation for the loss of their concession in 1873. As a result of his negotiations with Tehran, the de Reuter family was able to establish a national bank that was incorporated in 1889 as the Imperial Bank of Persia. The bank would play a vital role in preventing Persia from sliding further into a state of economic decay, Drummond Wolff felt, remarking that its foundation was 'a matter of capital importance to encourage the creation of commercial machinery'.

But as he left Tehran to return to Europe, Drummond Wolff's mind was ticking fast with a much more ambitious idea. For if Persia really did harbour the oil reserves that de Morgan felt sure it possessed, then could not a British investor take up the challenge of finding and exploiting them? This would be a huge coup for the British government and, if he could find the right person, for Drummond Wolff's own diplomacy.

2

The Great Investor

Even by the elitist standards of high society, a visit to the Epsom racecourses in the late Victorian or early Edwardian era would have been a very refined and expensive affair, one that would have been only for the most affluent. To own a private viewing box at the races, however, was the ultimate privilege, something that only royalty could ever afford.

There was, however, just one exception, and he was a middle-aged business-man by the name of William Knox D'Arcy. Plump, even stout, with a large walrus moustache, the 51-year-old D'Arcy had by the turn of the century acquired a vast fortune that had allowed him to hire his own personal viewing box at the Epsom racecourses and buy a house in Grosvenor Square, situated in one of London's most prestigious areas, a mansion at Stanmore in Middlesex and a private shooting estate at Bylaugh Park in Norfolk. Together with his wife Elena, whom he had married in 1872, and their five children, he lived life to the full. Socializing widely with the high and mighty, and entertaining them regularly at all three of his homes – sometimes inviting the great names of the day such as Enrico Caruso and Dame Nellie Melba to give private performances – he had by 1900 become well known, well established, well connected and popular.

D'Arcy's origins were always modest but never especially grand. His father was a solicitor who practised near Newton Abbot in Devonshire and who had been successful enough to send his son to a leading public school, Westminster. But when he first started his professional career, joining his father's legal business in his early twenties, young William would doubtless never have dreamed of amassing a personal fortune remotely as vast as the one he was soon to acquire.

His great turn of fortune had come about soon after he had left England to begin a new life in Australia, settling at Rockhampton in Queensland where he established his own legal practice. In 1882 he had made a chance encounter with three brothers, all locals, who needed financial backing to explore a derelict mine that was situated a short distance away, at Ironstone Mountain. Nothing much had ever been found there, they admitted, but they had found a few rocks nearby that seemed to be tarnished dark yellow, and since gold had been discovered elsewhere in the region, it was just possible that the site might still have more to offer. Desperate to find funding, the brothers offered half of their interest in the venture in return for an initial lump sum investment.

Sensing a golden opportunity and following his gut feeling, D'Arcy teamed up with a few other local businessmen, giving the brothers the funding they needed and then forming a syndicate to explore the mine further. Two years later, a considerable amount of underground caving work had yielded nothing, and the dispirited brothers had decided to sell their stake, accepting D'Arcy's offer of £100,000 for a mine that seemed to have nothing much of value left. But the young lawyer was not so easily dissuaded and, after a lot of hard work, his diggers eventually struck a rich seam of gold that made him and his fellow shareholders in the new Mount Morgan Gold Mining Company very rich indeed. By 1895, when he headed back to his homeland in search of new openings, William Knox D'Arcy had become one of Australia's wealthiest men.

It was at almost exactly the same time that, on the other side of the world, tens of thousands of would-be prospectors were infected by an epidemic of 'gold fever', prompting them to stampede to parts of America that were rumoured to offer real opportunities of finding quick wealth on a fabulous scale: many of these feverish individuals lay aside the comfort and security of their everyday lives to travel for months on end, often enduring terrible weather and gruellingly hard work in pursuit of what often turned out to be just a hollow dream. William Knox D'Arcy was certainly not easily led – far from it: he naturally possessed a supreme independence of mind – but it is possible that he was affected by a dose of the same condition, and far from being satisfied with the vast sums his Australian enterprises had afforded him, he was merely spurred on by them. He wanted more – much more – and had a keen and ready eye for any other opportunities that would make him richer still, or at the very least would help maintain his high social standing if the value of the shares in his Australian venture ever suffered a serious fall.

Besides raw financial power, William Knox D'Arcy had two formidable assets at his disposal to help him realize his dreams. One was intuition – an uncanny nose for making money when others were dismissive. The other was an aptitude for making friends in high places, establishing a good rapport with well-connected individuals who were often amongst the first to hear of tempting opportunities in various parts of the world, or who could pull strings to help him grab a chance. A great asset in this respect was his relaxed, jovial manner, for he was an individual who was wholly unassuming, one who tended to put people at ease despite his commanding presence.

One of his close friends was Lord Orford, a frequent visitor to Grosvenor Square, who had extensive contacts with diplomats and officials in every corner of Britain's vast empire. And amongst these contacts, it so happened, was London's former representative in Tehran, Sir Henry Drummond Wolff. In early November

1900, a few years after de Morgan's detailed reports on Persian oil prospects had been published, Drummond Wolff approached Lord Orford with an interesting proposition. The shah of Persia was cash starved, he pointed out, and open to suggestions for foreign investment. Above all, he continued, the Persian king was willing to offer a concession to a suitable foreign capitalist who would be allowed to drill for oil in return for taking an agreed percentage of the proceeds of its sale. Did he, Lord Orford, know of anyone who might be interested? Wolff had acquired this gem of information from someone he knew well and had always deeply trusted. For just a few days before, on 27 October, he had attended a Persian trade fair in Paris, where he soon met up with an old acquaintance from his Tehran days, General Antoine Kitabgi Khan, who told him all.

Amiable, well dressed and well versed in the ways of both the royal court and of Western society, the grey-haired Kitabgi, then in his early sixties, was widely regarded as a reliable source of both information and influence. As head of the Persian Customs service, he was superbly connected not just with the shah but with almost everyone of note within his kingdom, notably the Amin al-Sultan. The 'Amin', or the Grand Vizier as he was sometimes referred to in Western circles, was the shah's right-hand man and guardian, the kingdom's number two who made, or at least advised upon, almost every decision of note. He was, in effect, the Persian prime minister. Amin and Kitabgi had worked together on all manner of high-ranking issues, notably the de Reuter concession, the formation of the Imperial Bank of Persia and a number of other foreign schemes to develop the Persian economy.

But it was not just his contacts that made Kitabgi so valuable to Drummond Wolff. For he also harboured a lot of goodwill towards Britain in particular, and was anxious to find backing in London rather than turn elsewhere. Quite why he appears to have harboured such a relative Anglophilia is hard to explain. It is certainly true that, alone in the Persian court, he was originally something of an outsider who may not have shared the same narrow xenophobia from which others suffered. In fact, being of Georgian origin and a practising Roman Catholic, his whole background was very different from that of other court officials. His Armenian wife may well also have profoundly influenced his outlook on both Persia and the outside world. Whatever the reason, Drummond Wolff always felt that Kitabgi represented 'the European element of the Persian government ... for he was well versed in Western matters – being able to draw up a concession and initiate commercial movements'.[1]

Like Henry Drummond Wolff, Kitabgi had met de Morgan in Tehran and subsequently made a close and careful study of his writings. These had been sent specifically to him from Paris by one Eduard Cotte, one of de Morgan's relations and an individual who had negotiated closely with the Persians to secure a number of Western business interests. Kitabgi felt sure that the French explorer had made a find of real significance: 'the stretch of the oil fields at Kend-i-Chirin', he wrote, 'is a hundred times superior on the surface to the development at Baku', adding that 'in such a manner, that in taking a quarter or even less, we are in the presence of a source of riches incalculable to extension, without counting the great economy on the expenses of production and transport'.[2]

Drummond Wolff shared Kitabgi's confidence that considerable quantities of Persian oil were waiting to be discovered. Soon after returning to London he had written a confidential report for British government ministers that gave a very upbeat message about the kingdom's oil prospects. 'The Russian oil fields are getting exhausted at the present day', he wrote, whereas 'the virgin oil fields of Persia promise a good future as they may be made to engage the whole of Western markets in a short time if there be sufficient oil'.[3]

Kitabgi was also as painfully aware as the shah, and the prime minister, of just how desperately his homeland needed foreign investment. By this time the kingdom was badly in debt – to the tune of around £1,216,000, claimed the British Minister in Tehran, Sir Arthur Hardinge – and had an adverse balance of trade. The central government appeared completely incapable of keeping a tight grip on its own expenditure even though the economy's output, and its exports, were doing little more than stagnating. International lenders, who were only too well aware of the shah's poor track record of repaying debts, were keeping him at arm's length: as one newspaper observed in March 1900, 'the money markets of the world are closed to him … the reason is not far to seek. It is the old story: past breach of faith and disregard of obligations.'[4]

Not surprisingly an overwhelming malaise had long fallen over the shah's court. As Amin al-Dawla had remarked desperately in 1878, 'there is nothing we can do. Day by day we become more desperate … we want to become world famous for excellent outstanding deeds but we have no plan, no organisation, no money.' He felt sure he knew the reason. 'Alas! All were busy looking after themselves and reaching out for personal gain.'[5]

Within a week of arriving in Britain, Drummond Wolff had made several approaches to some of his closest friends and contacts in his London circle. But while most of them said that they would try to dig some names out, Lord Orford barely hesitated. He knew just the man, he said: an investor who had made vast sums in Australia and to whom he felt such a venture would appeal enormously.

But even for an investor as canny and self-confident as William Knox D'Arcy, this was an impossibly hard decision to take. De Morgan's writings, and the hearsay of numerous other travellers, all strongly suggested that oil was present in Persia, but this was not really the issue. The real issue was whether it lay there in sufficient quantities required for commercial exploitation, and the huge investment that this would entail. Even then, could it really be found quickly enough to stop the operation running dry of cash and leaving D'Arcy indebted or, quite conceivably, even destitute?

D'Arcy was under no illusion that the potential rewards would have to be considerable if they were to offset such enormous risks. After all, besides the obvious difficulties of the long distances that his men would have to travel and the hard terrain that they would need to cross, he knew from the geologists' reports that they would also be confronted by rock formations that would be formidably hard to drill through in order to reach any deposits that may exist far beneath. Not only that, but even experienced oil explorers could be deliberately misled by locals who maliciously told them what they wanted to hear. Such dangers had already become particularly apparent during the Baku oil boom, for example, when it had been said that among the 200 or so local oil magnates only a few were honest. All the rest soon courted a reputation for performing such tricks as digging a false oil well, filling it with petroleum and then selling the rights even to shrewd and experienced investors. In any case, D'Arcy knew that even if oil was eventually found in commercial quantities, there was no telling when it might start to dry up: by this time some of the Baku fields had already started to peak, while others elsewhere in the world had led only short lives, having quickly and unexpectedly turned from gushing oil to spewing water.

D'Arcy would also have been painfully aware that several other ambitious investors had already tried moving into the Middle East, holding their own high hopes of finding oil, fame and fortune that had eventually, sometimes quickly, been badly dashed. So in 1868 a French company, the Societé Soufriere des Mines de Gemsah et de Ranga, had been digging for sulphur in Egypt but unexpectedly struck oil. To begin with this seemed path-breaking, but the company later nearly bankrupted itself by making unsuccessful attempts to capitalize on these promising early findings. Further attempts to find Egyptian oil were made on the coast near the Mons Petroleus, where it was known to be present in considerable quantities. But these efforts, too, soon ended in disappointment, even though the well was drilled right down into the granite.

Other Western companies had had similar experiences in the region, if not quite so spectacular. In 1884, for example, the Dutch firm Hotz & Co, based in Bushire in Persia, obtained a concession to prospect for oil in the lands around Dalaki, but its small-scale operations were quite unsuccessful and were quickly abandoned. And at the same time that D'Arcy was first offered a chance to invest in Persia, a British aristocrat was also busy financing his own private expedition in the area, boring right down to the then exceptional depth of 3,000 feet, with disastrous results. By the time he was forced to concede defeat, giving up empty-handed and doubtless feeling empty-headed, he had become nearly delirious with stress and had wasted his personal fortune.

Most of all, however, D'Arcy would have been only too conscious of the miserable fate of the last major enterprise to explore for Persian oil. Little more than a decade before, in 1889, de Reuter had signed another concession with Tehran, one that allowed him to explore the kingdom's mineral resources. Before long he had established a company, the Persian Bank Mining Rights Corporation, that had exclusive rights to search for oil and which was obliged to give the Persian government 16 per cent of its profits. Shares in the company were soon sold, and its £1 million capital was widely expected easily to cover the costs (estimated at around £200,000) of undertaking exploratory operations.

It was not long, however, before things started to go badly wrong: costs started to soar far more rapidly than anyone had expected, while oil remained highly elusive. The company's engineers eventually succeeded in drilling three wells, one of which was bored down as deep as 800 feet, but burned up considerable amounts of cash in doing so. In 1896, five years on, only a fraction of the original capital remained. Soon company directors were forced to admit that their operations had been stymied by 'natural difficulties in the severity of the winter in the north and the extreme heat in the south ... the backward state of the country, and the absence of communications and transport'. The chairman, Lepel Griffin, added that:

> It is obvious in a country like Persia, with an autocratic Government and all authority directly emanating from the shah, no commercial enterprise of a new and strange character can be profitably carried on and it is still more certain that, if in the place of assistance and support, the Corporation meets with direct hostility, opposition and outrage from high officials of the Persian Government, its only recourse is to refuse to spend more capital on a fruitless endeavour and retire.[6]

By the time word of a new concession reached D'Arcy, the Corporation was on the very verge of being declared bankrupt and being wound up.

D'Arcy would also have known that finding oil in heavy, commercial quantities was in any case really just the starting point. If he was going to make a real return on his money, then he would also have to be quite sure that any oil could be readily taken first to the refineries, where the crude substance would be treated and then transported to international marketplaces. This was one vital factor in the success of both John Rockefeller in the United States and the Nobel family in Russia, who controlled not just the output of oil from the wells but the entire transit system for the process. Robert and Ludwig Nobel initially moved Baku's oil northwards towards the Baltic, from where it was shipped to foreign markets, and it was not until 1883 that a railway was built that linked the oilfields to the Black Sea, thereby giving these exports a much more direct route abroad. Funded by the hugely wealthy and powerful Rothschild family in Paris, its construction was a huge commercial breakthrough.

Anyone could have told D'Arcy that Persia was in this respect hardly an ideal place to tap oil. Unless it was located in reasonable proximity to the coast, any extracted oil would be extremely hard to move farther afield. The kingdom had virtually no infrastructure, as de Morgan had quickly discovered, and anyone searching for oil would have to fund the construction of road links that would allow the chosen sites to be both explored and, if anything was found, to then be exploited. Of course this assumed that roads could be built in the first place: but Persia's vast stretches of mountains and desert wildernesses meant that no one could make even this basic assumption.

Several things may have prompted D'Arcy to throw caution to the wind. He may have simply had an overpowering instinct, a gut feeling, that he should press ahead and risk losing everything in the process. Or perhaps his imagination was set alight by the stories of the fabulous wealth and power that other oil barons had found the world over, on a scale and magnitude that easily dwarfed his own.

After all, by the turn of the century, D'Arcy's assets seemed almost immaterial compared to those of John D. Rockefeller, who had managed to take control of much of America's oil industry by the early 1880s, when he was only in his early 40s. And the Baku oil boom had enabled a privileged few to acquire extraordinary wealth, even if many of them were not well suited to handling it. Astonishing stories reached the West – often quite true – of local oil barons building vast palaces, with one millionaire modelling his mansion on a house of playing cards, while another constructed a palace made of gold plate which, not surprisingly, was eventually plundered by brigands. The fabulous Armenian multi-millionaire Alexander Mantachoff – who had been a humble peasant before buying a small plot of land where oil was suddenly and unexpectedly struck, making him vastly wealthy overnight – also had unusual ideas about how to spend his windfalls. In his own palace he insisted on distilling kerosene in platinum cisterns and holding wild parties with a strongly Arabian theme: troupes of beautiful women from the world over were taken there, as well as dancers who performed some remarkable gyrations, highly skilled acrobats, a vast and exquisite cuisine and an unlimited flow of wine and spirits. On the same grandiose scale he collected art treasures and built an exemplary Armenian church in the centre of Paris, just off the Champs-Elysées.

This was a hard act to follow, but one or two Western entrepreneurs of the time seemed destined to do just that. The British businessman Marcus Samuel had by this time already acquired considerable wealth from his own investments in the oil industry. In 1892 he had made a commercial breakthrough, one that astonished the world, when he commissioned the construction of a special tanker, the *Murex*, and used it to ship a large cargo of Russian kerosene through the Suez Canal. Suddenly vast international markets seemed within reach of

European investors, and Samuel wasted not a moment in making the most of these new opportunities: within months he had set up a new tanker company, the Tank Syndicate, that was renamed the Shell Transport and Trading Company in October 1897. Already a wealthy man, he was by now becoming supremely rich.

But difficult, or even near-impossible, though such a Persia venture may have been, the great British investor was interested, and soon after first hearing of it Drummond Wolff felt compelled to tell Kitabgi that 'concerning the oil, I have spoken to a capitalist of the highest order, who declares himself disposed to examine the affair, and if you so desire I shall put him in communication with you'.[7] A few weeks after the idea had first been mentioned to him, decision time started to loom: D'Arcy knew that if he did not make a move, then Kitabgi may start to look elsewhere. Soon after the start of the new year, Cotte visited him at Grosvenor Square and urged him to meet with Kitabgi to discuss the proposal in more detail. This would be their first meeting and, Cotte hoped, the start of many more.

As the great investor took these initial steps towards the Persian concession and carefully weighed the case for and against backing the regional search for oil, he began to brief himself carefully about the state of local and regional politics. From his contacts he heard that the kingdom's ruler, Mozaffar al-Din Shah, had ascended the throne only four years before, at the age of 43, and that in sharp contrast to his father, Nasser al-Din Shah, he had always been a somewhat sickly, irresolute, good-natured and entirely uneducated man. His irresolution was understandable, for prior to his accession he had had virtually no experience of government, and was for this reason dependent on the wisdom and judgement of his prime minister, the only other individual of note within the machinery of Persian government.

He also knew that Persia differed fundamentally from many of its regional neighbours because it was, in theory at least, an independent kingdom that lay outside the Ottoman Empire. For more than four centuries most of the Middle East – including the Arabian peninsula, North Africa and Mesopotamia – had formed part of the vast Ottoman Empire and had been ruled by the sultanate at Constantinople. In practice this whole Middle Eastern region was always a remote and peripheral part of the empire, and the powers of its Ottoman suzerain were far more nominal than real. By 1900 Ottoman power was also on the wane, and the first dent in its Middle Eastern power had been made as early as 1798, when Napoleon had without difficulty succeeded in seizing Egypt from its grasp.

But while Persia lay outside the Ottoman Empire, its sovereignty was also more theoretical than real, because it had for centuries suffered incursions by, and been under the heavy political influence of, foreign powers. Over the previous few decades, by far the most important of these powers – Great Britain and its rival Tsarist Russia – both viewed the region as falling within their natural spheres of interest.

By 1897 Great Britain had reached the zenith of its power; it was said that a quarter of the world's map could be coloured in pink – the traditional colour of the British Empire – and that more than 450 million people fell under its sway. The entire Indian subcontinent, whole swathes of Africa and beyond: all of these vast lands were ruled from London, which was the heart of the largest empire ever established. The chief British concern about Persia was that it seemed to Whitehall to be perilously close to India – the great jewel in the British imperial crown – and could make a convenient launch pad for an enemy power that wanted to attack not just the Indian mainland but also harass the shipping that kept British troops there supplied.

But Britain's interest in carving out a sphere of influence in Persia conflicted directly with Russia's own ambitions. Persia lay immediately adjacent to Russia's southern borders, and ministers in St Petersburg had a strong interest in maintaining strong commercial ties between the two countries, exploiting any economic opportunities that cropped up and, above all, keeping any competitors out. This meant that the Russians would almost certainly try and block any bid D'Arcy made for an oil concession (viewing it as a move by the British government to win influence in the region) just as they had forced the Persian government to abort the concession granted to Baron Julius de Reuter in 1872. So D'Arcy became quickly aware that if he failed to seize his chance to get the Persian oil concession, the Russians would have no hesitation in taking it for themselves. He had to move now, before his enemies had a chance to act, and take the opportunity while it was there.

The first Paris meeting between D'Arcy and Kitabgi, with Cotte and Drummond Wolff at their sides, took place on 8 January and over the next few weeks several more followed. Accompanied by a highly respected geologist and oil expert, Dr Boverton Redwood, D'Arcy pressed the Persian official for details, discussed every aspect of what he and those working on his behalf might encounter both in Tehran and in the field, and then made up his mind about what to do next.

On 1 March, D'Arcy informed Kitabgi and all the others involved in the negotiations of his decision. He would, he told them, be willing to press ahead with the venture, and make a direct approach to the shah to secure the exclusive rights to drill for oil. Before securing such a deal, however, he wanted to take up Redwood's suggestion of obtaining the independent advice of a respected geologist, whom he would commission to explore the two areas that seemed most promising: Chiah Sourkh in the north-west and the vicinity of Ahwaz in the south-west. Moreover, he wanted to despatch a carefully chosen envoy to Tehran to strike the right deal with the shah.

The man whom D'Arcy chose to travel to the Persian capital on his behalf, 'to obtain from the shah of Persia a concession for the oil fields believed to exist in that country', was an individual he knew well and whom he judged to be 'worthy of every confidence'.[8] His name was Alfred Marriott.

3

Marriott Plays the Great Game

For the foreign visitor approaching from afar, the Persian capital could hardly fail to impress. Set in a vast, open plain that was bordered by spectacular mountains, their peaks snow-capped throughout the year, Tehran boasted a superb natural splendour that would have made as powerful an impression upon Alfred Marriott as it had on all the other Western travellers before him who had made their way southwards from the Russian border and seen it for the first time.

Marriott had been about seven miles away when he first caught sight of the distant city, but as he got closer he would have seen the newly constructed ramparts that were intended to ward off any would-be attacker, while also marking the outermost limits of a rapidly growing city. Being so used to London, he might also have been taken aback not just by the greenery that surrounded the city but also by its compact shape and size. Just a few years before, after all, Lord Curzon had paid his own visit there and remarked on how the 'belt of verdure [was] topped only by a few edifices ... it was difficult to believe that that green band could shroud a great city with a population of nearly 200,000 souls. The only buildings that rose to any height above the level of the tree-tops appeared to be a large mosque, with four tile-covered minarets, that looked from a distance like painted organ-pipes and, upon nearer approach, like sham Corinthian columns [and] one or two detached towers.'[1]

From the moment of his arrival there, in the third week of April, Marriott would have been immediately overwhelmed by the furious cacophony of the city's streets and bazaars. This comprised an almost frantic scene of merchants, vendors and buyers, camels, donkeys and horses, all fighting for attention and space. But it differed somewhat from other parts of the Middle East or the Indian subcontinent, for there was more sophistication here than in India and, amidst a few street lamps, tramlines and signboards, even a dash of Westernization. Some shops had doors and front windows that allowed them to display their wares in true European fashion. Amongst local people the turban had gradually disappeared and these days almost no one wore the long flowing robes that were seen elsewhere in the Islamic world and beyond. Instead they had tight-fitting clothes, invariably of a very sombre colour, that were cut in European, or semi-European, style.

From his conversations with Drummond Wolff and Kitabgi, Marriott would
have got some idea about what to expect and where to go on his arrival. He had
arranged his first stop to be the residency of the head of the British diplomatic
legation, Arthur Hardinge, who lived and worked in what his contemporaries described as 'a fine house, standing in a beautiful garden of several acres, full of roses
and nightingales, intersected by rivulets flowing on blue tiles and overshadowed
by weeping willows'. The residency was situated in a quarter where the city's small
European population – an assortment of diplomats, businessmen and engineers,
numbering probably no more than 300 or so in total – lived amongst local people.
It was here that he would be able to find an apartment, one that would allow him
to live and work quite comfortably over the coming weeks.

A short distance from here, about 20 minutes away by horse, was a confined
area surrounded by high walls. Known locally as the Ark, or citadel, it lay in the
very heart of the city, overlooking the roads that ran to Hamadan and Baghdad
in the west, southwards to Isfahan and the Persian Gulf, and along the eastern
road which had long linked the capital to Khorassan, Seistan and, beyond them,
which led all the way to Afghanistan and India. This was the very heart of the
capital, and it was here, amidst many fine gardens and ornate buildings, that Shah
Mozaffar al-Din and his ministers lived and worked.

Within a few days of his arrival, Marriott had made contact with the shah's
officials and was taken into the royal court to introduce himself. He was led
through a series of courtyards, admiring the elaborate paved flooring, sparkling
fountains, and the rows of poplars, pines and shrubs that lined his way. Before
long, at the upper end of one court, he saw before him a handsome, if not overtly
impressive building, at the centre of which was the Talar, or throne room, where
a white marble throne was positioned on a raised platform. This was where the
crown jewels were carefully locked away, and where during the annual celebration
of Nowruz, the Persian New Year, the shah followed the ancient traditions of
Darius and Xerxes by personally meeting many of his subjects and offering them
his greetings. The British traveller could not fail to be awed by the fabulous art
collection he saw around him. Everywhere were expensive paintings, designs,
engravings, mirrors, bronze sculptures, porcelain vases and armchairs covered
with a thin plating of real gold. In the centre stood a square glass case heaped full
of pearls that a visitor could plunge his hand into and scoop up great cascades
and handfuls and other gems that had been excavated from every corner of the
shah's empire and beyond.

Marriott knew that, as a visitor, he could expect some generous, occasionally
lavish, hospitality on entering the royal palace. Other Western visitors to the
kingdom had described how 'several rows of dishes heaped with confectionery
were spread across the floor, indicating, according to Persian custom, that the
guest was expected to have a pleasant taste in the mouth when he received a

welcome'.[2] Rice – known locally as *pilau* or *chillo* – was served at nearly every meal and was reputed to have a very distinctive flavour, prompting another visitor to comment that 'the grain is small and has a pungent odour I have never noticed in any other variety of rice'. A wide variety of other dishes, made of nuts, pistachios, dried fruits, confectionery and pickles, was also served. In the days ahead crucial discussions and negotiations would be played out over mealtimes, which as a result would take up much of the working day. It was quite usual for the two daily meals, together with the previous hour of chatting over the hors d'oeuvres and smoking in the reception room, to last more than five hours each day.

Before leaving London, General Kitabgi had tried to brief the young Englishman about how to negotiate with the Persian officials. It was of paramount importance, he emphasized, that he respected local customs at all times: there was 'a necessity', he claimed, 'of acting in Persia according to Persian ideas and not those of the English'.[3] No one he met there, he continued, should get the idea that he or anyone else wanted to change local customs or ways – 'to take their caps off their heads' – in any way.[4] Kitabgi had also emphasized that in Persia, more so than elsewhere, matters of tiny importance could sometimes shatter high hopes: 'it is often for trifles that the best enterprises have been destroyed in Persia'.[5]

Marriott was also well aware that he badly needed such advice, for the world of Persian politics into which he had now stepped bore no resemblance to the one he had left behind at home. There was no parliamentary body of any note, for the Persian parliament – the Majlis – had a role that was only low key and unimportant. The country had no formal elections in the way that was true of western European governments, and no constitution. The only individuals who really mattered were the shah and his prime minister, and if anyone else bore any importance it was only because at any one time they could whisper in the ears of these two key decision-makers.

The differences did not just stop there. In Tehran just a few years before there had even been stories of 'roughish horseplay' at the royal court that would have simply been unthinkable back home. Here some ministers were said to have indulged in 'wrestling with official colleagues, or pitching one another into a spacious pond, from which the servants dragged them panting and struggling not to sink, while their sovereign shook with laughter at the sight'.[6] A few years before the shah had bought some skates and bicycles from Western capitals and then made his senior advisers and ministers, all high-ranking Persian aristocrats, ride them around the court's ornate garden. When an English officer had presented the shah with a collapsible rubber boat, he was quick to seize his chance: after secretly unsealing the valve, he ordered a dozen of his senior clerks and officials to row along a nearby miniature lake, laughing hysterically as the boat slowly collapsed before sinking and leaving the richly dressed courtiers completely drenched. And just as one Roman emperor had famously made his horse a senator, so in a similar spirit had the shah granted one of his beloved cats a considerable private pension.

Bracing himself, Marriott prepared to meet the prime minister, Amin al-Sultan, of whom Hardinge, Drummond Wolff and other Western visitors would also have given him a careful description: 'he himself had begun life as a Georgian slave from Transcaucasia, and he had the blue eyes and the light complexion of his race', as Hardinge once wrote. 'He combined with an apparent frankness a cheerful, almost jovial, ease of manner, which frequently disarmed his most bitter and uncompromising foes.' In particular, he was 'versatile, resourceful, good-natured and a pleasant and persuasive companion', although he did have some idiosyncrasies, one of which was 'a curious trick or habit of describing himself in the third person singular, as "a certain individual": "the Russian minister is greatly displeased at the support which a certain person is, as you know, constantly giving to any demand made by England"' was just one of the instances of this habit that the British minister described.[7]

But the ultimate decision-maker – whose cooperation Marriott would have to secure if he was to win his concessionary prize – was of course not the prime minister but the shah, Mozaffer al-Din. Again, Hardinge would have furnished him with a good description: 'he presented a dignified appearance in his military uniform and black lamb's wool cap or *kulah*, looked well-bred, with good features and a straight, slightly aquiline nose, but rather older than his real age, for his brow and face were beginning to be wrinkled and his long moustache was already fast turning to grey'.[8]

From this moment on, as he entered the royal court and made his case for a concession, Marriott was, inadvertently or not, a key player in a game of international intrigue, espionage and rivalry. This was a 'Great Game' for power and influence in the region, and it was inevitable that the British government would to some extent be drawn into his quest to win D'Arcy the exclusive oil rights he so badly wanted.

The key rivalry for influence in Persia lay between Britain and Russia, although at first sight this may seem difficult to explain. Persia, after all, was at this time a poverty-stricken land that had little to boast about. Its population, around nine million strong, was overwhelmingly rural, and nearly everyone was employed in agriculture or in the embroidery trade that produced the kingdom's renowned carpets. Other than the capital, only Tabriz and Isfahan had sizeable populations. Much of the land was in any case barren or inhospitable and, as Marriott would quickly have discovered, completely lacking any real infrastructure.

For the Russians, however, none of this really mattered. Because Persia was so close, lying to its immediate south, it had a natural strategic value to the Russians, who could not afford to see a hostile power seize the reins of power in Tehran. Persia, in any case, had a rapidly growing population that had always been an important market for Russian traders. Most importantly, however, the Tsar and his ministers knew that control over Persia would win Russia a direct route to the Gulf, one that would give its generals enormous strategic power and its traders a vast commercial advantage.

To pursue these interests, the Russian government had gradually established an elaborate network of spies and informers in Persia, a network that at this time was run by their chief representative in Tehran, a Mr Argyropulo. The British officials who met him described him as 'an elderly man, a grey-bearded bachelor of Greek descent, as his name implies' who belonged to a particular, old-fashioned breed of Russian diplomat. This particular type, felt his British counterpart, Sir Arthur Hardinge, 'was distinguished by excessive reticence and therefore reluctant to allude to any local political topics' for 'cultivation of this absolute reticence was a tradition of the Russian "Oriental Section"'. Hardinge even claimed that 'his reserve was so great that it purposely impelled some of the diplomatic ladies to tease – and even to agitate – him by purposely asking him indiscreet questions, for the purpose of hearing his evasive replies about the foreign policies of Persia … I myself now and then touched on politics with my Russian colleague but was usually answered by evasive generalities'.[9] But Argyropulo's silence was understandable, for he had a lot to hide. His agents always kept careful watch over the shah's court, keeping particularly close tabs on its links with the British legation, which in turn closely monitored the Russians' own contacts and movements.[10]

There was one reason above all others why Hardinge, and his bosses in the British government back in London, were so concerned to ward off Russian influence. This was that the security of India was felt to depend on events within the Persian kingdom. Any hostile presence in Persia, it was felt, would be uncomfortably close not only to the border between India and Afghanistan but also to the Gulf straits, which could act as a highly convenient staging post for an enemy fleet to set sail. It was significant that at the height of the Indian Mutiny of 1857, for example, rumours had been rife on both sides that the Persian army was marching into Afghanistan and into India in order to link up with the rebels and join their cause, throwing the British out of the continent for ever: 'we cannot verify the news', commented one writer in a Delhi newspaper, 'but it is not an impossibility'.[11]

Over the previous few decades the British government had started to take a strong interest in the region as the Russians began seizing large parts of Central Asia and inching their way closer to India: after the capture of Tashkent in 1865, for example, the British foreign secretary, Lord John Russell, proclaimed his wish that 'both Powers would respect the independence of the Persian monarchy, would be careful not to encroach on the territory of Persia and not undermine the authority of the shah'.[12] There was, as Curzon wrote, an 'ever increasing proximity of Russian power upon the northern and north-western frontiers of India from the Pamirs to Herat'.

Curzon and his sympathizers were right that, among some extremist circles in St Petersburg, the idea of a march on India was an alluring one. In some sections of the Russian military, for example – particularly those where memories of the Crimean War still rankled – it was often discussed and written about. In 1898 a Captain Lebedev wrote a short book, *To India: A Military, Statistical and Strategic Sketch*, that seemed to anticipate Russia's occupation of Afghanistan, one that would bring its forces right up the border with British India: all that was missing, he and some others argued, was the perfect opportunity to launch such an attack against a distracted or divided Great Britain.

From a British point of view, the task of safeguarding India did not necessarily mean dividing or destroying Persia, let along occupying it. Curzon had written in 1893 that 'the continued existence of this country is bound up in the maintenance … even in the extension of the British Empire', while Lord Salisbury wanted 'to maintain the continued national existence and the territorial integrity of Persia and to develop her resources'.[13] It did mean, however, stopping the kingdom from falling into enemy hands: 'our ambitions are … to prevent it from being undermined or taken from us by others'.[14] No one in London minded the Russians doing what they wanted in Persia's northern provinces. But there was much more dissension about how much influence, if any, the Russians should be allowed to have, or how Britain should exert its own weight, elsewhere in the kingdom.

Tehran was the main theatre in which this fierce competition between Britain and Russia was played out. It was here that both sides had their respective sympathizers, as well as their enemies, spies and informers. General Kitabgi leant strongly towards London, but Amin al-Sultan, the prime minister, was often said to look more towards Russia. This may simply have been because he felt he had no choice when the Russians were so close to hand and could easily dispatch an armed force against Tehran if need be. Hardinge noticed that the prime minister and the shah 'were inclined to propitiate the formidable [Russian] empire', but regarded this as a far from unreasonable position since 'the Transcaspian Railway, constructed some years earlier by General Annenkoff, had a station at Duchak, an easy ride of two or three miles from the Persian border in that region'.[15] After all, it had been not many years before, in 1828, that the Persians had fought against their northern neighbour and suffered a terrible defeat that culminated in the humiliating Treaty of Turkomanchay. The Tsar's forces had also looked ready to step in much more recently, for during a minor disturbance at Tabriz in April 1897, the Russian consul had informed the Tehran authorities that 5,000 troops were ready to cross the frontier 'to protect the Christians in Tabriz'.

Now, at the turn of the century, St Petersburg could doubtless find some other way of flexing its muscle against Tehran. Amin had once told Drummond Wolff that 'Russia has a frontier of 12,000 miles on the country, and without declaring war she can at any time do great injury to Persia by raising against her some of the numerous Yamoot Turcoman frontier tribes'.[16] What's more, they had also stationed their own forces right at the very heart of Persia: 'the supremacy of Russia', wrote Hardinge, 'was in fact, though not quite as complete as our own in Egypt, already effective, for a well-armed and well-drilled force of Cossacks had been created by an able Russian officer, Colonel Kosakovsky, under whose orders it had been placed'.[17] Even this relatively meagre Cossack force could probably have quickly overawed Persia's own soldiers, whose miserable state often shocked those who encountered them: stories were legion of how street beggars had sometimes been given uniforms and taught to salute in order to buttress the army's size, of some soldiers asking passers-by for instructions on how to salute or use a rifle, and of others being sublet by their officers to work as gardeners and servants.

By the spring of 1901 the shah and his ministers were in what Hardinge called a state of 'complete vassalage' to Russia. Mozaffar himself, the British representative felt, was just 'a weak, childish and ignorant puppet brought up ... in an atmosphere of subservience to Russia'.[18] Although the British were well aware of Persia's desperate financial position, they were nonetheless caught wholly by surprise in early 1900 when news broke that the Persians had accepted a large Russian loan of £2.4 million at a low rate of interest. The Persian prime minister, it turned out, had been negotiating with his Russian counterparts for several months in considerable secrecy before signing up for the deal in St Petersburg. What really mattered to London was that this deal, which replaced and overrode an earlier loan made by the British-owned Imperial Bank of Persia, had also come with political strings attached. For its terms stipulated that Tehran could not take out a further loan with any other foreign power unless the Russian government had first been consulted and expressly given its permission for this. Not only that but by 1901 British diplomats had 'ascertained that the Grand Vizier was contemplating a new treaty of commerce with Russia, which would probably be detrimental to British interests'.[19] True, Britain may have struck a treaty with Persia that gave her 'most favoured nation treatment'. But this did not count for much when the Russian minister in Tehran had acquired such immense power in Tehran.

At the same time, some of the British government's own actions in the kingdom had heightened Amin's mistrust of its intentions: for example, the British 'occupation of the Customs posts at Bushire and Kermanshah, which had taken place just a few years before, had alarmed many thoughtful Persians, and raised doubts in their minds as to England's ultimate intentions', argued

General Thomas Gordon of the Imperial Bank of Persia.[20] So the rivalry between the two great powers for regional influence was immense, and every political stride that the Russians took into the kingdom, their British counterparts tried to match. 'I am determined to exhibit an outward and visible sign of the at least equal military resources of Great Britain', wrote Hardinge, 'and with this object, I obtained, through the Government of India, a small force of Indian *sowhar* or cavalry to act as an escort and guard of honour to the British minister and his successors in Persia'. Using them as the British equivalent of the Cossacks, who maintained such an impressive, perhaps intimidating, presence in the capital, this force managed to impose something of the 'might and majesty of the British Empire' and formed 'a brilliant guard of honour, not merely in the capital but in all the other chief consulates in important Persian cities such as Meshed, Isfahan and Shiraz'.[21]

But at the turn of the century the task of winning influence in Persia at Russia's expense presented the British with a formidable challenge. This was all the more pressing because the Russians had started sharply to step up their activities in the kingdom. In 1898 two Russian subjects, F. Enakiev and Alexei Goriainov, had entered into negotiations for a 70-year concession to mine the Qarajadagh area in the north, while the authorities in St Petersburg also obtained permission from Tehran to build a lighthouse and a residential quarter at Anzali.

It was such seemingly impossible odds that seemed to confront Alfred Marriott as he strode, that April day, into the great game of international rivalry that was being fought out so hard in the Persian capital. To win the concession, he would need all the help he could get from the British government, and because the stakes were so high, London was hardly in a position to look away. Before leaving London D'Arcy had formally requested diplomatic support for his mission and soon after, on 12 March 1901, a very senior official in the Foreign Office, Sir Martin Gosselin, had given him a formal introduction to Arthur Hardinge in Tehran. It ran thus: 'This letter will be presented to you by Mr Alfred L. Marriott, who is proceeding to Persia on business connected with mining. I have to request you to be good enough to afford him such assistance as he may require, and as you can properly render to him in furtherance of the object of his journey.'[22] The British government was certainly not in any way sponsoring Marriott's mission, but at the same time it was by no means indifferent to its outcome. 'I was given to understand in the course of the negotiations that a word from me might considerably assist their success', as Hardinge wrote to Lansdowne on 30 May.

When on 21 April Kitabgi had a chance to put the British proposals for a concession before Amin al-Sultan, he immediately discovered how much international competition they would be running up against. He already knew that the Russians were pushing hard to get more political and commercial concessions from Tehran, but was taken aback to hear Amin tell him of the political pressure he was under from St Petersburg, and expressed his wish to strike a 'balance between Russian and English governments'. But such qualms did not prevent Kitabgi from handing over a copy of D'Arcy's draft concession (which would now need to be translated into Persian) or stop Hardinge from formally introducing Marriott to the prime minister for the first time. The delicate, subtle, duplicitous and intricate process of doing deals in the very heart of the kingdom had now begun in earnest.

Marriott quickly tried to strike a powerful chord with the prime minister and in the course of this, their very first meeting, emphasized the point that, with royal cooperation and assistance, 'petroleum will be found in great quantities and that an industry may be developed which will compete with that of Baku'.[23] The Englishman knew that at the court there was a real sense of indignation at the strength of Russian influence in their realm, and that simmering deep down was a sense of injustice and resentment about the Persian loss of Baku, which had been annexed by the Russians nearly a century before. The Grand Vizier appeared impressed and left his British visitor feeling cautiously optimistic by replying that he would consider the proposals on seeing a translated version of the full text.

But as he waited patiently for news in the days ahead, Marriott heard not a word from the royal court. He knew that the translation of the proposed concession, which was a long and detailed document, would take some considerable time, and that throughout the holy month of Muharram, which had begun on 21 April, the entire kingdom would come almost to a standstill. As he waited he reassured himself that the indispensable Kitabgi, who was in constant touch with the royal court, was doing his best to get both influence and information. Kitabgi's efforts certainly lifted Hardinge's spirits, prompting him to report that the general 'has, I understand, secured in a very thorough manner the support of all the shah's principal ministers and courtiers, not even forgetting the personal servant who brings His Majesty his pipe and morning coffee'.[24]

But as days became weeks, he and his sponsors back in London – Sir Henry Drummond Wolff and William Knox D'Arcy – began to fear the worst. When Drummond Wolff began to wonder if the relationship between the prime minister and the shah was still strong, Marriott tried to strike an upbeat note, cabling back to London on 6 May that 'we are making slow progress with business. Present state of affairs unsatisfactory, doing all possible, must act with great caution. Undue haste would be to lose the business. Please do not be impatient.'

In fact the silence was fast becoming unbearable, and by mid-May Marriott and his British counterparts knew that the delay was due to more than just the time-consuming translation, or the onset of the holiest month of the religious year. The real reason the authorities 'are hesitating and want pushing', he wrote, was 'due to the fact that [Amin] does not know if he ought to grant this concession without first consulting the Russians'. Agreeing to the D'Arcy concession without prior Russian permission was, after all, a clear breach of their obligations under the earlier loan agreement and would have torpedoed their chances of getting the additional funding from St Petersburg over which they were currently negotiating.

It was at this crucial stage that Hardinge stepped in to venture a useful word: 'I took the opportunity, as an important British enterprise was at stake, of intimating to the Atabeg-i Azam my conviction that British capital in Persia would be granted. His Highness said that he had all along been favourably disposed towards the scheme, and that I might rely on his doing his best to promote this and all other British commercial undertakings.'[25] Such a 'favourable disposition' on the part of the prime minister was enough to prompt Marriott to send cables back to London that were somewhat triumphalist in tone: 'a very critical stage successfully passed', ran one of the messages, 'all is going on well and I have good hope of obtaining the concession in a week's time'.

But elated though Marriott might have sounded, the difficulties of getting the shah to sign the concession were still enormous. Above all, Mozaffar was supposed to get Russian assent for the enterprise, and to sign such a deal without it would have been an enormous political and financial gamble. 'Great secrecy was observed in preparing the necessary papers', as Hardinge wrote of Marriott and Kitabgi, 'as it was felt that if the Russian Legation got news of the project it would attempt to crush it and would almost certainly succeed in doing so'.[26] So when the shah balked from signing the copy of the concession that was put before him on 20 May, Marriott did not have to try hard to guess the reason.

Marriott knew that his best chance was simply to outbid the Russians. For St Petersburg's main leverage was the amount of money it had already lent to prop up the shah's order, and which it now looked ready to add to. If D'Arcy could rival these amounts, lending his own money without the political strings that the Russians always attached and at a comparable rate of interest, then Marriott knew that he could sorely tempt the shah to disregard the Tsar's ministers, or at least take some liberties. It was, after all, common knowledge that this was a land and culture in which money talked. In the world of Persian politics, as de Morgan had been well aware, public office and all manner of favours were openly bought by the payment of a commensurate fee. 'In no country that I have ever seen or heard of in the world, is the system so open, so shameless or so universal as in Persia', wrote one visitor, Lord Curzon, during his visit to the country in 1891.[27] Acquiring the concession, Marriott reckoned, would ultimately be a question of paying enough for it.

Marriott noted that, to begin with, the shah 'refused to sign unless we paid £40,000 down and £40,000 in formation of the Company, also 16 per cent instead of 10 per cent on net profits'. But under such pressure to make progress, Marriott decided to make a more tempting offer, allowing Kitabgi to 'promise his friends

£5000 in advance of their shares' because he 'had all the Ministers together discussing the affair (a chance which might not occur again) and delay might be fatal'. A few hours later he upped the offer once again, promising a further £5,000 if it would help his cause. But he was taking considerable risks by doing so, since D'Arcy had expressly forbidden him to make any early payments – in effect bribes – and knew nothing about what Marriot was now up to. For in the circumstances of the moment, Marriott was prepared to gamble, hoping that D'Arcy, when he found out, would still have as much confidence in his skill and judgement as ever. His tactics seemed to have reaped dividends when Kitabgi visited the prime minister and returned to report triumphantly to Marriott that the concession would be granted, and that the cash bonus had proved 'most useful' in winning royal assent. The shah's interest, it seemed, had been bought.

Marriott and Kitabgi were moving closer than ever towards their prize, but so too were their Russian rivals. On 24 May Kitabgi noted that there were 'substantial indications of the intrigues which surrounded the shah in order to prevent him from signing the act of concession'. From one of their informers inside the Foreign Ministry, it appears, Argyropoulo had got wind of the concession and demanded an immediate explanation from the prime minister. Assurances quickly followed: a British visitor had proposed an oil concession, confirmed Amin, but 'the conclusion of this affair, if it ever took place, would take many months and that during that time, he would have plenty of leisure to inform his government and to demand instructions'. But Argyropoulo was not convinced, and urgently cabled his bosses in St Petersburg for advice.

Quite what happened at this point has been the subject of some debate. Arthur Hardinge later claimed that the prime minister, though he was keen to go ahead with the project, was desperate not to offend the Russians and found an ingenious way of reconciling the competing interests. Amin's plan was to inform the Russian Legation, as he was supposed to, that the concession had been put before the shah, but would do so not by despatching a courier, who could tell them in person, or sending a letter written in Russian. He would instead write a letter in Persian, 'more especially in the written or *shikaste* character, which is illegible, owing to its peculiar abbreviations, even to scholars familiar with the printed language'. This was ingenious because he was well aware that there was only one person at the legation, the Oriental Secretary, a Mr Stritter, who could have translated it, and from his spies Amin knew that Stritter was about to leave Zergendeh, the Russian Legation's summer residence, to escape the summer heat by taking a short break in the mountains. So if he sent the letter to the Russian delegation at this carefully timed moment, then he could plausibly argue that, since he received no reply, he had assumed that Stritter had no objection.

Whatever the accuracy of this story, it is certain that, at this crucial point in the negotiations, D'Arcy was moving the staggering sum of £10,000 into the Imperial Bank and was ready to release the funds: the shah knew that all he would have to do would be to put his signature to the paperwork and, for the moment at least, his pressing financial problems would be solved. Then, on 28 May, during an elaborate dinner party at the official British residence, Marriott finally heard the news he had so wanted to hear: that the paperwork had just received the royal signature and that the oil concession, after weeks of delay and intrigue, had finally been granted.

The shah and his advisers, it turned out, had barely changed the terms of the draft agreement that Marriott had presented them with. Under its terms D'Arcy was given 'a special and exclusive privilege to search for and obtain ... natural gas [and] petroleum' anywhere within the Persian kingdom other than the five northern provinces, which fell within Russia's unofficial sphere of influence. He had two years, no more, to form a company that would exploit the concession, in return for which the shah's government was to be paid £20,000 in cash and a further £20,000 in shares, while also receiving 'a sum equal to 16 per cent of the annual profits of any company or companies'.

Marriott could hardly contain his delight, instantly cabling news of the breakthrough back to London. On 30 May, in a euphoric state, he paid a visit to Amin, who declared that he was 'very satisfied with the concession and said he was sure it would be a good thing for Persia, and at the same time promote the friendship already existing between his country and England'. A few days later, he met with the shah, who asked 'several questions about the manner in which the operations would be commenced in starting the petroleum works'. His business in Tehran was done. He arrived back in England on 23 June, expressing his deepest gratitude to all those who had been at his side throughout.

Euphoric though he was, D'Arcy appears to have received Marriott somewhat coolly, lavishing his highest praise upon General Kitabgi and Lord Lansdowne, the foreign office minister in London who had introduced Marriott to Hardinge. But although Marriott's mission had ended in such a spectacular and costly way, the challenge of finding oil in the kingdom had barely begun. Not only would he have to headhunt an individual of exceptional calibre to spearhead operations on the ground, working in the most arduous and demanding circumstances imaginable; he would also have to guard his concessionary rights against the determined efforts of the Russians to take them away.

4

The Spies Fight Over D'Arcy

One August morning in 1901, an obscure Russian official working in Tehran received an urgent telegram from St Petersburg. As the head of the Discount and Loans Bank, he had always had to deal with a constant flow of telegrams from various creditors and lenders who needed to arrange loans or repayments to and from Russian business interests in Persia. This particular telegram, however, was of a more unusual nature.

The official's name was Eduard Konstantin Grube, and ever since his arrival in the Persian capital, seven months before, he had been undertaking work very different from the sort he was used to. This unimposing middle-aged man had been working in international banking for at least 30 years and was well accustomed to negotiating all sorts of financial deals. Now, however, his portfolio had become wider and more varied than ever before. For he had started to work on behalf of a boss in St Petersburg who had instructed him to monitor any possible threat to Russian interests in Persia and, when prompted, to take necessary steps actively to thwart them. By this time, in other words, Grube was much more than just a banker. He had also become a secret agent.

The urgent telegram that reached him that scorching summer's day came from the highest level of the Russian government, dictated as it was by the man who had not only hired him but who was by this time wielding enormous political power, and was in effect subservient only to the Tsar himself: Count Sergei Witte. Described by those who knew him as 'ambitious, emotional and determined', and sometimes as brusque, even uncouth, in his manner and ways, the 52-year-old count had been appointed finance minister in 1892. Over the preceding nine years he not only made enormous efforts to transform Russia's wretched economy, but also established a vast personal power base. Such was his personal power – and such was the strength of his sway over Tsar Nicholas – that he often not only overruled fellow ministers but actively interfered in the workings of their departments. Before long he had even built up his own network of paid informers and agents who worked within other ministries and who kept him closely informed of what his fellow members of the Russian cabinet were up to.

This network of agents extended well beyond the capital, however, and reached as far as France and Germany, where local representatives of Russia's main lending banks kept him closely informed of events on the ground. Witte ran this personal network of agents quite independently of the foreign ministry, which had traditionally always been responsible for such operations, and by 1900 there was a great deal of competition and rivalry between the two services. One of the regions where the finance minister had been so keen to establish the influence of both the Russian government and his own secret service was Persia. This was an area that he had long regarded as a vital national interest, one upon which he felt sure an enormous amount would depend in the decades ahead.

For some years, the Discount and Loans Bank had helped to spearhead this political drive. In 1891 a Tehran-based Russian trader, Iakov Solomonovich Poliakov, had helped obtain a concession from the Persian government for the establishment of the Persian Loan Company that could help subsidize lending to the shah's government. Three years later this company had evolved into the Discount and Loan Company that St Petersburg wanted to promote for the 'peaceful penetration' of the region: in practice this meant acquiring further concessions, negotiating loans and financing Russo-Persian trade and transport at the expense of any foreign competitors. By now Grube and his bank had managed to get a stranglehold on all of Russia's main financial and commercial enterprises in Persia.

Having made such determined efforts to get a grip on the kingdom, Witte's reaction to the news that D'Arcy had won the oil concession was, not surprisingly, one of overwhelming fury. Not only had the British won a major interest, but the shah and his ministers had plainly kept a great deal hidden from him knowing that, under the terms of Russia's earlier loan, they were supposed to have gained prior permission from St Petersburg. 'A concession of similar sort had been granted to the English without our minister's knowledge', he fumed, and almost immediately he wrote a letter to the shah threatening that 'as long as he is in power, the repetition of anything like that will not be forgiven by the imperial government'.[1]

There was, however, a more specific reason why the Russians were so furious. For one of the explicit terms of the D'Arcy concession, Article 6, decreed that 'the Persian Imperial Government shall not grant to any other person the right of constructing a pipeline to the southern rivers to the South Coast of Persia'. It was this prohibition of a link to the Gulf, much more than anything else, that deeply alarmed St Petersburg. Superficially at least, the Persian Gulf would hardly strike anyone as a place worth fighting over. For much of the year it was almost unbearably hot, even for the locals who were well used to such climatic extremes, while sandstorms, insects, diseases, piracy, slavery and mass corruption were all just unfortunate realities of everyday life. But none of this deterred the Russians, who in the past few years had started to take a much more active interest in the region.

Two years before, in the summer of 1899, the British had begun to notice the strength of this newly founded interest when several Russian officials had unexpectedly arrived in the coastal town of Bushire. Their ostensible purpose according to the British political representative in the town was to inspect some nearby offshore islands 'as to suitability for a coaling station', but their real aim was much more likely to have been to reconnoitre as much of the region as they could, assessing the strength of local defences and the degree of British influence.[2]

When, soon afterwards, the Russian consul at the Persian city of Isfahan, Prince Dabizha, also paid a visit to the same place, British suspicions were stronger than ever. 'You should watch his movements and the movements of other Russians in the Gulf ports', cabled a concerned British Minister in Tehran, as he tried to work out what his opposite numbers were up to, and arranged for his spies to follow the prince's every move. When the prince eventually made a move to get home, the British spymasters appear to have found an ingenious way of trying to deter him from ever returning: given a routine health check during his journey, he was told by an English doctor that Bushire was rife with plague and that he would have go into quarantine – in effect into a form of imprisonment. Yet such tactics did not deter the Russians from sending two gunboats to Bushire a few months later when, at the height of the Boer War, they may have felt that the British were at their most vulnerable.

There was one interest that, far more than any other, lay behind this newly founded Russian interest in the Gulf region: oil. By 1899 de Morgan's reports about oil prospects in Persia had been read in influential circles in St Petersburg and had raised eyebrows. Some Russian strategists were concerned that if a rival foreign power won the race to find Persian oil, then their own petroleum industry would pay a very heavy price. For if Persian oil began to saturate the regional market, then the price of a barrel would inevitably drop, hammering Russia's foreign exchange earnings and conceivably even undermining its entire economy.

From the Russian point of view, there seemed to be a much better scenario worth pursuing. In this ideal situation they would not only keep their competitors out of the region altogether but also build a pipeline across Persia that could transport Russian oil into the Gulf and feed it to new markets, including those of the vast Indian sub-continent, at a much lower price than hitherto. At present, Russian exports could only reach these markets if they were moved over vast distances, to and from the Suez Canal, and the high transport costs made their products far more expensive than those of their rivals.

At the same time the international markets were becoming ever more competitive, mainly because of the fast-growing American presence in the region. By the turn of the century, US oil production already accounted for not much less than half of the world's total and, because oil exploration in North America had barely got under way, this proportion looked set to increase considerably.[3] The leading American oil producer, Standard Oil, had already acquired a fearsome reputation for its highly aggressive tactics in the market, and its commercial agents had been actively searching for new consumers in the Persian Gulf and beyond. With such formidable adversaries at its heels, Russia knew that it simply could not afford any complacency. Western visitors to the Gulf region had already noticed the strength of competition between oil companies belonging to the two great powers, commenting that 'the cheapness of the Russian oil enables it to compete against superior American qualities'.[4] But for how long could the Russians keep their rivals at bay?

In the Russian capital, the pipeline project had become fashionable over the past decades, ever since a clever and resourceful engineer, one S.E. Palashkovskii, had first thought of the idea and, in a series of articles published in the 1880s, made detailed proposals to build such a link. A pipeline between the Caspian Sea and the Persian Gulf, he argued, would offer Russia 10 million roubles in profit in its first year of operation and eventually far more, perhaps even increasing tenfold. He continued: 'Is it not simpler, leaving Constantinople to the jealous surveillance of our European friends, to turn where the goal is both nearer and more easily attainable? In Turkey we have to deal with all of Europe, but in Persia, where we can easily reach the ocean at the Gulf of Oman, we would have to deal with England alone.'[5]

By the turn of the century, the Russian government was coming under heavier pressure than ever before to take firm action over the pipeline as American exports started to saturate the markets, driving down prices and causing panic in the local oil industry. At the beginning of 1901 the market price of Baku oil began to fall dramatically as demand waned, falling by nearly half in less than twelve months. The reason for the fall in demand was that the Baku producers could not compete with their regional rivals, whose oil could much more easily reach big markets in India and the Far East.

Not surprisingly this dramatic decline was causing serious consternation: in a memorandum addressed to the minister of agriculture and state properties, the association of Baku oil producers complained bitterly of their plight and asked for something to be done.[6] These producers were highly dependent not just on exports for their profits but on the Indian markets in particular: in 1901 the leading journal of the Russian oil industry, *Neftianoe Delo*, even claimed that 90 per cent of the kerosene used in India originated from Russia, and pointed out that India was a main transit point for the supply of a much wider region.

In St Petersburg, Witte harboured a strong sympathy for the pipeline cause and did his own calculations. If it was built in just four years, he argued, and had a maximum capacity of around one million metric tons then it might just be profitable within twenty years, having recouped the costs of construction that would of course be vast – an investment of around 80 million roubles (about £8 million). The hugely reduced transportation costs it offered would mean that, even if it was operating at only half capacity, Russian oil could be sold considerably cheaper – by around 5–10 per cent per barrel – than it would otherwise be. For the finance minister, in other words, the case for the pipeline was overwhelming, and he was now prepared to give far more attention to realizing his dream. Before long he had set up a special committee to consider building trade links with the Persian Gulf, made recommendations that new lines of communication be established between Odessa, Bushire and Basrah, and established a new consulate and bank at Bushire that would be guarded by Russian soldiers with a naval vessel stationed permanently in the Gulf.

By the summer of 1901, a detailed business case for the pipeline had been put before the Tsar. This argued that such a pipeline would give Russia a 'brilliant position', allowing her to compete with her rivals, while also having powerful and important political repercussions: 'The laying and working of the kerosene pipeline would in any case create in the Persian Gulf real Russian commercial interests which no power would have the right to ignore ... and therefore would result in the growth of our influence in Persia and on the shore of the Indian Ocean.'[7] Before long Witte had won some sympathy from the Tsar, for in August Nicholas II approved his proposal with the commendation that it was 'a question of great importance which requires serious thought'.[8] But if the D'Arcy concession prohibited any such deal, how were they going to realize their ends?

By the time Tsar Nicholas nodded his approval, Witte thought that he had the answer. The key, he argued, lay in the Persian government's perpetual state of financial crisis. Although this crisis had been temporarily alleviated by the Russian loan of January the previous year, it had only been a few months before the shah had overspent his way back into serious debt, owing at least £1 million to foreign creditors, and was now standing on the verge of bankruptcy. But the shah was still contemplating a major trip to the capitals of Western Europe, a trip he much wanted to undertake, but which was currently beyond his means.

Witte was willing to offer Tehran another huge loan, on the clear proviso that in return it must renege the terms of the D'Arcy concession that prohibited the construction of the pipeline. Russia, as the foreign minister Count Lamsdorf put it, wanted 'politically to make Persia obedient and useful: that is sufficiently strong to be a tool in our hands – economically to preserve for ourselves the major share of the Persian market for free and exclusive exploitation by Russian efforts and capital.' It was to this end that, on that August morning in 1901, Witte telegrammed Grube, his Tehran agent, detailing him with the exact terms on which the loan could be made and instructing him to get negotiations with the royal court under way. Under his plan the Persians would allow the Discount and Loans Bank, of which Grube was the local manager, to fund and operate the pipeline and it was this role that gave Grube the ostensible authority to undertake such high-level discussions.

By acting as the finance minister's local right-hand man, Grube had considerable power, more so than the individual, Argyropoulo, who was ostensibly the figurehead of the Russian government in Tehran. There was, not surprisingly, considerable rivalry between the two men, one of whom was a relative newcomer to the Persian capital, the other a long-serving diplomat of an old school of diplomacy who recognized only a traditional means of doing business. Sir Arthur Hardinge, for example, noted how:

> KM Grube is inclined to talk rather too frankly, and I think that his consciousness of the important political position which he occupies here, as the de facto equal of the Russian Minister and holder of Persia's purse strings, may have led him to exaggerate the greatness of his influence, but the views expressed by him are I venture to think worth noting in so far as they indicate, which within certain limits they probably do, the inner mind of M. de Witte.[9]

Argyropoulo, however, was in no position to resist Grube since his own boss in St Petersburg, the foreign minister Count Lamsdorf, had in the past few years become increasingly subservient to Witte. So although Argyropoulo was personally opposed to any proposals to build a pipeline to the south, feeling that such a project was simply too expensive and too impractical, he was forced to drop his objections and assist Grube as best he could, even supplying him with information before reporting it to his own superiors in the foreign ministry.

At the beginning of September, Grube approached his contacts in the royal court and offered a loan of 10 million roubles at a low rate of interest. But in return he wanted a new commercial treaty between the two countries, an immediate end to British influence in the Tehran exchequer and, above all, the scrapping of Article 6. He also demanded that the negotiations be kept secret, knowing that the British would otherwise waste no time in trying to interfere. The prime minister, Amin al-Sultan, was quick to agree, knowing that he owed the Russians a lot of goodwill after granting the D'Arcy concession in such an underhand way and when, on 5 October, Arthur Hardinge asked him to confirm rumours that a new loan was being discussed, he was told quite simply that no such negotiations were taking place.

But as word of the Russian loan leaked out, it became increasingly clear that the D'Arcy concession was under a twofold threat. On the one hand, it was possible, although unlikely, that under Russian pressure Amin and the shah may have wanted not just to annul Article 6 but perhaps even to review the entire concession, offering it to the Russians in return for the payment of the same fee that D'Arcy had offered. The more immediate threat, however, was that if

Article 6 was scrapped, then St Petersburg would have a perfect excuse to deploy considerable numbers of its own soldiers and personnel in the key areas where drillers were at work: pumping stations, repair depots and other installations running along the pipeline would, after all, all need to be guarded. The Russians could, as Hardinge wrote on 29 January 1902, cover 'Southern Persia with surveyors, engineers and protecting detachments of Cossacks, and preparing a veiled military occupation'. They therefore had the means constantly to harass drillers and, if he did succeed in striking oil, to stymie the resources necessary to transport it to the outside world. It was even possible for the Russian force to attack and capture any oilfield, desperate not to let such resources fall into the hands of its great international rival.

This was the main reason why British officials objected to the construction of a Russian pipeline to the Gulf. Some did not object in principle to its construction: Sir Henry Drummond Wolff, for example, felt that 'the object of Russia seemed to be that of access to the Persian Gulf. I considered that object to be legitimate and praiseworthy, if carried out in a peaceable manner.'[10] But he and other diplomats all knew that such a project would allow the Russians to dominate whole regions of the kingdom that had hitherto been outside their traditional zones of influence and this, of course, was widely viewed as a clear threat to the security of British India: 'a Russian port in the Persian Gulf', as Lord Curzon once argued, would be 'a deliberate insult to Great Britain, a wanton rupture of the status quo and an intentional provocation to war'.

To thwart the Russians, the British foreign office and its intelligence service got to work. In St Petersburg, the ambassador, Sir Charles Scott, approached Count Lamsdorf and urged him to try to obstruct Witte's moves: any attempt to trespass into southern Persia, argued Scott, would be a serious escalation of tension in the region and could not fail to have damaging consequences. Meanwhile, back in Persia, the vice-consul of the British legation, a Mr Grahame, was giving serious thought to the same issue. Grahame knew that, somewhere in the hearts and minds of the shah and his prime minister was a weak spot. His search to find it was perhaps spurred by a conversation he had with a former chief of police, Mokhtar al-Saltaneh, who urged him to take decisive action against the prospect of a Russian loan: 'you should put heart into the shah, for he has none', urged Mokhtar. 'Throw a stone. Wake him up: he is asleep. Now is the time … make direct representations to him that a fresh loan from Russia means binding Persia hand and foot – the entire sacrifice of his own independence.'[11]

Clever, ingenious and well connected, the chief local representative of Britain's Secret Intelligence Service was convinced that he had found a subtle and ingenious way of making Witte capitulate. He was well aware that, back in 1892, a British businessman had been forced to renounce a hard-earned foreign concession to explore for tobacco in the kingdom because the deal displeased the mullahs, who were quick to see the incursion of outsiders as a threat to Islam. Since then the political power of the clerics had grown even more, and this had become abundantly clear when a cholera epidemic struck Kermanshah, forcing the central government to quarantine the city. Then, in blatant defiance of the ban, a leading cleric – a *mujtahid* – by the name of Aqa Fazal Mamaqani, had led a column of 800 pilgrims from Kermanshah to Tehran and Masshed, deliberately spreading the disease. Intimidated by the power of the clerics, the government had not lifted a finger to stop him and his followers from contaminating the rest of the kingdom.

How better to stir up trouble for the Russians, reasoned Grahame, than to get the clerics into the streets in protest at the loan? On 5 February he held a long meeting with one of the kingdom's leading clerics, Sayyad Abdullah Behbehani, presenting him with several gifts, notably an expensive silver clock, as a sign of goodwill. Eventually the British vice-consul steered the conversation onto the single issue that really mattered to him – the Russian loan – and asked the sayyad for his views. The cleric certainly disapproved of it but added that he, and his fellow *mujtahid*, would be unwilling to voice their disapproval since this would cause them unnecessary trouble and inconvenience. Unless, of course, they were amply rewarded for their trouble. A figure of around 2,000 tomans, added the cleric just as Grahame was about to leave the room, would probably do the trick.

On his return to Tehran Grahame immediately informed Hardinge of Behbehani's message, and soon the British Minister had informed Lord Lansdowne in London, writing a message that ran:

> Your Lordship will observe that the sayyad, after deploring the venality of his reverent brethren, suggested in a soliloquy, or 'aside', that the sum of 400 pounds, if placed in his own hands might enable him to bring them into line. I told Mr. Grahame that it was out of the question for me to give so large an amount out of secret service funds, with no security as to its proper employment, but that he might take an early opportunity of leaving 50 pounds (in Russian rouble notes) with the sayyad, hinting delicately that more might be forthcoming should any practical result, in the form of a clerical protest against the loan, appear.[12]

But being so much less than the cleric had originally suggested, would the British donation now do as they hoped? When, soon afterwards, the sayyad was invited to the royal palace to interpret a powerful dream that the shah had experienced soon before, the cleric had a chance to voice his disapproval of the Russian loan. He listened patiently as Shah Mozaffar told him what he had seen in this dream:

> I saw you appear before me clad in the Ihram ... and bearing on your back a heavy bag.[13] I was angry and rebuked you for entering my presence in such scanty attire, when suddenly

the sack fell from your shoulders and from its mouth flowed gold and silver. Immediately there was a dazzling light and I saw in the heavens a moon of extraordinary brightness. I awoke greatly agitated and now call on you to explain this vision.

The cleric's interpretation of the dream was music to British ears:

Your Majesty saw me in the primitive Moslem garb throw a sack at your feet whence flowed gold and silver. This means that my ancestor the Prophet bids you to make no fresh loans from unbelievers, but to trust for the restoration of your finances to your subjects and fellow servants of the faith. And the brilliant moon which Your Majesty beheld is His Highness the Atabeg-i-Azam [the prime minister], who draws his light from yourself as his sun.[14]

At the same time that Grahame was working so hard against the Russians, British officials in Tehran were also busily drawing up details of a new loan agreement that would woo the shah and make him ditch the Russian offer. The prime minister tipped off Argyropoulo, showing him the British letter, and within hours Grube had transmitted its text to Witte in St Petersburg. The finance minister replied that the British offer 'was a loan by a foreign government and that he would not authorize the Persian government to accept it', but his protests may have been unnecessary: soon afterwards Grube cabled him again and reported that Amin was urging the shah to reject the offer because, under its terms, the British wanted control over the Persian customs as security if the borrowers defaulted.

News of the British move spurred Witte to push even harder for the pipeline, making his loan conditional upon the revision of the D'Arcy concession. As Argyropoulo admitted, the finance minister 'absolutely refused to afford Persia any financial assistance unless the pipeline asked for to the Persian Gulf was conceded, and that Count Lamsdorf was powerless to alter this decision'.[15] But by now the issue was starting to reach crisis point: the Persian government was going to have to decide whether it was going to accept the Russian loan and on what terms it would do so.

Seeing how strong the threat to his concession was, D'Arcy stepped in, and on 31 January offered the shah a new loan of £100,000 at a special rate of interest. In return, however, he would want some new exploration rights in the vicinity of Ahwaz, in the district of Khuzestan. With such sums dangled before them, he reasoned, the shah and grand vizier would be in a position either to stand up to Russia, and perhaps refuse the loan altogether, or else be in a much stronger bargaining situation that would allow them to insist on keeping Article 6 intact. But Witte and Grube were also moving fast. On 4 February Grube cabled St Petersburg, stating that Amin had agreed to the concession, and a week later the shah himself signalled his agreement, provided that the Russians took sole responsibility for any violation of the D'Arcy concession and for the protest of the British government that would inevitably ensue. Then, on 17 February, Witte prepared the final draft of the loan agreement, putting his signature on the papers before forwarding them to Tehran for the shah to countersign.

Hearing just how close to completion the agreement now was, D'Arcy doubled his offer to £200,000 and then increased it again to £300,000. News of D'Arcy's move caused consternation in Tehran, prompting Grube to send an urgent cable back to Witte saying that 'the English concessionaire of the southern pipeline ... has paid up to 50,000 tumans' to win favour, and urging the finance minister 'to promise similar reward'. Witte quickly cabled back agreeing to Grube's request, stating simply that 'you can promise 50,000 tumans'.

But the following day, the Russian nerve appeared suddenly to snap. In Tehran Grube told Amin that St Petersburg would issue the loan without any strings attached: the repudiation of Article 6 was no longer part of the deal. In the Russian capital, Count Lamsdorf had pressed Witte to abandon the pipeline deal, fearing that it could force Tehran even closer into British hands and thereby jeopardize Russia's grip over Persia: it was vital, he argued, 'to ease some of the conditions of the loan and even exchange the ... concession for some other conditions'.

A number of different things, it turned out, had broken Russian resolve. Above all, news of D'Arcy £300,000 offer had staggered officials in St Petersburg, creating serious alarm that the British financier could call on a bottomless pit of money that could swallow up much of Persia at Russian expense: as Hardinge wrote, 'M. de Witte, fearing that the Persian Government might borrow from English sources, and this escape from this grasp, withdrew the demand for the pipeline to the Persian Gulf.'[16]

Sir Charles Scott had also made clear the strength of British objections, raising the possibility of a heavy diplomatic, conceivably military, clash between St Petersburg and London. The seriousness of the issue had become clear when Hardinge had also told Amin that the British government would view the pipeline condition as a clear breach of the D'Arcy concession: only a month or so before, D'Arcy had obtained a legal opinion from a top British barrister that 'the construction by Russia of the suggested pipeline from Baku to the Persian Gulf would, unless consented to by Mr D'Arcy, be an unlawful interference with the exclusive right conferred on him by the Concession'.[17]

The efforts of Witte and Grube to thwart the D'Arcy concession and build the pipeline to the Gulf marked the high tide of Russia's influence in Persia. For the moment at least, her ambitions there began to wane, all the more so when, the following year, Witte was dismissed as finance minister and Russia became embroiled in disputes in the Far East that were soon to lead to war with, and a humiliating defeat by, Japan. It was now the growing power of Germany that presented a serious threat to Great Britain.

5

The Great Explorer

At the same time that Grube and Witte had been trying so hard to obtain their pipeline agreement and overrule the D'Arcy concession, a middle-aged Englishman was slipping quietly into Tehran to begin his search to find Persian oil.

Other than his unusually dark black moustache, there was nothing about George Bernard Reynolds that would have attracted particular attention amongst the local people who watched him ride on horseback through the capital's streets on that afternoon of 10 September 1901. Of modest stature and build, and always dressed soberly, perhaps even slightly shabbily, the 48-year-old would probably have seemed somewhat less interesting than any of the other Westerners who at this time trickled to and from the Persian capital. Nor would everyone who spoke with the new arrival have been particularly charmed by him. His manner could often be brusque, occasionally slightly coarse, and those who worked with him had accused him of rudeness, or of being 'sarcastic and bitter'. He was no natural diplomat, preferring to speak his mind with others even though, like many insensitive people, he had a thin skin himself. He was quite often unable to control his ferocious temper, and not all of those who had worked at his side had always felt much loyalty towards him.

But this gruff and modest exterior disguised a remarkable individual. His acquaintances and friends knew that Reynolds had an enormous physical and psychological resilience that could allow him to live and work in places that most mortals would find insufferable. He picked up local languages quickly and was a confident horseman, a highly capable geologist and, above all, an excellent mining engineer. He pursued his goals with a single-minded determination, some would say obsession, and always led by example, refusing to ask others to perform tasks that he would not do himself. He had, in other words, all the makings of a great oil explorer. These skills had been honed in the very demanding environments where Reynolds had previously worked. After graduating from the Royal Indian Engineering College, he had served in the Indian Public Works Department and then gone on to work in the oilfields of Sumatra. This had been no easy posting: hot and humid, its climate was notoriously demanding even upon those who were well accustomed to it.

Reynolds had made a name for himself in Sumatra, and D'Arcy heard of this reputation with great interest. Even before clinching the Persian concession he had made enquiries about a suitable engineer who could lead the hunt for oil, asking his extensive network of contacts in London to help him find the best person. There were only a handful of individuals who had sufficient experience, and the right personal qualities, to do so, and by chance the leading contender for the job was in London and looking for work. Offered an annual salary of £1,500 to undertake the project, Reynolds readily accepted.

From his track record in Sumatra and elsewhere, D'Arcy must also have known about the faults of this abrasive, short-tempered, conceited and opinionated man. He would have known that Reynolds was apt to be particularly short with his seniors, who worked from the comfort of their offices and who, he felt, knew nothing of the extreme hardships he was obliged to endure: 'he kept his temper and the confidence of his staff but not always that of his directors at home, who were most reluctant to come upon the scene in person', as one visitor to his camp site wrote. 'His correspondence with his principals, and even with consular authorities, was marred by a strain of facetious acerbity unworthy of him'. The same visitor added that 'in the bitterness of his soul he said many hard things of the faint-hearted and peevish men at home who were so ready to abandon an enterprise which might mean so much to Britain and to Persia'.[1]

But Reynolds did have a human side too. He wrote regularly to his wife back in Britain, kept a pet dog that stayed faithfully at his side and smoked a pipe. He freely lent his men books, would often pay for their drinks and always jumped at a chance to play them at bowls, one of his favourite games. When he wanted to he could show charm that could leave a very favourable impression on those who met him: his 'constant courtesy and kindness will always make me his debtor', as one traveller, Edward Cunningham Craig, who visited him on site in Persia, wrote in his diary.

As soon as he arrived in Tehran, Reynolds followed D'Arcy's instructions by meeting up with Kitabgi, who was tasked with briefing him on Persia and its ways with the same thoroughness with which he had briefed Marriott six months earlier. 'Now you begin to penetrate into the grammar of Persian affairs', Kitabgi asked the new visitor in his heavily accented English, 'tell me if it is possible to manage a like enterprise in Persia with the experience acquired in London?' Reynolds returned his hospitality and expertise, initially making a 'favourable impression' on his host, and cabling D'Arcy, waiting back in London for news, that 'I have been able to converse with him and learn far more of the human methods in vogue in Persia than I could possibly have done had I hurried away'.[2]

On 21 September, after spending ten days with Kitabgi, Reynolds was ready to make his move. His first destination would not be Shushtar, where Kitabgi had wanted him to go, but to the village of Zuhab, near Qasr-i Chirin. Getting there would mean undertaking a long journey by horse and mule, first to Kermanshah and then heading on into a mountain wilderness. Reynolds had good reasons for wanting to begin his exploration work in this particular region. Not only was it the place where Jacques de Morgan had found such promising signs of oil, but it was also a locality that another geologist had looked at closely and commented on favourably. For as soon as he had decided to pursue a Persian oil concession, D'Arcy had commissioned his own independent survey of the region, hiring H.T. Burls, a leading expert of the day, to take a close look. Burls had arrived back in London in July, after a three-month stay in Persia, and announced his positive findings. Claiming that 'the territory as a whole is one of rich promise', Burls had mentioned that some regions, notably Qasr-i Chirin, Qaleh Darabi near Ahwaz, Shushtar and Masjid-i Suleiman, all had particular potential.

D'Arcy had given Reynolds permission to locate at least six sites that seemed worthy of exploration, although he had at any one time only enough money to fund drilling operations at one place. Before long the great explorer had visited several of them and made some initial surveys. At Shushtar, Reynolds met with the local tribesmen and visited some of the seepages where Kitabgi, back in Tehran, had urged him to start his drilling work. Not long afterwards he eventually reached Masjid-i Suleiman, making his way past feuding tribesmen whose bitter clashes had made some routes impassable. 'Oil found in Gypsiferous rocks. The rocks here are saturated with oil as at Mandali', he wrote to his assistant David Jenkin on 31 March 1904. 'The property is a very valuable one.'

At each of the different places he visited, Reynolds made careful assessments not just of the rocks and geological structures lying beneath, but also of a wide variety of more practical considerations. Many of the places that seemed to boast the most promising deposits, he felt, were of no real value unless his machinery and equipment could readily be moved there, and any extracted oil then transported away. Drawing up a detailed map of each site, complete with the various routes along which everything could be moved and depots established, was therefore one of the most basic tasks he had to complete.

Reynolds had years of experience behind him, and when it came to locating the best drilling site he had good reason to have a lot of confidence in his own judgement. Long before anyone else, for example, he noticed a place that seemed to be superbly sited for a refinery if oil was ever discovered in the quantities he hoped for. As he wrote to an associate back in London, a place called Abadan, which was a long and narrow island of mud flats and palm groves on the Shatt al-Arab, the delta of the Tigris and Euphrates, was just right for the task, since the water on the coastal side of the island was considerably cooler than elsewhere, and this difference of temperature could only benefit the condensers during the refining process.

But finding the most promising drilling site was not the most pressing problem that confronted the oil explorer. Right from the moment of his arrival at Qasr in late October, it was obvious to Reynolds that this operation would be arduous in

the extreme, even by the highly demanding standards he was used to. On arrival
he had a hostile reception from local tribesmen, who were quick to suspect him
of being an agent of the shah's regime and an enemy of their own independence:
'the authority of the shah was held in low esteem by our host', as the Englishman
wrote to D'Arcy on 22 March 1902. But everything depended on how cooperative
these tribes were going to be, not just because they controlled the routes to
and from the proposed drilling site, and could easily render any operations
impossible, but also because, more specifically, they claimed ownership of the
area and soon demanded a special fee for letting Reynolds get to work. As he put
it, the tribal chiefs had absolutely 'no idea of the mineral rights of the owner of
the ground being nil' but instead wanted payment 'over and above that laid down
in the Concession'.

There were other reasons why even starting any drilling operations, let alone
striking oil, looked like a very daunting prospect indeed. In his initial survey,
Burls had emphasized that Qasr was such a remote spot that moving the heavy
equipment needed for such an operation would be a very difficult task. Not
only that, but Burls also noticed the lack of other raw materials which would be
essential for the task, notably a supply of water, timber and fuel for the steam
engines that powered the drills and rammed them deep into the ground. It was
just such difficulties that had long deterred so many people from investing in
Persia. One H.W. Maclean, who had been manager of the Persian Royal Mint and
economic adviser to the British government on regional affairs, had never been at
all optimistic over trading prospects and in a report on the shah's administration
he specifically referred to the large number of businesses that had failed in recent
years. 'The great cost of installing machinery', he warned, 'on account of the heavy
freight on inland transport, the cost of fuel, the inefficiency of labour which,
although cheap, is unskilled and without energy, have been the chief causes of
our lack of success.'[3]

Reynolds, however, decided to take up the challenge and press boldly
ahead. Before leaving Tehran he had cabled D'Arcy to make arrangements for
moving the heavy equipment needed to start work, and had now heard back.
Everything required, he was informed, was being shipped on *The Afrikander* to
the Mesopotamian port of Basrah, from where it would be moved northwards
first to Baghdad and then eastwards over the border into Persia. This last leg of
the journey promised to be the most difficult as the cargo, valued at £1,250, was
moved by horse, mule and wagon over the mountains to the proposed drilling
site. At the best of times, this long, arduous journey would have been a daunting
challenge even for the most determined; this was extremely heavy equipment,
weighing hundreds of tons, that had to be pulled by a procession of horses, mules,
carts and people. Things would be made tougher still, however, because seasonal
rains were by now just starting to flood the tracks, making them too muddy to

move over. Reynolds knew that such a trek would inevitably take months, and sure enough it was not until the following summer that all the cargo finally reached the drilling site.

Reynolds arrived in Baghdad in mid-November, as planned, to organize the cargo's passage first past the Turkish officials, who could be notoriously obstinate, and then over the border. Reynolds' sense of frustration could only have boiled over when, on his arrival at Qasr, it quickly emerged that some important parts of the drilling machinery were either broken or missing. In some cases he was able to improvise, using spare pieces of metal, or even wood or rocks, to do so. This, however, was not always possible and Reynolds was forced to cable back to London to arrange redelivery. But as the wait for spare parts continued, and weeks became months, D'Arcy was by now becoming extremely concerned. His costs were mounting steadily, and on 15 April 1902 he cabled his oil hunter with a message that simply ran 'when probably commence drilling – delay serious – pray expedite'. By this time Reynolds had taken some steps forward: he had, for example, succeeded in winning some trust from Aziz Khan and Muhammed Karim Khan, the two main tribal leaders in the surrounding area, but could do no more than reply that it was 'not possible to estimate' when operations would get under way. He could only add that 'no exertion on my part shall be wanting'.

As he waited for the shipments to reach him, Reynolds busied himself learning the rudiments of the Persian language and recruiting the labour force that would soon be put to work, or so he hoped. To undertake some of the more menial tasks – supplying the food, water, fuel and transport facilities that would keep the operation running – he could recruit local villagers or those who had made their way from much farther afield, sometimes travelling very long distances to get there. The more specialized drilling work, however, had to be done only by those who had some experience with such tasks, and preferably by those who were also cheaper to hire than their West European counterparts. By the time drilling operations finally got under way, in November 1902, Reynolds' team was truly cosmopolitan. Two of his drillers, McNaughton and Buchanan, were Canadians while most of the others, and a number of his machine operators, were Poles. The doctor came from India, the surveyor from Turkey, while his two main assistants were British. The others at the camp – bodyguards, cooks and cleaners – were nearly all locals.

For any one individual to manage an operation like this on their own would of course have been out of the question. Reynolds needed a deputy at his side, one who could allow him to do what he did best: supervise the drilling through the highly complex rock strata that lay beneath while another supported him and, when he was away from site, stand in for him. He found just the man in an American engineer, C.B. Rosenplaenter, who joined the team in its early months. He, like Reynolds, was highly experienced at such exploration operations, having worked extensively on the oilfields of Assam and Baku, and was considered by those who knew him to be a clever engineer and a good leader of people: 'he has worked pleasantly with Eastern people', ran one commendation, 'and has had Persians under his control'.

Before he even arrived, Rosenplaenter was known to be unusually creative, ingenious and resourceful in a way that would quickly prove indispensable at a location as remote as the Qasr site, which was now known as Chiah Surkh. Even in the most congenial circumstances drilling equipment easily suffered wear and tear as drill pieces broke or were worn out, steel cables were pulled apart, and metal casing cracked or corroded. But here, in such a remote location, spare parts would take months to reach them and even then those that did arrive were either too damaged to use, or sometimes even bore no resemblance to what the oil hunters had requested. The difficult conditions also caused no end of trouble, particularly when the seasonal winter rains washed away the sides of the well and caused them to cave in. Rosenplaenter's willingness to use spare pieces of timber and metal to replace damaged machinery, and his skill at fishing out of the well any equipment that had fallen in, were particularly valuable assets to Reynolds' operation, but could not make up for basic supply problems.

Reynolds and Rosenplaenter worked together to solve a great many engineering problems and difficulties, and those who watched them at work were quickly impressed by the knowledge they soon built up of the land, as well as their skills in searching for oil: so E.H. Cunningham Craig also wrote that without Reynolds' 'guidance and knowledge of the country I should have found it quite impossible to have worked out the many geological problems presented in so short a time'. The two men were also confronted by all manner of personal issues amongst their workers. Some members of the workforce suffered from exhaustion, others from loneliness or homesickness. There were sometimes strong personal disagreements or antagonisms between individuals over all manner of things, while others simply became disillusioned by the hard and unremitting search for oil. To inspire a team to persevere in such difficult circumstances would, of course, have been a daunting challenge even for operators as experienced and determined as Reynolds and Rosenplaenter.

Given the sheer desolation and bleakness of their surroundings, it would have been surprising if some of the men had not started to feel intensely isolated and depressed. Set high on a tiny plateau at Chiah Surkh in the Kurdish mountains, the setting for Reynolds' operation may have had a certain grandeur but little more. A good description of the area was given by one Samuel Benjamin, who in 1882 had been appointed by President Arthur as the head of the US legation to Persia, and who had subsequently travelled around the country extensively.[4] Some areas of the region close to where Reynolds later worked, he noted, were very productive and quite capable of producing excellent crops. But he emphasized that much of it was also bleak and uninspiring, and it was all too easy to move suddenly from a green oasis into arid wasteland. 'Enormous tracts of this country are mere deserts', he wrote, 'often covered with sand, gravel and salt, unprofitable for cultivation, almost entirely destitute of water.[5] It was in these parts that Benjamin had particularly noted a silence and isolation that was overpowering, almost eerie, and made a particular impression on a visitor: 'it is with a sense of repose, a silent and solemn satisfaction, that he looks over the vast endless spaces', he wrote. 'The soul expands with the sense of space, and seems already in this life to gain an intuition of the infinite spaces in which it shall find scope for a fuller expression of its power in another existence.'[6]

Much of this region would have been wholly uninhabited. The only settlements were the villages on the plains below. Most of these, Benjamin wrote, 'were surrounded by square lofty walls, with battlements and corner towers. At first one imagines every village to be a fortress, and is surprised that such fortifications should be so numerous and planted in the midst of a flat plain – in the evenings flocks and herds gathered there.' Within the confines of these walls lay a collection of huts, usually made of mud, where local people lived and worked on the region's main industries – weaving, embroidery and the cultivation of wheat, rice and opium.

In such a remote setting, the oil hunters would of course have had very limited contact with the outside world. To send a message to London Reynolds had to dispatch a courier to Kermanshah, a journey that took several days by horseback, where a telegram could be sent. Occasionally, however, Western travellers managed to reach Chiah Surkh and visit the exploration team, who would doubtless have been overjoyed to see them. In February 1903, for example, an official in the Indian Civil Service, Henry Dobbs, passed by and described what he found at the drilling site. Reynolds, wrote Dobbs, was full of 'generosity and kindliness' and had a very good rapport with local tribesmen and with his fellow workers.

Reynolds had of course never expected his living conditions to be easy, even for a man of his proven resilience, and right from the start it was obvious that his worst fears were going to be realized. The drinking water was filthy and always had to be carefully boiled, and even then it could quickly become unfit for drinking: 'best described as water with dung in suspension', Reynolds once said. Even in midwinter their camp was alive with insects of every description, although of course things became much worse in the summer: on one occasions a vast black cloud descended on the drilling site, and within a short time swarms of grasshoppers had proceeded to eat their way through everything green and to colonize the nearby river, making its water stink abominably. Their rotting bodies later lay everywhere, forcing the men to tread on a squelching carpet of dead insects and regularly skim their floating carcasses out of the water tanks.

Smallpox and cholera were also endemic, and were sometimes known to have wiped out other labour forces in the region.

There were innumerable other problems. The boiler in the steam engine was often corroded by sulphurous water and then packed up; letters failed to arrive when the courier or his horse or mule collapsed and died en route, and the drillers were sometimes hurt or injured by their work: at one point Rosenplaenter developed a large boil on his ankle which he said 'interfered considerably with his locomotion'. The unvaried diet must also have been trying. To keep his team properly fed, Reynolds arranged for food to be ferried regularly to them from the markets of Qasr by horse or mule. But although food was only rarely in short supply, the diet was typically limited and repetitive, and many had the same meals – usually rice with a few pieces of lamb or else 'only cold boiled eggs and dry bread' – every day for months on end. Even Reynolds had to complain about their very basic eating conditions, and the rawness of the food: 'the materials afforded for food here are rather trying for any digestion', he wrote on one occasion, 'so that teeth natural or false, are essential if a man is trying to retain his health'. News that the workforce were living on such meagre resources and in such primitive facilities did not always go down well in London, where one investor in the project commented somewhat sternly that if the labourers were 'kept in good condition you will be able to get the maximum of work out of them' and urged Reynolds to improve the state they were in.[7]

The greatest challenge, however, was the extreme climate. In mid-summer temperatures would often easily soar well above 100 F almost as soon as the day started, and when some of the drillers had already been affected by heatstroke by 7 o'clock in the morning, Reynolds felt moved to comment that 'what the thermometer would read during the noon hours we cannot even guess'. In the simple stone structures that were built to house the workforce, temperatures could sometimes quite easily reach 120 F, and in several letters home Reynolds described the effect such conditions were having on his men and their work: 'as the nights are hot the men get very little rest and still sleep less', he wrote in one such note, while a week later he added that the pace of work had slackened considerably because of 'the infernal heat'. Nor were conditions much better in winter, for the oil hunters had to contend not merely with piercing cold that frequently froze the water in their tents, but also with heavy rains that were capable of sweeping away roads, earthworks and buildings, most of which were constructed out of mud: 'the water came down in torrents', recorded Reynolds on one occasion, as some of the huts and cabins around him collapsed and their occupants re-housed elsewhere.[8]

To get the best out of his men and inspire them in such demanding cir-cumstances, Reynolds also knew that undertaking work like this would require considerable skills with people. Above all he would have to know how to demand the highest standards from his workforce, perhaps just 'by the exercise of patience and a little tact and firmness', while also showing flexibility as and when the need arose. This was a difficult balance to get right. On the one hand he did not like anyone to complain unless they had extremely good reason to do so: 'the men have very little to growl at', he once recorded, 'and if they would look after themselves a little and their own interests instead of sitting down and growling they would do better'. When one of the men complained too much, Reynolds merely commented that 'he ought to have brought his mother out'.

He also demanded high levels of self-restraint, emphasizing that he could not tolerate any lapses of personal conduct. It was particularly important, he argued, that 'our men behave themselves as reasonable beings not as drunken beasts', that 'the women of the country must not be touched by our men' and that 'there must be no striking' of any local people 'if they do wrong'. Anyone who breached such standards risked an immediate sacking, although only very rarely did Reynolds have to do this. His rules on the consumption of liquor, for example, appear rarely to have been broken.

Reynolds' tough, almost ruthless, line may have been understandable, for not all his personnel were cut out for such demanding work. There was one occasion, in 1905, when Reynolds sacked a Canadian driller, C.H. Locke, for striking a Persian while drunk, while Rosenplaenter commented of some of the Canadians that 'a more helpless crew I seldom saw' and pointed out how one of them complained that he could not eat gooseberry jam, while another was 'too casual to readily make a substitute out of wheat or rice, or any amount of both being available' when the camp ran out of some provisions. Rosenplaenter felt that his own fellow nationals would make even worse employees than these, and prayed that he would not have to employ any. 'The average American driller is quite unfit to be sent to a country like this', he wrote, 'as he will not suit himself to new circumstances and conditions.'

But at the same time Reynolds was flexible and sensitive when the need arose. Whilst working in Burmah, he had always had to respect the religious sensibilities of his Muslim and Hindu workers and now, when he recruited several Poles into his drilling team, knew that all of them would probably be devout Roman Catholics. When he discovered that they often downed tools on the grounds that the day was devoted to the worship of a particular saint, Reynolds took immediate action, cabling London to request a Roman Catholic calendar that would allow him to plan for these special days and work around them. Similar tact was needed with the native workers and the camp's various Persian visitors, all of whom were Muslims: knowing their strong sensibilities about food, Rosenplaenter set up 'a separate Mohamedan Kitchen for such native chiefs and Prominent Persians'.

It was not just to their workforce that Reynolds and Rosenplaenter needed to show tact and diplomacy. All around them, living in the surrounding mountains and watching their every move, were the same wild, unpredictable tribes that Jacques de Morgan had encountered more than a decade earlier, and from whose wrath he had on occasion only narrowly escaped. The threat these tribes posed also meant that the early oil explorers needed an abundance of one other quality: raw courage.

During a brief visit to Chiah Surkh in January 1904, the British Minister in Persia, Sir Arthur Hardinge, quickly noticed the precariousness of their situation. 'One of the greatest difficulties attendant on Mr D'Arcy's enterprise lies in the lawless character of the region in which he has to work ... the real Rulers of the country are the tribal chiefs, great and small, who are constantly engaged in petty feuds and warfare with one another.' He added that his two fellow nationals had managed 'by conduct at once straightforward and tactful to remain on good terms with the turbulent and constantly warring native elements'. So far, he continued, 'no single untoward incident of any importance has troubled their relations with them'.

For a time, Reynolds and Rosenplaenter were cautiously optimistic about maintaining good relations with the tribesmen. Local tribal and religious leaders were sometimes invited to the drilling site, where they were offered, if not luxury and comfort, then various other inducements to goodwill: 'they seemed very keen on receiving a substantial present from us, especially in the shape of some shares of our Company', wrote Reynolds. But both men knew how easily things could change: 'the Mullahs in the North are exciting the population as much as they can against the foreigner', wrote Rosenplaenter to Jenkin on 25 October 1902, as political tension in the kingdom started to mount. 'The real fight is now between the Shah and the Mullahs for the control of the public affairs.' In time, heavy internecine feuding between different tribes badly interrupted the regular flow of food and supplies to the camp and at one ominous moment fighting threatened to force the explorers to abandon their camp altogether.

Also ominous, however, was the fact that neither men could trust the individual, Shaikh ul-Mulk, who had been assigned to work alongside them as an intermediary with the tribes. Shaikh was an associate of General Kitabgi, who had sent him to accompany Reynolds in order to iron out 'the number of small difficulties inevitable in all beginnings', but it was not long before it became clear that, like his master in Tehran, he was full of dangerous intrigue. Dobbs, for example, had noted that Shaikh 'tried to get all the payments of gift, salaries etc. into his own hands with the obvious desire of enriching his friends and acquaintances' and was making false allegations about Reynolds who he claimed 'was exciting hostility in the neighbourhood by not employing Persians exclusively and by not dispensing money with sufficient liberality'. He went on to note the dangers these machinations could so easily cause, pointing out that 'apart from the question of the existence of oil, the undertaking will certainly fail, if the Concessionaires at home refuse to trust the man on the spot and undermine his authority by listening to the tittle-tattle of interested persons like the Shaikh ul-Mulk'.

At the beginning of April, after nearly eighteen months in Persia, Reynolds was at last able to take some leave and return to London. By the time he left, the well at Chiah Surkh had been drilled down to a depth of just over 900 feet, and his Turkish surveyor had been drawing up plans to build an overland pipeline to the coast in the event that oil was struck. Yet, although he and his team had worked desperately hard over the past five months, they still seemed no closer to finding what they wanted, and by the time he arrived back in Britain, D'Arcy's concerns were starting to mount considerably. Earlier he had cabled Reynolds that: 'Our time is getting short, and I cannot get one day's extension from the Shah. So this means that either you must find oil in quantity soon enough to enable me to form and float a subsidiary company before May next, or I must either pay the Shah the amount due under the concession out of my own pocket or abandon the whole thing.'[9]

D'Arcy and Reynolds were, in other words, in a race against time to discover Persian oil before the money ran out. But the odds were stacked against the oil hunters, not least because conditions on the ground were steadily becoming ever more dangerous.

6

The Oil Hunters Take On the Tribes

From his spectacular vantage point set high in the mountains of south-west Persia, George Reynolds looked down into the valley far beneath and searched for any signs of movement. For two whole days he had been waiting for his key contact to arrive but now, after carefully scanning the horizon, he would have to resign himself to waiting even longer.

It was 15 October 1905, and Reynolds was still recovering from the rigours of a three-week trek into what was undoubtedly one of the most remote areas of Persia. This was true tribal territory, a vast stretch of mainly mountainous land that sprawled between the city of Isfahan in central Persia and, in the west, Shushtar and Masjid-i Suleiman, the small settlements where he hoped soon to start drilling for oil after losing hope elsewhere. Getting to the heartland of the tribal belt at Shalamzar had been no easy task, for he had set out from the coastal town of Ahwaz, far to the west, on 26 September, and the subsequent journey had been physically very demanding.

This was the land of the Bakhtiaris – 'the people of the west' – and it was their tribal leaders, the khans, that Reynolds had now come to visit. They alone could grant him permission to explore for oil in these wild parts, and they alone could protect the explorers from the multitude of robbers, bandits and rapacious villagers ready to pounce. The future of the concession, in other words, now rested in Bakhtiari hands.

As he travelled through the region, Reynolds saw why this was an area over which the central Persian government had never succeeded in stamping its authority, and why the tribes here had always enjoyed so much autonomy. Nearly all the tribesmen he had passed were armed, their rifles slung round their shoulders, and most were highly expert in the arts of mountain warfare. Given sufficient determination, a mere handful of these warriors could have rendered many of the mountain roads completely impassable, inflicting intolerable casualties on any attacking force that was brave or foolhardy enough to advance against them.

Only a handful of Western travellers had ever crossed this remote region before, and more than a few of those had met a grisly end. A century earlier, two British soldiers, Captain Grant and Lieutenant Fotheringham, had been butchered in cold blood by tribesmen who had promised them their hospitality.

The two men and their Persian companions were 'seized and being bound together were, after the most insulting and barbarous usage, shot one by one, by the Khan's own hand, in unsparing, unrelenting and unprovoked cruelty'.[1] But amongst those who had safely returned, a fair few, notably Major Henry Rawlinson, Henry Layard and Baron Clement de Bode, had all written about their experiences. From these writings Reynolds had built up an idea of what to expect on his arrival. De Bode, for example, who travelled there in the early 1840s, had described the people's appearance:

> They look rather fierce, owing probably to the mode of life they lead; the features of their face are cast in a rough mould; but although coarse, they are in general regular. Their black eyes look wild and expressive. The complexion of their face, as well as the other parts of the body, which happen to be exposed to the sun, is exceedingly dark, with some nearly of a mahogany colour. The two black tufts of hair behind their ears give them if possible, a still darker appearance. The Bakhtiari are muscularly built, and are chiefly of a middle stature.[2]

By the time the great oil explorer made his own visit, more than 60 years later, the tribesmen's appearance, dress, ways of life and reputation would not have been much different. Most of them would still have worn the short-sleeved felt coat with the round cap that de Bode had commented on, and nearly all would have subsisted on basic farming and shepherding, regularly heading to the markets of Isfahan to sell their wares. Above all, Reynolds would have been aware of the tribes' temperamental shortcomings. De Bode mentioned, for example, that 'my new acquaintances, the Bakhtiari, were not very hospitably inclined; nor were they half so civil as I had invariably found Persians to be' and added that 'the feuds which exist between the different clans create inveterate hatred and keep up an unquenchable thirst for revenge ... (and this) extinguishes all feeling of humanity in their breasts'.[3] Furthermore, 'to this already sufficiently dark picture of their character must be added that they are such notorious thieves and robbers, that the name of Bakhtiar is become synonymous with both these words'.[4] In general this meant that 'the Bakhtiari bear a very bad reputation among the Persians. Although the latter are themselves not over and above scrupulous as regards veracity, they are outdone by the Bakhtiari in duplicity and bad faith.'[5]

Both Reynolds and D'Arcy had always known that if they were to have any chance of striking a fair deal with these tribes, then the close support of someone who knew their ways, their language and, above all, their mentality would be indispensable. Just as important was that they needed to have complete trust in this individual, whoever he happened to be. There were not many candidates, but in Tehran several people put forward the same name: John Preece, a British diplomat of great repute who was said to be more familiar with the tribes and their ways than virtually any other Westerner alive. For a number of years Preece had been working in Isfahan as the British consul, and liaising with the Bakhtiaris had long been part of his daily practice. But by a cruel twist of fate he happened to be making a rare visit to Britain, taking an extended period of leave, just when he was so badly needed in Persia. By the time he had made his way back to the kingdom, in late September, Reynolds had been waiting for him for more than four months.

The challenge facing both men was all the more daunting because the khans knew that the wider political situation in Persia was leaning heavily in their favour. In Tehran, the dying Shah Muzaffar al-Din was confronted with a political crisis, as popular demands for parliamentary representation steadily grew. Although the dying Muzaffar had agreed to these demands, his successor, Muhammed Ali Shah, was strongly opposed and the ensuing political disagreements had effectively paralysed the Persian government. Above all, this crisis seriously undermined the government's ability to enforce law and order in the very regions where Reynolds wanted to explore for oil. Without the support of the central government, Reynolds and D'Arcy were more dependent than ever on the cooperation of the Bakhtiari tribes that dominated the particular area of Persia where the exploration operation was based. Everything would depend on them if Reynolds was going to make progress in his bid to find oil, a bid that was becoming increasingly desperate.

Back in London, the great investor was becoming painfully aware of the perilous financial situation that his Persian operation was in. Though he knew that Reynolds had spared no effort, D'Arcy did not have limitless amounts of cash to throw at the project, and could not fund drilling operations forever. 'Every purse had its limit', as he had confessed to David Jenkin on 28 February 1903, 'and I can see the limit of my own and I want first to know what sum Mr Reynolds thinks he can get oil for and then whether that money can be supplied.'

To make things worse, D'Arcy still could not be sure that Persia really had any oil, at least not in commercially exploitable quantities. For while Reynolds had been hard at work, D'Arcy had hired another geologist, W.H. Dalton, to travel to the region and make a further independent report, hoping that his findings would reassure both himself and any would-be investors. Without this reassurance, he admitted, the task of finding backers 'to take shares in any company that might be formed for working it' would be a hopeless cause. But Dalton's mission was not only an expensive one, costing over £2,000, but failed to help matters, for he returned home armed with conclusions that were annoyingly vague: in Persia, his report ran, there was a 'continuous recurrence of accumulations of oil the commercial value of which can be determined only by test drilling at judiciously selected points'. Only a few of his points caught much attention, notably his recommendation that Reynolds should move his work to the two other sites that both men had surveyed. Of these, Dalton felt that Shardin was 'by far the best' and the other, Masjid-i Suleiman, 'the next best'. But to work in these places the explorers would need the permission of the tribes who ruled them, and it was to this end that Reynolds had now travelled into the Bakhtiari heartland.

As his debts started to mount and no news came of a breakthrough, D'Arcy must have been painfully aware of the grave financial risks he was running. When, some twenty years previously, Dutch explorers had searched for oil in the East Indies and drilled their first discovery well, they had had a much better knowledge of local geology and a far clearer idea of exactly where to concentrate their efforts. It did not take them long to strike black gold. Nor was D'Arcy offsetting these high risks with the promise of a particularly generous reward. While Article 10 of the shah's concession allowed the Persian Government to receive 'a sum equal to 16 per cent of the annual profits of any company or companies', other foreign concessions had typically been much more generous to the oil hunters: so in Russia, for example, it was quite usual for the government to auction off oil-bearing state lands in return for a lump sum payment and a relatively low yearly rental charge.

The warnings and dire predictions of others who had wanted to invest in Persia but failed to do so must also have been ringing in his ears. Lord Curzon, for example, had been bitten badly by his own Persian experiences. A few years previously he had accepted the directorship of the Persian Bank Mining Rights Corporation, which had spent vast sums on haphazard drilling operations before going bust. In 1901 Curzon had said that he saw no chance of D'Arcy's plans to find Persian oil reaping any rewards and now, two years later, reaffirmed his views that the operation was most unlikely to be profitable. Nor, he added, was there any particularly compelling strategic reason why D'Arcy's bid should be supported with the funding of the British government: it was highly unlikely, he argued, that the Russians would at this stage be sold the concession.

D'Arcy had won a temporary financial reprieve in May 1903 by setting up an operating company, just before the expiry of the two-year deadline that had got under way when he first signed the concession with the Persian government. The First Exploitation Company, of which D'Arcy was chairman, was now established with an issued capital of 350,000 £1 shares that allowed him to keep the operation running and to pay the Persian government the £20,000 that he was obliged to give them. But still the financial strain he was under was by any standards enormous. When, on 25 November 1903, he hired a suite at the Coburg Hotel in Grosvenor Square and held a conference before his business associates, the full extent of the financial damage emerged: by the time he was forced to admit that he had come to the end of his financial tether and would now have to seek 'outside' help if his company was to survive, his overdraft with Lloyds was standing at the vast total of £176,548 and 14 shillings, of which £4,158 was made up of interest. The bank began to demand the whole company as security for the overdraft, which by April 1904 had swelled even more to £186,366 and 9 shillings.

It occasionally seemed as though his nerve would snap. At one point, when the exploration operations hit technical snags, D'Arcy became very concerned at the complete lack of progress: 'this Persian business ... apart from my large money interest in it, I am most anxious that it should succeed. I am aware that the finances are running and [we] will have to find more money.'[6] Not surprisingly he began to live on hope, even at the expense of being altogether truthful with himself: when Reynolds had drilled down some 900 feet or so, D'Arcy was quick to express hope that the news 'may soon be followed by another wire saying oil in quantities is really found'.[7]

Very occasionally D'Arcy and Reynolds appeared to have achieved a real breakthrough. On 14 January 1904, for example, oil had started to gush freely from the 756-foot well at Chiah Sourkh, prompting an ecstatic D'Arcy exultantly to proclaim the arrival of the long-awaited turning point in his fortunes. 'Glorious news from Persia ... and the greatest relief to me', he exclaimed in one letter, as it seeped at a steady rate of 600 barrels a day. But his hopes were soon dashed when the seepage started to dry up and the explorers found brine mixed in with the oil, clearly indicating that the find was in any case of poor quality. He must have felt all the more dejected when Boverton Redwood, the top adviser in the Burmah Oil Company who had advised D'Arcy from the start on his Persian venture, warned him that because the wells were most unlikely to be commercially viable, and because any oil would in any case have to be transported 400 miles to the sea in a mountainous region, it would be better completely to shut down Chiah Sourkh and concentrate instead on the more promising districts of south-west Persia. Months of work at Chiah Sourkh had, in effect, been a complete waste of time and money.

Reynolds had at this point shut the site down, plugging the wells and locking the two main drilling engines away in a workshop. There were two places he could head to now, one near the village of Shardin, the other about 50 miles away, outside Maidan-i-Naftun. With desperate energy, Reynolds had cabled London and asked for permission to explore both of them: 'you must understand that if you do drill there my work will be more than doubled on account of the travelling required between the two places, but I came out here to see this business through and unless you let me drill there I shall not think I've done so'. D'Arcy assented and the remaining drilling machinery, camp equipment and tools, which together weighed 40 tons, were now taken south via Baghdad, down the Tigris, to Basrah, across the port to Mohammerah and put on board a ship that was then towed further down the river. At the same time a convoy of twenty men and hundreds of mules and horses was also heading for the new sites, moving on foot to cut down on transport costs.

But although D'Arcy's financial situation was becoming increasingly tight, he was just beginning to get an initial show of interest from one immensely powerful corner: the Admiralty. It was at this time that some senior figures were starting to show a serious interest in fuelling the ships of the Royal Navy with oil, replacing the engines that had always been stoked with coal. And if the Admiralty became interested in D'Arcy's Persian project, then it would not be long before the British government threw its full weight behind it.

As a fuel for ship engines, oil had considerable advantages over coal. Above all, to keep an engine running on oil required only a small working party to undertake the relatively simple task of connecting up hoses. A coal ship, by contrast, not only had to return to harbour first but also required far more hands for reloading. But the task of converting so many engines to take oil was in itself a massive operation, daunting in both scale and cost. Furthermore, while Britain produced coal in vast quantities, it had no oil reserves of its own and would become dependent on foreign sources of supply.

By the time drilling operations were getting under way in Persia, the mass conversion of ship engines to oil still seemed a long way off. Naval engineers had undertaken only a few experiments, and all of these had quickly ended in disaster: in June 1903, for example, the battleship HMS *Hannibal* had suddenly become engulfed in thick black smoke when its prototype engine overheated. D'Arcy had also gathered from various sources of information that 'the professional engineers at the Admiralty are advising the head not to commit themselves too deeply to Fuel Oil, as in their opinion the next few years will probably see a development in internal combustion engines worked by coal gas'. But some of the top brass and senior officialdom were starting to recognize oil's potential, most notably Admiral Sir John Fisher, then the Second Sea Lord, who had been interested in the idea ever since the early 1880s: 'I am thinking of going to Persia instead of Portsmouth', he once joked to D'Arcy. If the great investor was still a long way from getting the firm backing of the Admiralty for his exploration work, then his work and enthusiasm were nonetheless starting to raise eyebrows.

When D'Arcy sought to sell part of his company to raise enough money to support the crippling costs of exploration work, he spoke to a senior Admiralty figure, Edward Pretyman, to see if the British government would be prepared to make him a loan. In return for an undertaking to supply naval fuel oil, he could offer the Royal Navy an exclusive, long-term and guaranteed source of supply. If Whitehall was already building such links with the British-owned Burmah Oil Company, then why could it not do the same with his own organization?

Pretyman was just the right man for D'Arcy to approach. He was, after all, the chairman of the Admiralty's Oil Fuel Committee, which had just been set up to examine the availability of oil and take all possible steps to bring additional supplies under British control. And he was not only influential but sympathetic, recognizing the importance of D'Arcy's plans: 'it was clear to us that petroleum would largely supersede coal as the source of the fuel supply for the navy', as he once remarked, adding that 'it was also clear to us that this would place the British Navy at a great disadvantage, because, whereas we possessed within the British Isles the best supply of the best steam coal in the world, a very small fraction of the oilfields of the world lay within the British Dominions, and even these were situated within very remote and distant regions'.

Almost straight away he gave the great investor an encouraging response. The best thing for D'Arcy to do, he advised, was to write to the Admiralty, giving details of the prospects for Persian oil and of any progress made, while spelling out how much money he needed. Pretyman added that if his initial enquiry merited favour, then he would push hard to get a fuel oil contract for the First Exploitation Company. D'Arcy's letter, which explained that he needed at least another £120,000 to continue with the search for oil, won some sympathy with the Admiralty but was then forwarded to the young Chancellor of the Exchequer, Austen Chamberlain. It was at this point that his proposal ran into serious obstacles, for Chamberlain had strong reservations about his request and flatly turned it down, feeling sure that parliament would find the venture too risky. But Chamberlain recognized that without his support the concession might well lapse, perhaps then falling under Russian control, and these concerns prompted him to pass D'Arcy's request to the Foreign Office, where senior officials immediately asked Sir Arthur Hardinge to carry out his own inspections of the exploration sites on the ground and to make some assessment about their viability.

British officials knew that for the moment the Russians' attention was turned to the Far East, but felt that it was only a matter of time before they resumed Witte and Grube's quest to build a pipeline running from Baku all the way down to the Persian Gulf. In St Petersburg important figures such as Moshir al-Mulk, the Persian representative in the capital, were certainly warning that 'the failure of Russia's attempt to obtain access to warm water in the Far East could only result in increasing her desire to obtain command of a port in the South'.[8] Influential voices in or close to the British government concurred: Major H.R. Sykes, lecturing before the Central Asian Society on 1 March 1905, not only agreed with this viewpoint but felt that Britain was powerless to stop Russia from advancing.[9] Curzon also certainly took this viewpoint, arguing as vehemently as ever that Russia was striving to acquire 'supreme political influence and unchallenged economic control' within a country that was 'so weak as to be dependent but not so weak as to fall absolutely to pieces'.[10]

This meant that Hardinge's findings were leapt on in Whitehall as soon as he arrived back from his trip to Reynolds' drilling sites. The oil exploration operations were extremely promising, he reported, and one of the Russian banks in Tehran would be only too glad to buy D'Arcy's concession – regardless of its commercial value – as a means of extending Russian influence to the whole of Persia and then into neighbouring Mesopotamia: the shah, he continued, might then agree to the pipeline project that the Russians had been pushing for only shortly before. For these reasons alone he recommended that the British government should do its best to support the oil venture and even buy its own stake in D'Arcy's operation.

But though D'Arcy had received Hardinge's blessing, Whitehall just could not commit itself as quickly as he needed. To stem the flow of cash, he needed urgent action, and it was not the British government that now baled him out but the Burmah Oil Company, whose directors, Charles Wallace and John Cargill, were first introduced to him by Pretyman in August 1904. Both men had become concerned about the lack of new exploration opportunities in Burmah, and in October Cargill had been forced to admit to an adviser that 'for a considerable time past we have been devoting much of our energies and a very large amount of capital in prospecting work over a large extent of territory, with a view to endeavouring to prove fresh deposits of oil, but unfortunately up till now with no success'.[11] The Burmah directors were also unsure about the Indian government's willingness to grant further licences for exploration, even though they had previously always been cooperative. Never before had the task of finding new openings been more important for Burmah Oil.

D'Arcy did not mince his words about the full extent of the financial crisis that was facing him: he reckoned that he would now need the astronomical sum of £500,000 if his operations were to strike black gold, and another £150,000 to repay the expenses he himself had incurred. In return he could offer Burmah Oil half of his company shares. Cargill and Wallace agreed to take the risk, and in May 1905 the First Exploitation Company was dissolved and replaced by a new Concession Syndicate. Everything would now depend on how much progress the oil explorers were making on the ground. On 16 October 1905, Preece and Reynolds finally met up at Shalamzar, the main residence of the Bakhtiari leader, Il Khani, raising D'Arcy's hopes of making some progress at last. Negotiations over the rights of the British exploration team got under way almost immediately, but right from the onset it was obvious that the chief negotiator, Sardar Assad, was going to demand a hard bargain.

The task of haggling with the Bakhtiaris had always promised to be an exasperatingly slow one. Reynolds had already got a taste of their obstinacy the previous year when making some initial surveys of Shardin and Masjid. In the course of one meeting he had noted how the tribal leaders were totally oblivious to the terms of the shah's concession and were only interested in getting a separate deal of their own that would give them 'practically 10 per cent of net profits of working the oil in their country'. This was way more than D'Arcy could allow unless he renegotiated the entire 1901 concession from scratch. A minor consolation, however, was that not all the local tribes were quite as demanding as the khans: the Sayyid tribe that inhabited the area around Shushtar, for example, had a much more modest request, wanting to take only the annual delivery of eleven tons of crude oil, eleven of bitumen and a £100 payment.

Undeterred, the Englishmen remained locked in long discussions with the four main Bakhtiari chiefs. Reynolds quickly noticed how 'Sardar Asad … took, I may say, the entire role as spokesmen of the Chiefs, no other chief having it seemed a word to say in his presence … He, I should say, was masterful and has seen more of the world than most Khans, and has a greater flow of language, so it may have been a pre-arranged affair that he should hold the platform.'

To make matters worse, the British explorers appeared to have other enemies in Persia who were now trying hard to make their life as difficult as possible. One day Sardar Assad, the Bakhtiari chief who was heading the negotiations with Reynolds and Preece, received a mysterious, handwritten letter, posted anonymously from Tehran, that conveyed an emotive, even vitriolic, message: at all costs, the message ran, should he 'prevent the Foreigner interfering in his country' and recognize that the British explorers were trying to advance their sinister ends 'by intrigue, if they cannot gain their ends direct in the former, they do it through the latter'.[12] The writer was clearly well informed about events on the ground, making references to the earlier drilling operations at Chiah Surkh and warning Sardar that elsewhere the British team would try to repeat the tricks they had played there: its members had stolen fuel instead of paying for it, warned the anonymous writer, and they had hired foreigners instead of local people, while George Reynolds was guilty of harbouring 'a natural enmity with Persians'. It was clear that the hunters had a determined enemy in Tehran, probably one of the officials who had at some point been employed by the team before being laid off.

After four days of haggling Sardar demanded a 5 per cent share in D'Arcy's company and, though this was considerably more than he was supposed to give away, Reynolds was forced to nod his assent. But Preece's experience at dealing with the tribes soon came in handy, for it was not long before he had knocked them down to 3 per cent. This initial agreement now formed the basis of a formal deal that was signed by several leading tribal elders at Junaghan, one of their main residences, on 15 November 1905. Under the agreement, the Bakhtiaris would allow D'Arcy's company to 'search for oil, make roads, pipelines, build houses, etc.' over the next five years in return for the shares and for payment 'at the fair price of the day' for any arable or irrigated land that was used. The tribes also agreed to give the explorers constant, round-the-clock protection, and 'to assume responsibility for any robbery and for any damage to the Company's property' in return for an annual fee of £2,000. This was, of course, a very considerable sum, but Reynolds and Preece felt they had little choice but to agree.

Even with the khans on their side, the security situation in Persia could still be somewhat perilous, posing a real threat to the future of exploration operations there. On one routine journey from Shardin to Ahwaz, Reynolds was physically assaulted and his surveyor, an Indian, threatened. Part of the trouble, he felt, was that the individual guards upon whom their safety depended received almost nothing for their services from the khans, who were the real beneficiaries of the November agreement. 'The poor wretches sent out as guards, taken away from their usual means of livelihood, are at once reduced to starvation', Reynolds sighed, later bemoaning the fact that 'we did not reserve to ourselves the right to pay these Guards … The Spark of discontent is there, and only needs fanning by our well-wishers to cause trouble.'[13]

The British consul at Ahwaz, Captain David Lorimer, now came to their assistance. Lorimer was a relative newcomer to Persia, having arrived there on secondment from the Indian Political Department only two years before. But he was dedicated to his job, and had a great love of the local languages that he had quickly learned, and of exploration and adventure. Those who met him in person were invariably impressed by the way in which 'he lived frugally but kept good horses and good books', and by 'his one-eyed Persian clerk [who] was a character worthy of Haji Baba'. His cooperation and assistance, Reynolds and Preece felt sure, would be a considerable asset to their cause.

Reynolds now opened up negotiations with some of the other tribes in the vicinity of Shardin, whose cooperation would be vital 'as should it ever become necessary for our men to be withdrawn, owing to disturbances among the Tribesmen and insufficient guards, the results would be disastrous to the enterprise'. On 23 February 1906 talks began at the tribal camp at Ram Hormuz and a new guarding arrangement was set up.

This agreement, however, was only a very temporary respite, for soon afterwards came a much more ominous development. At the beginning of May, the khans announced that they wanted to scrap the existing guarding agreement and instead get much more generous terms from the British. On 15 May the khans met Preece and gave him a detailed list of all their objections to the present arrangement, claiming, in particular, that £2,000 was not sufficient to cover the expense of guarding them round-the-clock. For a time things looked dire, as the Il Khani withdrew all guarding arrangements and left the British to fend for themselves. But after yet more haggling, and Reynolds' offer of an extra payment of £500, their disagreements were resolved and the previous arrangement continued as before. As D'Arcy pointed out: 'I can see no cause for alarm, as unreliable as the Bakhtiaris are, they are no such fools as to attempt to kill the goose that lays the golden egg, and the increased amount that they have agreed to take and are presumably satisfied with, will, let us hope cause them to continue in this frame if mind until Reynolds gets oil – and I do not think this is very far off.'[14] At last, after months of delay, Reynolds' exploration work could continue, and the hunt for Persian oil was once again properly under way.

Reynolds' men started to drill two wells at the new site at Shardin within three months of their arrival. But this was far later than he or anyone had hoped, for once again work had been held up by faulty and damaged equipment. When a hole was bored into the ground, its sides were held firm by steel casings screwed together and protected at each end by steel caps. Reynolds had always made doubly sure that these casings were properly protected and held together, and was dismayed when a consignment arrived which were made of wood, not steel, and whose casings were in any case badly mangled. He could not carry on, he decided, until replacements arrived. Even then progress had been painfully slow. This was not because of any geological obstacle but because this was an area where wood – which fed the steam engines and kept them running – was notoriously hard to come by, and when it was obtained in any real quantities it was often spirited away by local villagers or corrupt guards. To begin with the team could drill no more than 50 feet each month, and by early 1907 the two wells had been dug down to a depth of only about 300 and 100 feet. And still no oil, or even any glimmers of its presence, had been found.

The operation was still burning up cash extremely fast and Cargill, who had never been remotely as keen on the whole project as his fellow director Charles Wallace, was now openly warning his colleagues that providing extra funds for Persia would simply be throwing good money after bad. Persia, he added, was in any event looking like a risky market and, since Burmah oil was booming, probably an unnecessary one. It was Wallace's intervention that saved the venture, however, and in late February the Burmah Oil Board offered to put up all the extra cash that D'Arcy so urgently needed.

But throughout these long months, the stress on the Syndicate's directors – and not just on D'Arcy – was always enormous. Urgent cables were being sent to Persia by the Syndicate's directors from its headquarters, now based in Glasgow, desperately hoping for some sign that would lift their flagging spirits. 'When do you expect to strike oil?' asked company secretary James Hamilton urgently in May 1907, a question that Boverton Redwood reiterated soon afterwards, adding that the Glasgow directors were 'fully entitled to more information than they have hitherto obtained'.

But Reynolds was forced to concede that he saw little prospect of locating any oil before his men had managed to drill much farther down, reaching right through the thick gypsum layer that was covering any possible oil deposits. It was not until September, when they were down to a depth of more than 1,500 feet in both of the two wells, that Reynolds was able to use surface indications to make some assessment of just how deep this gypsum bed really was. He calculated that its thickness was around 4,500 ft and at the current rate of drilling it might take many months to get through it and finally strike oil. Put bluntly, the Shardin site, like its predecessors, was far less promising than he had at first hoped and it would now be pointless to continue drilling. Nor, he continued, was there any location nearby that seemed to offer any potential, and he and his men would have to undertake a time-consuming and costly move farther afield if their hopes were ever going to be fulfilled.

To make matters even worse, the security situation was also starting to deteriorate rapidly. The extra £2,500 that D'Arcy and Reynolds had agreed to fork out to the khans appeared to have made little or no real difference to the number or quality of the tribal guards they were supposed to be supplying. Lorimer held meetings with tribal chiefs in a bid to resolve the situation, but could do nothing to improve things: the tribal leaders, he said, only wanted 'to secure the whole £2,500 and not spend a penny ... no cash payment is ever made. Payments are merely effected by remission of taxation.' Things became even more serious in June 1907, when Shahab al-Sultan, the one Bakhtiari leader who had some sympathy for the British position, was ousted from power. Unfortunately, a rival who harboured no such sympathy then stepped into his shoes.

In political terms, the kingdom of Persia was certainly in a turbulent enough state to pose a real challenge to the future of oil exploration work. In Tehran the murder of the prime minister was felt to be 'a sad blow' for the future of the oil concession, while in the south-west the explorers were attacked by men loyal to Ali Murad Khan, who was well known as a local rebel. Reynolds' faith in the goodwill of the khans was fast failing, and in one letter, penned on 29 May 1907, he described how they struck him 'as full of intrigue as a nightingale's egg is pregnant with music'. Exasperated, Reynolds also wrote back to London that 'you will please understand that all these visits and worry with workmen and tribesmen take up time, and I find it difficult to do what I would wish and visit and examine some sections of rocks exposed in the neighbourhood'.

Such a tense situation was also having serious repercussions on D'Arcy's never-ending quest to find new funding for his operations. Burmah Oil had already declared that its reluctance to invest more heavily was due to 'Persian unrest', and James Hamilton now travelled from Glasgow to London to give D'Arcy an ultimatum: the Syndicate would be wound up, he argued, unless D'Arcy obtained a guarantee from the Foreign Office of government protection against 'trouble caused by and the demands of the tribes in Persia'. Hamilton was fully aware of the state of the Concessions Syndicate's financial crisis, and the political trouble in Persia was tipping the balance even further against it. Burmah Oil's extra funding was virtually exhausted, and its directors were now putting D'Arcy and

Reynolds under immense pressure. Shortly afterwards, Hamilton also despatched a letter to Reynolds saying that 'we would like if possible to put the two wells at Masjid-i Suleiman down to 1500/1600 feet, and if no oil is found at this depth, to abandon operations, close down and bring as much of the plant as is possible down to Mohammerah'.

Back in Tehran, British officials had been having doubts of their own. Arthur Hardinge remarked, as he left the capital and headed for home, that 'it is as yet too early an opinion as to whether this oil enterprise will be crowned with success. The promoters are very sanguine but they have perhaps inadequately appreciated the difficulties attending all commercial undertakings in a country possessing no regular or efficient administration, where authorities' one idea in relation to commerce is to levy blackmail on it for their own personal and immediate profit.'[15]

Reynolds had now started to shift his exploration operations to Masjid-e Suleiman: the two Shardin wells had eventually reached a depth of 2,172 and 1,942 feet without showing any signs of oil, and he felt that now, in June 1907, it was once again time to move on. But as his team headed towards the new site, they were approached by a number of villagers who seemed to regard their mysterious visitors as a threat and started hurling stones at them. Some of the drillers, their tempers already frayed in the scorching summer heat, picked up some of the stones and began hurling them back, and for a while serious disorder seemed about to break out. Not long afterwards, Reynolds heard that Ali Murad's men had also begun to appear in the vicinity and were posing a real threat to his team, who were now increasingly concerned about their own fate and that of the entire operation.

D'Arcy was also deeply alarmed by the telegram that reached him soon afterwards, telling him about the bandits, tribes and troublesome villagers that all posed a serious risk to the lives of individual explorers and to the future of the entire operation: it was quite possible, for example, that the camp could at any time be looted and the valuable machinery damaged or destroyed. Recognizing that 'the unsettled state of S. Persia is a Danger to our Business', D'Arcy got in contact with his old acquaintance in the diplomatic world, Sir Charles Hardinge, who was by now a permanent secretary to the Foreign Office, to get his advice and, if possible, his support.

The initial British response did not quite work out as planned. Acting on Hardinge's construction, the British consulate at Ahwaz despatched the gunboat HMS *Comet* to sail up the Karun river and come to Reynolds' assistance. The story of this relief force was not worthy of a classic romantic tale, however, for it had moved only a short distance before sliding onto a mudbank a few miles outside Ahwaz and grinding to a sudden halt. In London, Hardinge held urgent consultations with colleagues and came up with another idea. Instead of relying on local tribesmen as guards, he argued, he could despatch a small military detachment from British-ruled India to look after them. He knew just the man who could lead such an operation, and he would not waste a moment in getting in touch with him.

7

Lieutenant Wilson Rides to the Rescue

For a young British lieutenant called Arnold Wilson, life in the Indian Army had gradually become a bit too familiar. He had already served four years as a junior officer with the 32nd Sikh Pioneers, and in this time he had certainly developed a very deep attachment to his regiment and a certain love for the land and its people. But it was not long before he began to want more than the habitual routines – the daily drill, occasional night-fighting exercises, trench digging, peacock-shooting, pig-sticking and language training – that made up so much of his life at the regiment's main base at Ambala in the very far north of India.

One afternoon in late November 1907, however, life was about to change drastically for the 23-year-old officer. For while he was at work at Chandigarh, a short distance from Ambala, a courier arrived bearing an urgent telegram that, quite out of the blue, had been despatched from the Foreign Office in London. Ripping open the envelope, Wilson was astonished by what he had been instructed to undertake. For he had now been asked to take command of twenty men of the 18th Bengal Lancers, taking them by rail and ship to the Persian Gulf port of Mohammerah and then overland to Masjid i-Suleiman. The ostensible purpose of this tiny force was to reinforce the guard of the British Consulate at Ahwaz, which in the previous months had come under attack from robbers and bandits. Its real mission, however, was to protect Reynolds and his drillers from the trouble that was by now posing a dire threat to the success of the oil-exploration operations.

Wilson was not under any overriding obligation to commit himself to this particular mission: it lay well outside his ordinary duties and so he could, if he chose, turn the offer down and simply continue his service in India. But he immediately leapt at the chance. Not only would such a mission break the tedium of his military service, but it would also help him realize his career ambitions of eventually becoming an officer in the British consular service. He remembered the advice of a colleague – 'never refuse a job unless it is a soft one' – and now saw this offer as a perfect, almost God-given, opportunity to get the experience that he would need to move up the career ladder. Within hours the young lieutenant was on his way, leaving Chandigarh for Ambala, which was a 25-mile drive by mule tonga. The next day he took a train from Ambala for the southern port of Karachi, where he would soon be boarding a ship bound westwards for the Persian Gulf.

Over the next two days the train made its way through Bhatinda, Samosata and Sukkur, crossing areas that were 'mostly desert, with occasional oases of green crops, palms and tropical plants in brilliant contrast to the quieter shades of the desert'.[1] This long journey at least gave Wilson plenty of time to get himself ready, and brace himself for his Persian itinerary.

It was unlikely, however, that he needed very much time to do so: it was not long, after all, since he had returned from this region, and it was because he had some basic familiarity with the land that he had now been chosen to undertake this particular mission. It had been just eight months before, in early March, that he had followed the same route from Ambala to Karachi to make his way by ship to Bandar Abbas, on the Persian south coast, with an army friend. Both men had been granted several months' special leave to make their way through Persia and Russia back to London. And as they travelled from Bandar to Shiraz and then Isfahan they had acquired a basic knowledge of Persia's languages, conditions and customs that he knew would now stand him in good stead.

From his earlier travels to Persia, Wilson also knew that he would inevitably be embroiled in games of international rivalry. He remembered how, as he and his companion had left Bandar Abbas for the ancient town of Lar:

> at the first stage on the road we were overtaken by a mysterious Persian, mounted upon a single mule, who announced that he would keep us company. Suspecting him to be an agent of the Russian consul and, in any case, disliking the look of him, we tried politely to dissuade him. He insisted on remaining, so we waited till he slept and then untethered his beast, which bolted back to Bandar Abbas. When he awoke next morning we mildly suggested that he should do likewise, so soon as he could obtain, from a neighbouring village in a date-grove, a donkey to carry his saddlebags. He took the hint and we saw him no more. Long afterwards we heard from the British consul that he had, in fact, been sent by the Russian consul to spy upon us.[2]

Now, eight months later, memories of such encounters must have come back to him as the train continued its long journey southwards towards Karachi, and he must have been gripped by a certain sense of excitement, or danger, as he arrived there on 1 December and boarded the SS *Kola* to start the five-day trip to the Gulf.

Wilson certainly had excellent company during this leg of his journey, for on board was none other than Jacques de Morgan, who by this time had been appointed as head of the French Scientific Museum at Susa, and with whom Wilson shared many of his meals and evening conversations. The world of the oil explorers was in some ways a small one. Although he had seen it before, he was also still taken aback by the natural splendours of the regions he passed through:

'the Persian Gulf has its glories, black heartlands towering from deep blue water, blue skies and at night phosphorescence stronger than I have seen elsewhere', as he wrote in a letter home.[3] And after landing at Mohammerah he was struck not only by the beauty of the landscape but also by the region's historical resonance: the view from the Shatt al-Arab waterway, he felt,

> is something to treasure in the mind. Deep date-palm groves on either side: the turbid reddish stream of the Karun mingles with the clearer waters of the main river just below the Consulate. In 1856 we bombarded the place and sent ships to Ahwaz: there are men still living who have vivid memories of the vent and cannon-balls are sometimes picked up in the ditches. It is, to me, a new and fascinating world … Sindbad the Sailor started his journeys close by: so did Abraham – from Ur of the Chaldees. King Darius and Ahasuerus sat at Susa only 100 miles north. It is the oldest historical centre on the face of the earth.[4]

After several days of hard travelling, Wilson and his men arrived at the drilling site, pitching their tents and establishing their separate camp close by.

Wilson's immediate impression of the site was its overwhelming sense of desolation. It was set on a barren plain that was a long way from any settlement or village, and the nearest sign of civilization – or former civilization – lay nearly two miles away. These were the ruined walls and stone staircases of a building, the Masjid-i-Suleiman or 'Mosque of Solomon', that had been built over 2,000 years before, and which the drillers adopted as a name for their venue. This was his first glimpse of an oil-exploration site. As he looked around, Wilson saw the small stone houses, built specially for the drillers, that lay close to a shallow stream that trickled down from the mountain heights above. Reynolds had chosen this location because the stream offered a regular supply of water that kept the boilers topped up and the drillers clean if the simple showering units packed up. The stream also played a part in keeping their spirits up, for in one particular place the water was stained black by an underground oil seepage that constantly reminded everyone of how close to their goal they seemed to be. A short distance away from the simple stone houses was the derrick, which protected and housed both the drill and the hole it bored deep into the ground.

The basic processes of extracting oil would have differed little from the day in the late spring of 1859 when the American pioneer Edwin Drake had changed things forever. Up until then explorers had dug out special trenches at venues – often randomly chosen 'wildcat' sites – that were thought to harbour some promise. They then used spades and pickaxes to try to tap any oil deposits into them. Drake, however, recognized how primitive this technique was and worked out a much better way to drill underground. To begin with he built a 40-foot wooden derrick that was equipped with ropes and a winch that hoisted a large drill above the ground. A large tubular boiler and a six horsepower steam engine then powered the drill, lifting and then dropping it repeatedly so that it pounded the rock beneath. Drake knew that when the drill penetrates a stratum of rock beneath the ground, then the pressure of the rock structure, and any underground natural gas and water, would force the oil from the sand or porous rock to the surface and cause the well to flow. This was 'Drake's Folly', and it very closely resembled what Reynolds and his team had been using in Persia from the outset of their operations.

Using all this equipment, and indeed the task of drilling for oil in general, was not only highly arduous but typically also very hazardous. On one occasion a driller recorded an accident to one of the poles that hammered the ground, describing how it 'broke on the upward stroke close to the top and when the tools dropped, another near the bottom broke. We fished fifteen poles out of the hole that were turned into corkscrews.' Reynolds was also concerned about 'the increasing quantity of perfectly odourless inflammable gas' that could seep out from below, suddenly overwhelm the crew and then quite easily kill them. This danger seemed all the more immediate when the team's safety lamps were broken and replacements took some considerable time to arrive.

Setting up the camp at Masjid had certainly been no easy task for the exploration team. It was only a relatively short distance from Shardin, about 50 miles or so, but the very remoteness of the site and the inhospitality of the surroundings made the task of relocating the heavy equipment a very demanding one. Well before moving his operations there Reynolds had employed whole teams of local men who worked hard to build a road that could at least link the place up to the outside world. Two teams had laboured from dawn to dusk on this project, using explosives to blast the mountainside and shovels and spades to then lay the road surface. It was not 'all beer and skittles', as Reynolds wrote back to London, adding that it was very difficult for those 'who have never set foot in these parts to realize that it is impossible to get a native whom one can put in charge of a gang of men to do earth work or any such work there may be to do'.

Things became much harder for everyone when, in the winter rains, the River Karun broke its banks, overflowing onto the road and sweeping everything away: at one point, a whole section of the track that crossed the undulating Tembi river, a tributary of the Karun, was washed away on no less than fourteen separate occasions. But the team persevered, and by the spring of 1906, nearly nine months after it had got fully under way, the road was virtually completed. But even when it had been built, moving heavy equipment to Masjid along its uphill and tortuous track was a near insuperable task. The team had worked ferociously hard to move as much of their materials as they could before the winter rains began, and eventually succeeded in relocating the derrick by the end of October.

All this had been done under so much pressure of time that the team had had no chance to undertake a proper survey of the Masjid site before drilling started. The chief surveyor, Edward Cunningham Craig, had to draw up his report about Masjid's oil prospects without the aid of a topographical map, and his main assistant, Bradshaw, had been too busy building the road to help out. But having made his own initial assessment of the site some time before, Reynolds was always adamant that such efforts would eventually bear fruit. 'I do not think justice would be done to the place if you did not decide to drill there. To the best of my judgement it is the better of the two.' He added that the costs of relocating to Masjid were by this time insignificant: 'You have incurred the cost of the plant and the extra cost of drilling there will be a trifle in comparison to the expenditure incurred already.' Something told him, whether it was rational insight or gut feeling, that it would not be very long before the operation yielded firm results: 'a definite result will be obtained one way or the other before it becomes necessary to pay the 15 May instalment to the Khans', as he cabled at the end of February, a short time after drilling had got under way at Masjid.

Wilson was taken aback by the high calibre of the oil hunters who were keeping the operation going in such arduous circumstances. Reynolds, he felt, was in many ways 'the ideal man for such a post'. He was remarkably resilient, being 'very active in mind and body' and 'accustomed to long journeys on mule or horseback'. Although 'intolerant of opposition', he continued, Reynolds had a habit of 'getting the best out of the staff he employed', because he was 'patient in negotiation ... dignified in negotiation, quick in action and completely single-minded in his determination to find oil'. The great explorer also appears to have showed exemplary patience when he encountered obstinacy or extortionate greed on the part of the locals: 'if he required wood', recorded the young diarist, then 'a local chief would be pleased that trees were so scarce that he could not allow them to be cut: if he wanted labour, he would find that every able-bodied man was busy – until he had agreed to an exorbitant wage'.[5]

Wilson also soon met the site doctor, Morris Young, who he judged to be 'something of a genius at his work', not only a very fine doctor but also one who had adapted brilliantly to local conditions, conversing well in the native language and nearly always dressing in local garb. Young had by this time been at the site for a few months but had much longer experience at working inside Persia. He had at one time studied in Glasgow to become an eye surgeon but, burdened with student debts and inspired by a strong sense of adventure, had spotted an intriguing job advertisement: a railway survey party that would be based in the Middle East needed medical staff, ran the advert, and needed someone to join them as soon as possible. Young jumped at the chance and enjoyed the year-long experience enormously, particularly the leg of the journey in Persia. On his return to Britain he had badly wanted to make his way back there.

When, some months later, Young had been offered an opportunity to work as camp doctor at the drilling site, he knew that this would be a very demanding role, and as soon as he arrived back in Persia his worst fears were realized: he happened to return during a serious outbreak of bubonic plague, and for ten long days he had to endure quarantine at a house in Mohammerah, where he was forced to live in the most basic conditions. When he was finally out of quarantine, he headed north to Ahwaz and was introduced to George Reynolds, who greeted him curtly with the comment that 'you've been a devil of a long time getting here'. Young was taken aback not only by Reynolds' abrasiveness but also by the sheer austerity in which the oil explorer lived: his house, situated in one of the poorest quarters in Ahwaz, comprised a living room that was furnished only with a camp bed and table, a couple of chairs and a bookcase, while an adjoining office had only a large table, a typewriter, a few chairs and a couple of trunks. That was all.

But despite this difficult start the two men subsequently got on well, and by the time Wilson arrived they had become close friends. Young felt that Reynolds had 'a whole-hearted devotion to his work and an unwavering faith in the ultimate success of his quest for oil', while Reynolds must have been taken aback by the skill and energy of his camp doctor who, after just seven months at the site, had personally treated nearly 4,000 cases. It was not long before Wilson's contingent had started to settle into a steady daily routine. Much of the day was spent watching over the camp from afar as 'the work went on steadily [as] two rigs pounded day and night'. Such a task was not appetizing, for the site was full of 'heavy smells', the work 'monotonous' and the drillers covered 'in the oil and grease which surrounded them'. They did get some gratitude from the drillers, however, who were pleased simply to have the contingent's proper protection: 'they are glad to have the guard and not less to know that I am map making much further afield, for I can this way make contact with small tribal chiefs from whom we want to draw labour, pack animals and even supplies of straw, barley, wood for fuel and other local supplies'.[6]

The only real chance Wilson had to mix with fellow Westerners came at mealtimes, which were a simple affair. For the most part he lived on much the same diet that had kept him going during his trip in spring the previous year, a diet that was made up of locally produced barley bread, dates, lentils and rice with either goat meat or, if he had used his shooting skills on local wildlife, something more exotic. Fresh vegetables were hard to come by: it was 'brought now and then on mules from Shushtar, in stone houses, but the supply was irregular', as he bemoaned in one letter. Occasionally he would follow the example of the drillers, who were wary of local food and instead relied on the tins of food that were transported to the site by mule or horse. These men, he continued, 'are good, independent, rough men, unceremonious and curiously self-conscious, a good hearted lot', as he wrote, 'full of prejudices about food and drink, eschewing fresh food in favour of "Canned" provisions. They live uncomfortably ... small grievances bulk largely in their talk.'[7]

Despite the monotony, it was not long before Wilson and his men had a taste of the danger that had brought them here in the first place. His tent was on one occasion peppered with bullets, and was twice broken into and ransacked by thieves. Such risks prompted him to make immediate changes to his daily routines: 'I ceased to use a camp-bed and slept always on the ground: whence it was easy to rise, and easier to hear any suspicious sound', as he wrote in one letter home.[8] But such attacks were rarities, and the mountain tribes and bandits who had been posing such a risk to the oil-exploration operations appear to have been quickly warded off by the presence of Wilson's men.

But although the visitors may have been untroubled by the attention of robbers and bandits, there were nonetheless a great many other sources of discomfort that made their lives difficult, sometimes almost unbearably so. On occasion Wilson admitted in his letters that he sometimes badly missed his life back in India. 'I am still rather homesick for my Regiment', he wrote in early March, 'particularly today, when I found on the back of half a dozen labels on packages sent from Ambala as many messages, written in Gurmukhi or Urdu, from sepoys wishing me well and asking me to come back soon because "your place is empty". And there were some letters to the same effect put inside the packages.'[9] Similar sentiments were doubtless felt, if perhaps very rarely expressed, by his soldiers, all of them native Indians.

The local climate was also arduous even by the testing standards that this Indian Army contingent was used to. By the early summer Wilson was finding the sun scorching: 'the shade temperature in my tent was 110 degrees from 9 to 5', he wrote home, 'and following local custom I had deep caves dug in the hillside' for reading and rest. This set the tone for most of his subsequent letters: 'the heat of the summer made life in camp irksome. The only available lamp oil had a low flash-point and burned badly in summer'. A few days later he recorded how 'it was 124 degrees in my tent every day: a hot wind blew continuously from the north-west. My men, hardy Punjabi Mussulmans, found it hard to endure – their mounts found it ever harder and lost condition.' Others at the site concurred. Dr Young also complained about 'this awful last summer, which could have had nothing more than a paper wall between it and hell', while even the hardy Reynolds admitted that 'we are all feeling it'.[10]

But Wilson felt that such demanding conditions gave Persia a certain majesty. 'There is something terrible and grand in thunder and lightning when one is in camp in the mountains; in flooded rivers which like the Karun will rise 40 feet in a few days; in hail which will kill cattle; in sun so hot that eggs will cook in the sand; and in a moon and stars so bright that they make travel by night a joy.' He was often taken aback by the sheer natural splendour of his surroundings.

> The dawn comes slowly and the clear-cut outlines of bare hills of literally every colour are revealed against an upper background of grey changing in succession to delicate shades of blue, green and finally pink. Then the golden disk of the sun comes over the shoulder of the hill and the camp begins to stir as the hoar frost vanishes from the surface of my little tent and meagre pile of baggage.

And writing on the slopes of a mountain that looked out across the Karun river, more than a 1,000 feet below, he felt compelled to describe 'the snow-clad peaks are 100 miles distant but perfectly clear – it is the sort of view one may see in Switzerland and on as big a scale'. In March the spectacular blossoming of spring flowers – jonquil, nightstick, tulip and anemone – lasts only a few weeks before the summer heat overwhelms them, but Wilson got his chance to witness this particular sight, describing how 'the hills and plains are carpeted with flowers: in the valleys here and there are great beds of wild narcissus: my men, like Persians, bend low to their stirrups to smell them as they ride slowly through'.[11]

Wilson was also fascinated by the local wildlife, and on one occasion described what he saw in the course of a mountain hike:

> As I scrambled down a gorge, leading my nag, I saw a bear with two cubs – the small cinnamon bear of these parts – shambling down the track ahead of me. I had a rifle with me but did not shoot. Why should I? This is their home and they do no manner of harm. Later on I saw a leopard and in the plains or foothills hyenas, ugly beasts with very small haunches and heavy forequarters and chests. I often saw on the outskirts of a camp the large bones of buffalo freshly cracked by their jaws. Wolves were not uncommon north of the Karun and the Karkhah, but I heard them in camp oftener than I saw them.[12]

But back in London, financial pressure on the drilling operation had all this time been continuing to mount steadily, for the funding agreement struck the previous year was now nearing an end and money was once again becoming desperately short. One of the directors of Burmah Oil informed D'Arcy that 'money is exhausted … unless I find half of the expenditure in future the work must stop … of course I cannot find £20,000 or anything, and what to do I know not'. On 15 April 1908, the Burmah Oil directorate asked D'Arcy to pay up to £20,000 to subsidize operations out of his own pocket, adding that if he refused by the end of April 'the Board would then consider whether they would not at once abandon the operations in Persia entirely'. Shortly afterwards, the company's General Meeting passed a resolution that decreed that 'unless satisfactory results are shortly obtained this enterprise will be abandoned'.

As ever D'Arcy was trying his best to keep his hopes alive – 'I do not think it very far off … until Reynolds gets oil' as he had written a few weeks before – but this new moment of crisis now presented him with a clear dilemma. On the one hand he simply could not afford to raise the extra thousands that would be needed to carry on with operations; but on the other he had recently been told by James Thompson, Cargill's solicitor and cousin, that Burmah's threat to cancel the whole operation was really just a bluff, since the company would not want to waste so much time and effort, or want to risk watching the Russians step into their own empty shoes. Heeding his advice D'Arcy gambled and refused to pay up.

But at the beginning of May, after Wilson had been at the site for more than five months, a telegram from London reached the drilling team bearing the news that Burmah Oil was pulling the funding. 'Funds were exhausted and the decision reached finally and irrevocably', wrote Wilson, 'was that he was to cease work, dismiss the staff, dismantle anything worth the cost of transporting to the coast for reshipment, and come home.' Wilson was personally dismayed by the announcement for a number of reasons. 'The news was to me quite unexpected. I knew nothing of such matters but it seemed clear to me that no wells had been drilled to anything like sufficient depth to "prove" the field and that it would be necessary to drill many more before its value could be assessed.'[13] And as he wrote to a British attaché in Tehran, this was 'a short-sighted decision. What is to stop a Russian controlled oil company from getting a new concession from Persia? What is to prevent CS Ltd from selling D'Arcy's rights to an America or German company? Cannot Government be moved to prevent these faint-hearted merchants, masquerading in top hats as pioneers of Empire, from losing what may be a great asset?'

Reynolds knew that he could afford to ignore the telegram, perhaps claiming that he had received it much later than he really had, or that its terms had been too vague, or full of typing errors, to have any real meaning. Casting it aside he ordered his team to carry on with their work regardless, pressing ahead until or unless they got written confirmation that operations were to be stopped. Now, more than at any other time, the drillers must have prayed for signs of a breakthrough, hoping that they might strike oil in the same dramatic, sudden manner with which it had been discovered elsewhere in the world. Just eight years previously a number of American workmen, worn out by a fruitless nine-month search, had been seized by an overwhelming sense of despair and thrown their tools down the open borehole, only to be blinded minutes later by the sudden gush of oil: the weight of just a few pieces of iron, it turned out, had happened to break some underground rocks and smash open an oil deposit lying right underneath them. Alfred Stuart, one of the oil explorers of the Caucasus during the 1870s, had once light-heartedly drilled a well into the shallow seepages of a Grozney hillside and struck a great spout of oil that proved impossible to control as it poured down the hillside, polluting streams, ruining houses and eventually flooding the whole countryside. And at Burkesville near Kentucky, in 1829 two men pierced into a rich reservoir of natural gas and oil and then had to flee for their lives when the huge upsurge not only swept away the wooden derrick but caught fire, burning whole swathes of forest for miles around.

But more often than not there were giveaway signs that oil was close at hand. For it generally lies deep below the ground, trapped between layers of sand or porous rock where it is often mixed with natural gas bubbles or brine. So if brine floated to the surface, or if there was a noticeable smell of gas, then something might well be awry. It was two weeks later, in the third week of May, that the men who were working on well no. 1 noticed a 'most distinct smell of gas'. This gave them a clear sign that something might be afoot and it spurred them on to work harder – almost manically so – than they had ever done before. To their frustration they had to stop for three days when a part of the steel drill bit became unscrewed, forcing them to abandon everything while they searched for it and undertook necessary repairs. But when drilling resumed, the strong smell became almost overwhelming, and in the strong sunlight gas could clearly be seen rising from the well. Success seemed so very close at hand but they were still not quite there, for the drill now hit a layer of very hard rock that promised to be very difficult to penetrate.

In the early hours of 26 May Wilson was suddenly woken in his tent by the sound of shouting and 'unaccustomed noise'. He got up and ran towards one of the two wells, and to his astonishment and delight could make out a jet of oil spurting upwards into the air: 'it rose 50 feet or so above the top of the rig, smothering the drillers and their devoted Persian staffs who were nearly suffocated by the accompanying gas'. At a depth of 1,180 feet, No. 1 well had struck oil and the biggest oilfield then known had been unearthed.

Mixed with sulphur the oil stank abominably, but at this moment of supreme jubilation and euphoria no one would have cared and would perhaps barely have noticed. They would certainly not have had much time to do so, for the drillers were now desperately trying to save as much of the oil as possible. Reynolds had run over to the scene as soon as he heard his men shouting and helped them cap the well while diverting the flow of oil into a great pit or reservoir that had already been dug into the hard red clay about 200 yards away. Once the situation was in hand, with the well flowing steadily at a rate of 300 barrels each day, the great explorer finally had a chance to declare his news. 'I have the honour to report that this morning at about 4am oil was struck in the No. 1 hole at a depth of 1180 … Particulars re gravity and quantity of oil flowing will follow but unless I get this away at once I shall miss the post.'

At the same time Wilson sent his own cable to Major Cox, the British consul at Bushire, wiring a message that simply ran 'See Psalm 104, verse 15 third sentence, and Psalm 114, verse 8 second sentence'. Cox immediately reached for his copy of the Bible and was astonished by what he found: 'that he may bring out of the earth oil to make him a cheerful countenance ... the flint stone into a springing well'. Almost straight away the news then reached the British legation in Tehran and was cabled to London.

In his private correspondence, Wilson recorded his reaction to the event, and noted what he felt was the vast significance of the discovery. 'It is a great event', He wrote to his father. 'It will provide all our ships east of Suez with fuel; it will strengthen British influence in these parts. It will make us less dependent on foreign-owned oilfields; it will be some reward to those who have ventured such great sums as have been spent. I hope it will mean some financial reward to the engineers who have persevered so long, in spite of their wretched top-hatted directors in Glasgow, in this inhospitable climate.' The reaction of London's stock markets proved that Wilson was not alone in grasping the huge importance of the find. Almost immediately 'oil fever' raged as the prices of D'Arcy's company's shares soared. In Glasgow, where the Burmah Oil Company was based, there was a huge, unprecedented rush for applications to buy shares. For days there were long queues at the bank counter where stock could be purchased, and many would-be applicants were forced to concede defeat and give up. Soon the Company could afford to reimburse D'Arcy for the expenses he had incurred, and to give him shares in the company that were valued at the then staggering sum of £900,000.

Perhaps the only disappointed person in this long story of Persian oil was D'Arcy's wife. She saw the prospectus of the newly formed Anglo-Persian Oil Company and was greatly disappointed 'to see that they have left my husband's name out of it absolutely. This, I think, is a great mistake, as his name is associated far and wide with this Persian business. He will not do anything, of course – I have talked to him for months but quite uselessly, so I am making a last bid for fame to you.'

In Persia the search to discover oil was over. But elsewhere in the Middle East it was barely beginning.

8

Admiral Chester Eyes Mesopotamia

While Reynolds was on the verge of making his dramatic breakthrough at Masjid-i-Suleiman, an elderly American was just beginning a race to find oil in neighbouring Mesopotamia.

Grey-haired, heavily moustached and bespectacled, the 63-year-old Colby M. Chester had arrived in Constantinople in January 1908 at the instigation of his employers, the Chamber of Commerce and the State Board of Trade in New York. His prior stop had been Geneva, where he had attended a week-long international trade conference. After that he had boarded a train and headed east to the capital of the Ottoman Empire.

Chester must have been full of memories as the train reached the city and pulled into its main station. For this was not his first trip there. He cast his mind back to the events of November 1895, when American missionaries in Harput and Maras had been repeatedly fired on by Ottoman troops as they fled from their burning homes.[1] The damage to their property had been extensive, costing around $84,500, and an infuriated Washington administration had immediately demanded reparations. But when officials in Constantinople denied all responsibility, one senior official recommended that some American battleships be sent 'to rattle the Sultan's windows', giving him a gentle reminder that the question of reparations was a serious business. Eventually, in 1899, the USS *Kentucky* arrived on the coasts of Constantinople, although its mission soon turned out to be anything but warlike: Ottoman officials cordially received the officers, who were then personally invited by Sultan Abdul Hamid to attend an elaborate dinner at the royal court, known for centuries as the Sublime Porte. The person who had the greatest honour of all – to sit at the sultan's side throughout the meal – was *Kentucky*'s captain, none other than Colby Chester.

Up until this time he had known nothing other than the navy all his professional life, having joined up at the age of just fifteen, in 1859, and subsequently seen active service in the American Civil War and the Spanish–American War of 1898. After the incident at Constantinople he had deeply impressed his seniors and quickly climbed the ranks, eventually being promoted from captain to rear admiral in 1903. But in 1906 he had decided to move on and find new openings while he still had the chance, and using his contacts in the American government, found his way into the world of business and international trade. With his travelling experience and leadership skills, many leaders of industry felt that the former rear admiral would have all the makings of an excellent overseas trade representative.

The purpose of his trip in 1908 was not specifically to ask for an oil concession but to propose and discuss an idea borne by two American travellers, Arthur Moore and Homer Davenport, who had journeyed to Arabia the previous year. They had initially gone there to buy horses, but had soon become interested by a somewhat more ambitious idea. If a railway was built between Aleppo and Alexandretta, they argued, then it would dramatically reduce transport costs for regional trade and prove hugely lucrative.[2] Such a line would cross stretches of land ruled from Constantinople, having formed part of the Ottoman Empire for several hundred years. The various investors they discussed their idea with back home were equally enthusiastic, and Chester, recently appointed to represent his New York sponsors, was asked to outline the idea to Ottoman officials when he next had the chance to visit the Sublime Porte.

Although he expected to encounter a lot of hand wringing, excuses and delay, Chester got a broadly positive response from the officials, who asked for more details about the proposal. Chester cabled the request back to New York, and some weeks later his son, Commander Arthur Chester, also arrived in Constantinople to lay out detailed plans about what was involved. After travelling to Aleppo to take a close look at sections of the proposed route, the young American then submitted a formal proposal for a concession.

Everyone knew that building a 900-mile stretch of railway like this would be a hugely time-consuming and costly business, but some years before a certain Dr Pasdermadjian, an Ottoman official from Erzerum, seemed to have found a new way of making such projects financially self-sufficient. For if the concessionaries had exclusive rights not just over the railway route but also over an area immediately surrounding the line, then they could also explore for minerals within this wider vicinity and, if they found any, exploit and sell them to fund the railway venture. So when the Ottoman Ministry of Public Works offered the Chesters these broader terms, allowing them to dig underground within a 24-mile radius of the railway, news of the decision caused alarm and consternation in several foreign capitals. For in this situation winning a railway concession would also give the Americans exclusive rights to search for the single substance that, more than any other, almost everyone else wanted: oil.

On his first visit Colby had toured the Ottoman capital with enthusiasm and a sense of wonder, walking through its bazaars and taking in the glories of the great Byzantine and Islamic buildings – St Sophia, St Irene, Constantine the Great's own monument, the façade of St Theodore Tyrone – that he had read and heard so much about. But wonderful though many of its sights were, the Ottoman Empire hardly promised to be a particularly appealing place to search for oil. Its whole infrastructure was certainly anything but ideal, since many of its laws were badly drafted, out of date and barely enforced by corrupt courts and by police forces that were either grossly inefficient or, in many areas, completely non-existent. There were also a whole host of local laws that considerably complicated matters, or at least seemed to: whenever a European or Western geologist appeared in a particular region, all manner of dormant claims and interests were sometimes aired by local officials or noblemen who started talking about their 'exclusive rights' to anything that was found there. Some of these claims were made by the optimistic, such as one Faud Pasha, who tried to persuade Western geologists that he was in fact the ruler of one area, near Mosul in Mesopotamia, where oil seepages were flowing freely. Other claimants should have known better, such as some members of the Egyptian royal family who argued quite unconvincingly that they had unquestionable proprietary rights to much of the Turkish lands.

Many areas of the empire were also as geographically remote as the areas of Persia where Reynolds had worked, and were almost wholly unconnected with the outside world by any real formal transports links. The main obstacle, however, would be wilful obstructionism on the part of the officials in the capital. It was common knowledge that the empire desperately needed financial investment, for politically and commercially it was fast falling apart. But the Turks were also deeply wary of any foreign involvement in their domestic affairs, and for the past century or more had had to suffer the indignity of watching the British, French and Russian governments and their armies making increasingly audacious encroachments within their borders.

Yet this scarcely mattered to entrepreneurs who were sufficiently wealthy and brave to fund oil-exploration operations. For over the past three decades their appetites had been whetted by the findings of several scientific missions, like those of Jacques de Morgan in Persia, that had gone to the region in search of oil and invariably returned with broadly positive findings. In the whole Ottoman Empire there was one region above all that seemed to harbour particular promise. This was Mesopotamia, which covered a huge expanse of the Middle East that not only included the land between the two great rivers the Tigris and Euphrates, but which also stretched eastwards all the way from southern Turkey as far as south-west Persia, and then as far south as the kingdom of Kuwait.[3] The Ottoman armies had captured the whole region in the course of the sixteenth century, and by the turn of the century still ruled over the two great cities – Mosul and, to the north, Baghdad – where most of the oil seepages were to be found. A work party of German experts had visited the surrounding areas in 1871 and had found signs of a plentiful supply of petroleum. The only real disadvantage, these visitors felt, was the area's inaccessibility, since there would be considerable difficulties moving any oil to foreign markets. Shortly afterwards a French geologist had been taken to see seepages near Mandali that the local *wali*, or ruler, Midhat Pasha, had made some initial moves to develop. This area also seemed very promising, and the geologist was also taken aback by just how much oil was flowing from these seepages.

By the turn of the century, several other voices had added further weight to these upbeat reports. In 1901 a German technical commission led by Baron von Oppenheim ventured the most favourable opinion on Mesopotamia to date, stating that it was essentially a vast 'lake of petroleum'. It would be advisable, ran the report, to develop these oilfields if for no other purpose than to break the stranglehold of the 'omnipotent Standard' – a reference to the Standard Oil Company that, together with Russian exporters from Baku, was at that time threatening to establish a global monopoly. Soon afterwards a well-known German geologist, Dr Paul Rohrbach, visited the Mesopotamian valleys and wrote that they were 'virtually soaked with bitumen, naptha and gaseous hydrocarbons', and in his judgement harboured far greater potential than the Russian Transcaucasian fields had ever done.[4] 'From the German point of view', ran his report, 'it would be unparalleled stupidity if we did not most energetically do our part to acquire a share in the revival of the ancient civilization of Mesopotamia, Syria and Babylonia'.[5]

Not surprisingly it was not long before the Ottoman officials began to see these regions as a potentially lucrative source of revenue, and in 1888, after reading Jacques de Morgan's reports about oil prospects in nearby Persia, they made an important change to the way in which two of the most promising districts were ruled. To allow the central government in Constantinople to gain most from any oil that was found in Mosul and Baghdad, the authorities in Constantinople changed the provinces' legal status in such a way that any oil profits would go directly to the sultan's purse. This also meant that potential investors would have to bargain for a concession with the sultan's closest advisers, who administered his private income, known as the Civil List. Chief among these advisors was the Grand Vizier, who at that time was one Ibrahim Hakki Pasha.

Harbouring a particularly strong interest in developing these resources was the German government, not least the state-owned Deutsche Bank. In 1888 the top Ottoman officials had promised to give the bank a helping hand in developing any mineral resources, including oil, that were found in the empire. Soon afterwards the Anatolian Railway Company, which was owned by the bank, obtained a concession not only to build a rail link through Anatolia to the head of the Persian Gulf but also to have preferential mining rights over a 20 kilometre strip of its either side.

The German government in Berlin had always strongly supported these tentative moves by Deutsche Bank to build up links with the Ottomans, even if they had not as yet borne commercial fruit. This was because since the mid-1890s the Kaiser had been keen to establish the sultan as a firm strategic ally. There were all manner of considerations lying behind this. An alliance with the vast Ottoman Empire would give the Germans access to the Persian Gulf, and this access would not only bestow them with immense prestige but also enable them to threaten vital British interests if, as many were beginning increasingly to fear, war should ever break out between the two great powers.

By the beginning of the twentieth century, Berlin had made several moves to cement this relationship. In 1898 Kaiser Wilhelm had made his second visit to the Ottoman Empire, a visit that did much to impress both the people who saw him and the rulers he met with. Greeted with great fanfare at Constantinople, he made a special tour of the Holy Land, making a triumphal entry into Jerusalem, hoisting the imperial standard on top of Mount Zion, visiting the grave of Saladin at Damascus and then making a speech that assured Muslims the world over of Germany's good faith towards Islam. But the Germans also had another plan to build a relationship with the Ottoman Empire. This was to make the 1888 railway agreement part of a much more ambitious project – the construction of a railway line that would run all the way from Berlin to Baghdad. In 1903, after several years of surveying and negotiation, the Ottomans and representatives of the Anatolian Railway Company signed an initial deal to build the link.

Right from the start, oil was central to the project. Under the terms of the deal the company would have a right to explore for oil around the track – the same rights it had under the 1888 agreement to build a railway that, if completed, would form one section of this much more ambitious project. The role of petroleum had become even more pronounced in the summer of 1904, when the Ministry of the Privy Purse also granted the company an opportunity to explore for oil around Mosul and Baghdad. This was an opportunity to undertake only 'preliminary investigations', but if any oil was found in the course of this twelve-month exploration period then the agreement also offered the company an exclusive 40-year concession to exploit the reserves. In his report Rohrbach had argued that 'we ought to attach the greatest importance to the circumstances that the Baghdad railway will pass close to the petroleum districts', and added that 'the only thing to be feared is that foreign gold and foreign speculation should succeed in securing a preferential right in the exploitation of Mesopotamian naptha before any effective German initiative has been taken'.[6]

Mainly because of the huge initial costs such an operation would incur, the company never made any real efforts to explore the region and had merely renewed its option every year until 1907, when it quietly lapsed. Nonetheless such moves were watched with alarm by the British contingent in Constantinople, where Ambassador Sir Nicholas O'Conor, a man of dry wit and formidable personal presence, argued that 'discoveries of bitumen and naptha would greatly increase the productiveness of the line'. But the Germans were not alone in eyeing a concession to explore for Mesopotamian oil. As early as 1901 William

Knox D'Arcy had felt that the region probably shared the same geological strata as Persia, and that it would make much more sense to explore both regions rather than just one. When in the summer his key negotiator, Alfred Marriott, finished his work in Tehran, having signed and sealed an oil concession with the shah, D'Arcy cabled him from London and asked him if he would travel to Constantinople to undertake some preliminary negotiations with Ottoman officials about a similar venture. Over the next eighteen months Marriott based himself at the Sublime Porte, but the going soon proved far tougher than either he or his sponsor had expected, and in 1903 D'Arcy replaced him with another contact, H.E. Nichols, after wasting a great deal of time and money.

The British Foreign Office had always been aware of Berlin's ambitions in the region, and was anxious to thwart its bid to establish a strategic alliance with Constantinople. London was particularly concerned by the prospect of a Berlin–Baghdad railway, which would have given the Germans direct access to the Persian Gulf and conceivably posed a threat to the security of British India. But Whitehall was also desperate to prevent any Mesopotamian oil falling into German hands, and was therefore anxious to give D'Arcy's ambitions in the region a helping hand. As O'Conor argued, 'There is every ground for believing that this concession, especially as Mesopotamia is developed by the extension of railway communications and irrigation works, will prove exceedingly valuable, and … the creation of such important British interests in that country will greatly enhance our influence and general position.'[7]

In March 1904 the British foreign secretary, the Marquess of Lansdowne, instructed O'Conor to provide Nichols with any information about Mesopotamian oil that he happened to have, notably the rumours that British spies had by this time heard about the Anatolian Railway Company's bid to win a concession in Mosul and Baghdad. Nichols and D'Arcy declined the offer, however, thinking that the involvement of the British government would bring a lot of unnecessary politics into their negotiations and seriously compromise their chances of success. It was not long before they probably came to regret their decision, however, since the truth behind the rumours emerged a few weeks later, and by this time there was nothing that either man could do to dislodge the strong German position in Constantinople.

The sheer difficulty of bargaining with the slow and obstinate Ottoman authorities soon began to tell. As the negotiations lingered on, O'Conor wrote to Hardinge complaining how 'Nichols is still hammering away at the Mesopotamian oilfields negotiations, but as he is on the point of closing something goes wrong'. The British ambassador felt that Nichols' best hope was 'to sweep the board by offering terms far beyond the greed of avarice' while also withholding any payment until any deal was properly signed for. But still the discussions went on and on without result, and in October 1908 O'Conor braced himself to make his own direct approach to the sultan, sidestepping Nichols altogether, until he was talked out of the idea by D'Arcy.

O'Conor's frustration was understandable, for every time Nichols took a step forward the Ottoman officials seemed to find new obstacles with which to block his path and then force him back to square one. The Turks were certainly expert at finding all manner of difficulties to make a foreign negotiator's life difficult. They would, for instance, often insist on the government having some rights of access to certain places within a proposed concessionary area, and then haggle endlessly about the circumstances in which they could exercise any such rights. And if an agreement was ever struck then they would demand a long interlude, perhaps of several months duration, before going any further: such a pause for thought, they argued, was necessary in order properly to air details of the agreement, find out if there was anyone else interested in making their own rival offers, or any other third party whose interests might in any way be at stake. All manner of other issues could complicate matters even more, such as the fate of other concessions in the region, which the Ottomans sometimes insisted had to be settled first before any agreement on oil could be properly considered.

In the meantime D'Arcy and Nichols were facing new competition from another party with a rapidly increasing interest in the Ottoman Empire. In the USA presidents William McKinley and Theodore Roosevelt had been quietly instigating a new policy of commercial diplomacy that mirrored their keen enthusiasm to find new markets for American exports, and the Ottoman Empire seemed to have much to offer. By the turn of the century some tentative steps towards building these links had already been taken. In 1899 a new direct steamship service had been established between New York and Constantinople, breaking the monopoly enjoyed by British ships. This direct service did not last long but it did encourage other countries, notably Germany and Italy, to arrange their own shipping lines that could transport American goods to Turkey much more easily and cheaply than ever before. All of a sudden a huge new market seemed to be beckoning.

By the time Admiral Chester stepped into the scene in 1908, the American government had been busily building up its political ties with the region, and in 1906 it established its first embassy to Constantinople, appointing John G.A. Leishman as its representative. But what had really changed everything was the political revolution of July 1908, when a group of 'Young Turks', committed to sweeping aside centuries of antiquated tradition and introducing drastic social and political changes, seized power in Constantinople. This had important consequences for the oil hunters, because an administration that had hitherto been strongly pro-German was now actively looking elsewhere – to Britain and perhaps the United States – for guidance, support and trade. Seeing a chance, President Roosevelt soon despatched a telegram expressing sympathy for their cause, while Ambassador Leishman wrote of his high hopes for the future: the revolution, he said, 'enhances the opportunity of extending our commerce many fold, as the development of the country, which was retarded and almost strangled by the methods of the old regime, will be encouraged to the greatest extent possible by the new Government, which is sure to result in a great wave of prosperity'.[8]

Chester had strong support from the American government – or at least from certain quarters within it – by the time he arrived at the Sublime Porte. His strongest supporters were in the corridors of the State Department, notably from Under Secretary Oscar S. Straus and Secretary Knox, who penned a letter to Ahmed Rustem Bey, the Ottoman charge d'affaires in Washington, emphasizing that his government was attaching the greatest importance to the proposed Chester Concession, and added that he was keen to establish growing commercial relations between the two countries.

The game for Mesopotamian oil had by this time become much more complicated because over the preceding few months a good number of other contestants had also stepped forward to join the fray. There was a Belgian group, represented in Constantinople by the somewhat eccentric Colonel Schaeffer, and a British organization comprising a firm of merchants in Constantinople and the Euphrates and Tigris Steam Navigation Company. Back in London, a Member of Parliament, R.L. Harmsworth, had also declared his wish 'to pursue this matter to the utmost of my ability and resources' and wrote to the Foreign Office asking for official support to his own claim for a Mesopotamian concession. Yet another British contender was the Euxine and Marmora British Development Syndicate, whose representatives proposed building a railway that would cover more of north Anatolia than the German plan and which would give them sole mining rights on 15 kilometres either side. The Syndicate's officials approached the Foreign Office in London for advice but were quickly told that they would run into obstacles: their plan would fall foul of a Russo-Turkish agreement struck in 1900, Whitehall officials warned, and therefore had almost no prospect of success.

At the same time another American, a Mr Bruce Glasgow, also turned up in Constantinople and was preparing to outbid Chester. The Admiral knew that he would have to take Glasgow's bid seriously, for he was representing a company, the Anglo-American firm of J.G. White & Co, that had considerable financial clout and which also boasted some powerful supporters in the American Embassy in Constantinople. But Glasgow could still not quite match the political and financial resources that Chester had at his disposal, and by the autumn of 1909, less than nine months after it had first been aired, his scheme was pushed right out of the picture. For a while a British aristocrat, the Earl of Denbigh, also entertained plans to resurrect the Glasgow scheme and contacted the Foreign

Office to obtain its support. But these plans also came to nothing, so that Chester was by this time assured of a huge head start over his rivals.

Being in such a strong position, Chester made yet more ambitious demands in the course of 1909. Instead of wanting to build a railway link between Aleppo and Alexandretta, as he had originally proposed to the sultan on his arrival in Constantinople, he now advocated building one that would move eastwards from Sivas all the way to Suleimaniya. The plan was then to build separate lines that would branch off to Samsun on the Black Sea, Youmourtalik on the Mediterranean and to Lake Van. At the same time he offered terms that he felt would be more appealing to the Ottomans, who of course wanted to give away as little as possible. Under this revised concession, the Chester group would now have exclusive rights to look for oil and other minerals only within a ten kilometre area on either side of the railway line.

Now represented by the admiral's two sons, Colby M. Chester Jr and Commander Arthur Chester, and their brother-in-law C. Arthur Moore Jr, the American contingent pushed their claims forward, and a draft of the proposed concession was drawn up by the Ministry of Public Works. In November Chester went on to co-found the Ottoman–American Development Company that would help fund the operation (with his eldest son acting as company secretary), and in March 1910 a senior minister in Constantinople took things a stage further by signing a detailed preliminary agreement between them.

But although the company was backed by the might of the American government, it was also up against a very determined German bid to block the Chester Concession. News of the admiral's move had caused considerable consternation in Berlin, where it was seen as a serious threat to German political and commercial interests in the region. So seriously did they take this threat that Berlin officials and their agents in the Sublime Porte, notably the formidable German ambassador Marshall von Bieberstein, tried all manner of tactics to scupper it. For a time they tried spreading a rumour that they felt sure would raise eyebrows in the sultan's court: Chester was secretly working on behalf of Standard Oil, ran the story they invented and then planted, and any such links meant that the Ottoman Empire could easily be dominated by a hugely wealthy oil conglomerate that had enough capital at its disposal to carve a vast sphere of influence throughout the wider region. The Turks, however, were not convinced, and the Germans instead used the threat of economic retaliation if the sultan went ahead and granted Chester his concession, while also promising to support Ottoman territorial claims on the disputed island of Crete if they cooperated in return.

The British were equally keen to try to block Chester's moves. Behind the scenes, unknown to the Americans, British diplomats in Constantinople were trying hard to wreck its chances, busily pointing out the concession's various hidden snags and hitches, while favourably comparing the advantages of the D'Arcy scheme. Nichols had the full backing of the Foreign Office to step in and do everything he could to demolish the rival proposals, and Gerald Lowther, the new British ambassador, recorded that D'Arcy's representative was 'doing his best to achieve the destruction of the Chester scheme'. In November 1908 D'Arcy also wrote to Whitehall, requesting renewed diplomatic support for his own concessionary proposals. His message reached an old contact from his Persian days, Sir Arthur Hardinge, who thought very highly of D'Arcy, regarding him as 'a man of substance, both physically and financially [who] deserves encouragement', and who now instructed Lowther to redouble his efforts to help the great investor.

But Whitehall officials felt that, even if the worst came to the worst, not all would be lost if Chester won the day. His proposed concession, after all, would not have given him the right to explore for oil in the most promising area of all, the province of Mosul, even if he could nonetheless 'take the pearl out of the oyster'. At the same time D'Arcy was taking his own precautions. In April 1910 he formally applied for his own concession to explore for oil in the areas that fell outside the scope of the Chester Concession, while also requesting exclusive rights to build and operate pipelines in the same regions: if he had the sole right to build and operate pipelines in Mosul, he argued, then any organization that did find oil elsewhere in the region would be dependent on his goodwill to move it to foreign markets. And if the Chester Concession should ever fall through at any stage, then he, as the sole pipeline operator in the region, would be supremely well placed to step into the Admiral's shoes.

Any British hopes about elbowing the Americans out, however, were misplaced, for unknown to London the Germans had been working hard to thwart D'Arcy as well as Chester. In June 1909 the head of the Anatolian Railway Company had formally written to the Ottoman authorities emphasizing that his own oil 'rights' were imperilled. He followed this up two months later with a formal complaint: there would be legal action, he claimed, if Constantinople refused to recognize his rights in the region under the 1903 agreement. Everyone, it seemed, was out to thwart each other.

Back in Washington, the State Department was well aware of the strength of German pressure on Constantinople. Senior officials arranged for 'very discreet but strong oral representations' to be made to the German Government, but started to think of alternative strategies if Berlin won the game: 'failing German cooperation and the removal of German opposition in this instance', ran one memorandum, 'it might be necessary for this government to cooperate in Turkey with other powers'.

In the meantime a succession of American diplomats were also pushing their case. When, in 1910, John R. Carter was appointed as the new American ambassador to Turkey, he was instructed that the Concession was a matter of paramount importance, one in which 'the President takes a keen interest' and one that he needed to pursue vigorously. Soon afterwards an Assistant Secretary of State, Mr Huntington Wilson, was despatched to Constantinople, ostensibly on a courtesy trip but really 'to create an atmosphere favourable to the Chester claims'. He raised the issue in talks with the sultan and received an encouraging reply: the Chester proposal would have to scrap the idea of building a railway as far as Yuomourtalik, he stated, since this violated the Baghdad Railway Concession which guaranteed the Germans prior rights to all branches on the Mediterranean coast between Mersin and Tripoli. But provided the Americans gave way on this point, and on a couple of other more minor matters, then the project could proceed. Meanwhile the new American president, William Taft, was most keen to support him, telling Congress that 'the United States has gained markedly in its commercial standing with certain of the nations of the Near East. Turkey, especially, is beginning to come into close relations with the United States through the new interest of American manufacturers and exporters in the possibilities of those regions, and it is hoped that foundations are being laid for a large and mutually beneficial exchange of commodities between the two countries'.[9]

Once these issues had been resolved, the grand vizier, the Committee on Public Works and the Council of Ministers approved the Chester Concession and in May 1911 sent a copy of the draft to parliament for ratification. A two-day debate followed but the proposal met stiff opposition. Defeated by a clear majority, the bill's sponsors were now forced to postpone any action until the autumn. Over the next few months Washington lobbied hard to push the concession further forward, instructing Ambassador Rockhill to study the proposal carefully 'with a view to the prompt consummation of the concession upon the reopening of the Ottoman parliament'. But when on 20 November the bill was presented back to parliament, it was not political opposition that it ran up against. It was severe financial hardship. For in the intervening few months the Ottoman–American Development Company had started to waver financially as shareholders began to lose faith in the project, and on 11 December Ambassador Rockhill informed the grand vizier that the Company had withdrawn its caution money as well as its application for the Concession. The bill now slipped away from the parliamentary agenda.

For the moment at least, the Chester Concession may have turned to dust, but it bequeathed a legacy. On the one hand it had stirred up a lot of international interest in the region and its natural resources. On the other, it had also illustrated just how elusive such concessions actually were: anyone who tried to obtain them not only faced immense competition from other countries, but was also confronted by the agonizingly slow and inefficient Ottoman bureaucracy. The

Americans had been negotiating the terms of the Chester Concession for three whole years and had always encountered an infuriating amount of procrastination and evasion. So far, Mesopotamian oil had remained just a mirage.

9

The Great Gulbenkian

As their own efforts to win the concession continued to flounder, Nichols, Chester and all the other participants who were playing the great game for Mesopotamian oil became aware that someone else had entered the race and, eerily, seemed also to have been keeping careful watch over their movements. For as early as 1907, this particular individual had quietly opened a small office in Constantinople and tasked his local representatives with tracking his rivals' every move. His name was Calouste Sarkis Gulbenkian.

Had they at this stage known that Gulbenkian was hot on their heels, every one of the other contestants would have felt an enormous sense of alarm and dismay. For by the time he turned his attentions to Mesopotamia, this extraordinary man had already acquired a formidable reputation as an investor who possessed an astonishing, almost uncanny, degree of foresight and judgement. True, he had missed out on Persian oil even though he had briefly been offered a golden opportunity: he had long been well acquainted with General Kitabgi, but on hearing of the concessionary proposal had decided that, given the lack of any clear evidence that oil was present, the risks of exploring Persia outweighed the benefits. But the sense of fury he felt when Reynolds had struck oil in May 1908 merely made him all the more determined to stop his great rival William Knox D'Arcy from snatching another Middle Eastern crown straight from out of his own grasp.

Although of diminutive height and slight build, Gulbenkian nonetheless looked the part of a formidable oil investor. By 1910, at the age of 41, he sported the thick beard and the long, twirling moustache that was fashionable in Edwardian times, and was always impeccably dressed. But perhaps his most striking attribute, one that many of his contemporaries commented upon, was his unusually piercing, pale blue eyes, which somehow seemed to notice every move and always seemed to hide immense calculation.

Gulbenkian's financial expertise and his remarkable knowledge of oil had been nurtured from an early age. He had been born in Armenia where his father, Sarkis, had become an early pioneer of the local kerosene industry and had eventually succeeded in winning a highly prized contract to supply the sultan and his court. So successful and efficient did Sarkis prove to be that he not only amassed a considerable personal fortune, but was generously rewarded with the governorship of Trebizond, a port on the Black Sea that acted as a transit point for vast quantities of Baku oil.

Besides acquiring considerable knowledge of the kerosene trade and the commodity's uses, the young Calouste also heard much about the workings of the sultan's court, where Sarkis had spent considerable time haggling with officials. He knew that he could use his racial origins to good advantage, since the sultan generally liked to discriminate against upper-class Turks (who could perhaps pose a threat to his rule) in favour of other nationalities from within his empire, including Jews and Greeks as well as Armenians. And Calouste had always been well aware how in Constantinople, as in Tehran, money talked. In such a place every man had his price and almost everyone of any note would have to be offered *baksheesh*. Not only that but the right amount of *baksheesh*, for if you tried to bribe too much then officials became wary and their superiors jealous, but if you offered too little you just insulted them and instantly lost favour.

In fact there were a lot of ways in which wheeling and dealing in Constantinople took real know-how and experience. From his father and his own contacts, the young Calouste learned of just the right moment to approach a minister for negotiations: when the official had eaten, or when he had just seen his mistress, then the chances were that he would be in good humour and open to approach. But if he was ill, perhaps after overindulging at table, or exhausted after a long journey, then it was best to keep well clear. He would also have to remember that in a world like this all sorts of tiny details, although seemingly insignificant, could sometimes reveal a surprising amount about one's ulterior motives and give the game away. The sultan, for example, ensured the loyalty of his ministers by making them eat fine meals, knowing that they could not turn the invitation down because it was a great honour to be offered food in the royal household and a great insult to refuse. But the ministers also knew that the sultan could easily hide poison in their meals: so if a minister refused or avoided any of the food that was given to him, then the Sultan would assume that he was fearful of poison because he had a guilty conscience, and had something to hide.

By the time he arrived in London to start his university studies, the young Gulbenkian was well versed in the politics of the Ottoman court as well as the ways of the kerosene trade. Formidably motivated and immensely hard-working, he now sought to acquire a more scientific expertise that would help him realize his ambitions to work in the oil business, and in 1887, at the age of just 19, he graduated from Kings College, London with an outstandingly good degree in civil engineering, a course in which petroleum had been particularly closely studied.

All sorts of different interests, and fears, seemed to drive Gulbenkian towards great things. His immense ambition was partly a product of his upbringing and a characteristic of his fellow Armenians, who had reputation for being extremely hard working. Calouste in particular, however, was also a lover of fine things and needed a lot of money to fund such tastes. By the turn of the century he had developed an interest in French classical art, and in 1907 had made his first purchase of a major work of art – the *View of Mira on the Brenta* by the Italian artist Francesco Guardi, his favourite artist whose works he was always looking for.

Armed with so much knowledge and expertise, and already speaking several foreign languages with reasonable fluency, Gulbenkian had set off to make his fortune in the world of oil. In 1888 he returned to Constantinople and from there made his way to Baku and then Batum, carefully researching the workings of the oil industry in both towns before publishing his findings in a highly prestigious French journal, the *Revue des Deux Mondes*, that was widely read in very influential circles throughout Europe and beyond. Within a year these articles had also been expanded into a book that had given its author outstanding cachet as an oil expert. This would have been a remarkable achievement for anyone, but Calouste had done it at the prodigiously early age of 21.

His obvious intellectual powers, and the originality of these early articles, immediately caught the attention of the many Ottoman officials who read them, and before long the young author was invited to visit the Sublime Porte. 'My publication attracted the attention of the Minister of the Civil List, Hagop Pasha, who was a great friend of my father, and of the Minister of Mines, Selim Effendi', as he later claimed, 'and they wanted to get as much information as possible about Mesopotamian oil prospects'.

Years later Gulbenkian was not ashamed to admit that the reports he now compiled for the Ottomans were not based on his own travels and first-hand researches, similar to those that were then being undertaken by Jacques de Morgan. On the contrary, he instead ploughed through the journals and reports written by other geologists who had made their way through the region, sometimes contacting them to ask for further information. But however second-hand and imperfect the means he employed, the report he subsequently wrote deeply impressed the officials in Constantinople who read it, and helped to so convince them of Mesopotamia's potential as an oil-producing region that they quickly moved to change its legal status to ensure that the sultan, not the local governments, would benefit from any oil revenues that flowed.

Grateful Ottoman officials paid him well for this work, but the young Calouste was also able to use the influence of his key acquaintance in the capital, Djavid Bey, to find further reward. For Bey recommended him as an adviser to Constantinople and as its chief financial agent in Paris and London. Born and brought up in Armenia, he was, after all, an Ottoman subject, even though he had by now also spent considerable time in both France and England.

So by this time he was a true internationalist with many friends in high places. By 1902 he had become a naturalized British citizen, even though he spoke English with a very strong guttural accent that was sometimes very hard to understand. He travelled almost constantly, regularly crossing the English Channel to make his way to and from his homes in London and Paris, both of which were near the epicentres of power. His Paris home was at 27 Quai d'Orsay, close to the government ministries where he was a regular visitor, as well as to the permanent suites of top hotels where he arranged for his many successive mistresses to stay. His house at 38 Hyde Park Gardens in central London also gave him easy access to the capital's high and mighty, and was close to his favourite sojourn at suite no. 420 of The Ritz, on the fourth floor overlooking Green Park, where he collected and housed all manner of luxurious and expensive items, not least an exquisite Persian carpet that invariably impressed visitors.

Besides his own oil expertise, a superb asset in building contacts on both sides of the Channel and beyond was his wife Nevarte, whom he had married in 1892. Nevarte came from one of the leading Christian families of Constantinople, one that had long had immensely useful contacts throughout the whole of the Ottoman Empire. In particular, she happened to have a cousin who was related to the longstanding ruler of Egypt, Nubar Pasha, and although this was only an indirect association, it was one that nonetheless greatly assisted Gulbenkian's professional career. Nubar turned out to be a great help because he had for some time been a friend of the royal heir, the Prince of Wales – later Edward VII – and was well networked with all the leading financiers and businessmen of the day. Not only that, but Nubar also had enduring links with the Baring brothers, the famous City of London merchant bankers who were later to give strong financial backing to Gulbenkian's business ventures, as well as with most of France's top business names, most notably the Rothschilds. With such acquaintances to boast of, Calouste Gulbenkian was well connected almost everywhere by the turn of the century.

Nevarte was also determined to make their Hyde Park home into something of a hub for London's business elite, knowing that this would be indispensable to her husband's professional success. When it came to this side of things, Calouste was almost entirely dependent on his wife, for although he had many remarkable abilities, socializing was not one of them. This limitation was, of course, bound to prove a handicap in the world of business where impressing would-be financial backers counted for all. Fortunately, however, his socially energetic, ambitious and personable wife had an unmistakable glamour and excellent social graces that stood them both in good stead. 'She collected a rich, cultivated and influential set around her ... her plans to break into high society were deliberate', as her children later recalled.

Two business contacts that Gulbenkian had made by the early years of the new century were the Samuel brothers, who had founded what had by this time become one of the world's most famous oil companies – Shell Transport and

Trading. Recognizing that the brothers would probably have a strong business interest in the region, he persuaded them to open an office in Constantinople that he would be prepared to fund and operate on their behalf. Its ostensible purpose was to deal with oil shipments from Russia for the Samuels' newly formed venture, Royal Dutch Shell. But in practice the great Gulbenkian wanted to use it as a cover for his own dealings in the capital, where he was prepared to spend vast sums on *baksheesh* and keep careful watch on his competitors in pursuit of the great prize that he felt sure was waiting to be discovered and exploited: Mesopotamian oil.

So if anyone was qualified to make headway through the sultan's court and win a Mesopotamian concession, it was Calouste Gulbenkian. Backed with the Samuel family's vast financial assets as well as his own, he must have seemed to be something of an unstoppable force. But if there was any obstacle lying in his way it was the sheer strength of German pressure, the same obstacle that had blocked the separate bids made by both Admiral Chester and William Knox D'Arcy to win the sultan's favour.

Both Gulbenkian and Marcus Samuel had had their appetites for Middle Eastern oil whetted not just by D'Arcy's experiences in Persia but also by news of yet more discoveries in the region. For just shortly before, in 1907, one of the Samuels' family friends and business colleagues had heard of oil seepages in the Red Sea and made his way to the region to find out more. Although most of his fellow directors in the Shell group wanted nothing to do with this risky venture, Marcus trusted his instincts and decided to sponsor a respected Dutch geologist, a Dr Erb, to visit the area and make an independent report. His initial findings were very disappointing, as was the survey subsequently carried out by Kruisheer, yet another expert who was shipped out to take a further close look. But still Samuel refused to give up, partly because he had heard so many stories and rumours of oil in the region, but also because he knew that any oil found in British-ruled Egypt would be classified as 'a source of oil within the British Empire' and therefore be likely to win the military protection of the Royal Navy as well as sponsorship and backing from within Whitehall.

Like the other oil explorers, Marcus Samuel seemed to be gifted with superb, almost uncanny, foresight, for in 1909 Egyptian drillers finally struck a large seam of oil at a site near Gemsa. Marcus was determined to seize his chance and asked his brother to work on his behalf in the region. By chance his brother happened to have a deep love for Egypt – its people, culture and sites – and often travelled there, usually to escape the British winter and find sanctuary in the most luxurious apartment that Cairo's highly prestigious Shepheard's Hotel could offer. So he was now well qualified to base himself in Egypt and help form the Red Sea Oilfields Ltd, which took over the Gemsa site in 1910 and began to exploit it to the full.

By the time Samuel and Gulbenkian were stepping up their operations in the search for a Mesopotamian concession, rumours about vast quantities of oil lying undiscovered beneath Egyptian sands had started to set the British press alight. On 18 January 1911 it was widely reported that huge new wells had been found at the Gemsa site, while shortly afterwards the *Financial Times* announced that 'the Anglo-Saxon Company will establish an *entrepot* [trading centre] supply of oil at the convergence of the world's greatest shipping trade'.

But even if his appetite had been whetted, Gulbenkian must have known that the prospect of winning a Mesopotamian concession would still be a formidably difficult task. Even he was still confronted by the same obstinacy, delays and excuses that had always dogged his competitors. But by 1912, there was one reason above all others why none of the European governments – British, German and Dutch – could afford to let the issue grind on fruitlessly as before. This was, quite simply, the heightened risk of American competition. For it seemed quite possible that, at any minute, Standard Oil of New Jersey or any other giant American firm could appear on the commercial horizon and use their massive financial muscle simply to extinguish any rival European. So while there was increasing mistrust, rivalry and suspicion between London and Berlin on the wider international stage, they were nonetheless being pushed ever closer together in this particular arena.

The two main contestants, Britain and Germany, also had other reasons to want to resolve the Mesopotamian question quickly. The Germans were particularly keen to get funding for their plans from the world's great financial centre, the City of London, but had so far failed miserably to find any interest there. No matter how much cooperation they got from Ottoman officials, it seemed most unlikely that their project would go far unless it won the confidence of international investors. The British, meanwhile, knew that by this time there were a number of interested parties other than the Americans that might start to get involved in the Mesopotamian scramble, thereby jeopardizing their own prospects for winning the concession. From the Ottoman capital one of the British representatives, Sir Henry Babington Smith, wrote to the Foreign Office warning about the arrival of a 'third party' in the negotiations that was complicating matters. This, it seems, was a reference to the somewhat eccentric Thomas de Ward, a self-styled aristocrat or 'baron' who had recently arrived in Constantinople and who had started to make numerous visits of his own to the Ministry of Mines in order to stake a claim to the concession.

British though the maverick 'baron' was, he was strongly distrusted by Whitehall, who felt that he might think nothing of selling his interest to the Germans or to any other rivals. Their fears were confirmed when he was informed by the Ottomans that a Mesopotamian concession could only be granted to an Anglo-German group, for within a few weeks Baron de Ward had risen to the challenge and formed just such an international organization, mustering a number of eminent supporters in both London and Berlin before renewing his bid to win favour in Constantinople. This unexpected move made Whitehall officials even more determined to thwart him, and when it emerged that he had supposedly offered the Turks £500,000 in return for the concession, the Foreign Office protested to both the grand vizier and to Hakki Pasha, who both denied having made Baron de Ward any promises at all.

Yet another Englishman who had by this time joined the Mesopotamian fray was one Roland Silley. He had arrived on the scene in 1910, but had not asked the Foreign Office for support until 1913, by which time he was feeling as thoroughly exasperated as all the other contestants by constant delays and excuses. But his bid for concessions in Mosul and Baghdad never had a chance of finding favour with London, which had already promised its support to D'Arcy and saw no reason now to change its mind. Nonetheless, the ambitious Silley had also fixed his eye on Basrah and Nejd, where his fellow Englishman had no plans to look for oil, and for a time it looked as though his bid for these regions might get the diplomatic backing he wanted: his attempt to get these two particular concessions would be looked at favourably, explained British officials, provided he gave them a written undertaking that his own commercial enterprise would never be transferred into non-British hands without their consent. But Silley's hopes were soon dashed, partly because the prospect of oil around Basrah soon aroused D'Arcy's interest, and partly also because Silley could not in any case provide the written undertaking that Whitehall demanded.

Soon afterwards, the India Office wrote a despatch to London that complained of the way in which 'other, and independent, eagles have gathered about the carcass'.[1] This was a reference not just to de Ward but to a whole host of other contestants. These included the Russian ambassador, working on behalf of ambitious fellow nationals, but also, most worryingly, the American Embassy, which represented the hugely wealthy and powerful Rockefeller as well as, perhaps, Admiral Chester. All of these interested parties, it turned out, had been making their own approaches to the Ottoman Ministry of Mines, and the Russians had already even offered to make an advance of ten million francs in return for the concession.

By now the obvious way forward seemed to be for the British and Germans to join forces. This appeared to be an even more promising avenue when the Turkish ambassador in London told Whitehall officials that if the British would agree to an amalgamation of their own interests with those of their rivals, then the grand vizier would, after all, go ahead and grant the concession. What was more, he was prepared to let the British take a majority stake in any such joint venture. It was at this point, in the summer of 1912, that a leading British-German financier of the day, Sir Ernest Cassel, formed the Turkish Petroleum Company, whose sole purpose was to bring rival parties together in order to win and then exploit a concession to search for oil in Mesopotamia and, if possible, elsewhere in the Ottoman Empire. Under this initial agreement, half of its shares would be held by the British-owned Turkish National Bank, which had been formed in 1910, while the rest was to be divided between Deutsche Bank and the Anglo-Saxon Oil Company, which was a subsidiary of Royal Dutch Shell.

There were two real winners and losers from this initial agreement. Although his name was hidden away, an undoubted winner was the man who, more than any other, had negotiated the entire project and steered it towards completion: Calouste Gulbenkian. He was a joint founder of the Turkish National Bank and, as an owner of 30 per cent of the bank's shares, therefore had a 15 per cent stake in the new company. But a loser was the Anglo-Persian Oil Company, whose directors were unhappy about the terms of the deal and refused to commit themselves. And without Anglo-Persian at its helm, the British government was also far from happy.

This was because there were by this time fast-growing links between Anglo-Persian and the British Admiralty. Within months of becoming First Lord of the Admiralty in September 1911, Winston Churchill had formally taken the decision to power the Royal Navy not with coal but with oil, and had soon begun the long and costly process of converting the ships' engines. This meant that finding a guaranteed source of long-term oil supply was of paramount concern to Whitehall, and because the Persian oilfields seemed to offer this, the Anglo-Persian Oil Company and the British government now started to come closer together. In June 1913 Churchill had presented his cabinet colleagues and parliament with a case for securing long-term sources of oil supply that would sustain Britain and her navy in the event of any national emergency. The British government, he wrote, should 'acquire a controlling interest in trustworthy sources of supply' and prevent the Admiralty 'from becoming dependent on any single combination'. Shortly afterwards, in a statement to Parliament, he elaborated further. Buying oil supplies from the open market, he claimed, was simply 'an open mockery', and this meant that it was essential for the Admiralty to become 'the owners or, at any rate, the controllers at the source' of the oil they used. At the same time he emphasized that 'on no one quality, on no one process, on no one route and on no one field must we be dependent. Safety and certainty lie in variety and variety alone'.[2]

In particular the deeply patriotic director of Anglo-Persian, Charles Greenway, was always quick to present his company as a major national asset, while senior figures in the Admiralty and the Foreign Office argued that the Persian concession, 'embracing as it did the entire oilfields of Persia ... should not pass under the control of a foreign syndicate'.[3] But both the British government and its new protégé were not content with just ensuring their grip over Persia alone.

Other Middle Eastern regions, most notably Mesopotamia, were also beckoning. In the words of the foreign secretary, Sir Edward Grey, 'evidently what we must do is to secure under British control a sufficient oil field for the Royal Navy', and by 1912 the Foreign Office's policy was to 'continue to endeavour to obtain the Mosul and Baghdad oilfields for the Anglo-Persian Oil Company'.[4]

By contrast, the Admiralty viewed Anglo-Persian's chief competitor, Royal Dutch Shell, with considerable suspicion since this company – predominantly Dutch owned – clearly had a strong foreign element that was felt to be under the sway of the Germans. Not only that, but most of its sources of supply, which were mainly in the Dutch East Indies and Romania, were so far away, and covered such vast areas, that they were reckoned to be highly vulnerable to enemy attack in the event of a national emergency.

News that Anglo-Persian had been pushed out of the initial agreement on the Turkish Petroleum Company caused dismay and consternation in Whitehall, and over the coming months the British government and APOC directors protested vigorously about the new arrangement and sought entirely to renegotiate the company's formation. Fortunately for them, however, they had more chance to do so than they had initially expected, for by May 1913 the Company's long negotiations for a concession had reached stalemate. After a long delay the Turks eventually turned down its representatives' request for a concession in the area between Mosul and Takrit, proving that the Company was not nearly as strong a contestant for Mesopotamian oil as it had wanted Anglo-Persian and the British government to believe: 'the German group are *not* now so confident as they pretend', wrote Charles Greenway in London.[5]

The British had a window of opportunity through which they could press their claims, and eventually, in a meeting that took place in London on 24 March 1914, a deal was struck. D'Arcy's group would now take a 50 per cent interest in the venture, putting the Turkish National Bank right out of the picture, while Deutsche Bank and the Anglo-Saxon Company took 22.5 per cent each. Gulbenkian would take the remaining 5 per cent of the 'beneficiary interest', a far smaller stake than before, but one from which he would of course still acquire enormous financial benefit if Ottoman oil was ever found.

Needless to say, this arrangement now suited Whitehall extremely well. For at just the same time Churchill had been negotiating closely with Anglo-Persian's directors, working out the details of an arrangement that would make the British government a majority stakeholder in the company. On 17 June he gave details of the new deal to the House of Commons: the government would acquire 51 per cent of the Anglo-Persian Oil Company, he announced, and spend £2.2 million to buy the shares. Not only that but it would also have a right to nominate two of its directors, each of whom would have a power of veto over all of its main affairs outside the narrowly commercial ones.

In the meantime, Calouste Gulbenkian had given up his interest in the Turkish Petroleum Company with a show of magnanimity, as though he was doing his duty for Great Britain, whereas Admiral Chester, who was now pushed right out of the picture, renounced his own draft concession with an indignation that was plain to see. But years later Gulbenkian did not conceal his own anger about the way in which his own business interest had been ousted:

> My stupefaction was great when a copy of the Agreement was handed to me and I discovered that at the last moment and without consulting me or asking for my consent, this important 1914 document, bearing the signatures of most eminent personalities, usurped my rights – in spite of the fact that I had been throughout the conceiver, founder and artisan of the Turkish Petroleum combine. This was a preposterous usurpation of power, crushing a minority without even consultation or seeking advice.[6]

But still there was one last hurdle for all of the interested parties to cross – the concession's ratification. They had been granted the concession but, as Chester had found out four years before, could not just assume that it would be ratified. Unfortunately by the summer of 1914 this looked just as remote a prospect as ever. For six years after seizing the reins of power, the Young Turks were no longer on good terms with the British government, having fallen out with London when news broke of the mass persecution of the Christian Armenians. Suddenly the Young Turks seemed to have a much darker side than anyone had realized: one of the leaders, Talaat Bey, had threatened to 'deal the Armenians such a blow as would stop them talking autonomy for fifty years', while another, Javid, may have had immense personal charm and wit, but was also known to have pulled out a knife and cut someone's throat without flinching; and then there was Enver Pasha, who was always well dressed and debonair but who had been the driving force behind the mass killings of innocent Armenians. Tension between Constantinople and London was high.

The man who saved the day was the great Armenian. Having already brokered the formation of the Turkish Petroleum Company in 1912 and subsequently kept it going – not least by renouncing a large part of his own stake in the venture – Calouste Gulbenkian now helped it along a crucial last lap of its journey. In June 1914 he managed to acquire a crucial letter from the grand vizier that, although amounting to less than a legally sanctioned concession, was still a formal and solemn promise granted by the highest of all Turkish authorities, one that came close to ratification. As he put it years later, it guaranteed 'the acquired rights promised to the Turkish Petroleum Company by the Ottoman Grand Vizier ... to the British and German ambassadors at the Sublime Porte'. The letter, written on 28 June and sent to the German ambassador in Constantinople, ran: 'The Ministry of Finance being substituted for the Civil List with respect to petroleum resources discovered, and to be discovered in the vilayets of Mosul and Baghdad, consents to lease to the Turkish Petroleum Company, and reserves to itself the right to determine hereafter its participation as well as the general conditions of the contract.'

One of Gulbenkian's great gifts was a remarkable persuasiveness, an ability that was partly borne of his uncanny ability to see the viewpoint, with its particular strengths and weaknesses, of those he was dealing with. His son, Nubar, later revealed how his father had deployed this skill in order to overcome the obstinacy of Turkish officials and obtain what would prove to be a vital signature: the Turks, he wrote, were 'persuaded to back Britain in writing because Turkey was broke as usual and urgently needed to raise the Customs Duties', which were fixed by international agreements. So 'father traded an increase in tariffs [with the support of the British government] for oil rights. He could rely on the British government because of his association with Lord Revelstoke who had the full confidence of the Foreign Office in financial matters. He also had the confidence of the Turks as he was their Senior Financial Adviser. He was on the inside at both ends of the negotiations.'[7]

But by a cruel twist of fate, the letter was sent on exactly the same day that another, much more momentous deed was carried out. On 28 June a Serbian extremist assassinated Archduke Franz Ferdinand of Austria, setting into a motion a deadly train of events that would lead to the outbreak of the First World War. Once again, the fruits of Mesopotamia turned out to be just beyond the grasp of the oil hunters.

10

The Irrepressible Admiral

In the mid-summer of 1920, officials in the State Department in Washington were astonished to find an unexpected visitor turn up on their doorstep, someone who had at one time been a highly familiar figure, but one whom they had neither seen nor heard of since before the outbreak of the First World War. For completely out of the blue, more than eighteen months after the end of hostilities and at the venerable age of 75, the irrepressible Admiral Chester had unexpectedly stepped back into the race to find Mesopotamian oil, and was once again pressing State officials to help him resurrect his concessionary claims and render their full support.

The rules and the entrants of this particular race, like the rest of the world, had been transformed over the preceding six years. Most of the oil syndicates formed before the outbreak of the war had simply vanished or changed beyond recognition, and there had in the meantime been a few minor bids to find oil in the region. In the south of Syria, German engineers, attached to the Turkish army, had tried without success to dig for oil, while some Russian soldiers had explored seepages when their armies had invaded eastern Turkey in early 1915. And in Mesopotamia, the Germans had also started to exploit the seepages at Kirkuk, Tuz and, above all, Qaiyara, where they carried out shallow drilling and used specially adapted lorries to remove some of the oil they had unearthed.

At the end of the war the entire political picture of the Middle East, as well as Europe, had of course also been completely changed. Having sided with Germany and been decisively defeated, the Turks had signed an armistice with the Allies on 30 October 1918 and then suffered the humiliation of watching British and French troops occupying much of their land. The question of what to do with their vast empire in the Middle East after the collapse of the central order had vexed the rest of Europe for decades (since at least the middle of the nineteenth century), but its resolution could now no longer be postponed.

One of the most vexing questions was the fate of a region that was widely thought to be the most rich in oil: Mosul in Mesopotamia. The Turkish leader, Kemal Pasha, had publicly renounced any claim to areas where Arabs were dominant, but strongly disputed that the majority ethnic group in Mosul – the Kurds – were in any sense 'Arabs' at all. On the contrary, he argued that, in allegiance and culture, the Kurdish population was much closer to Turkey, which he claimed had a very strong historic right to rule over the region. This put the Turks on a direct collision course with Great Britain, whose forces had overrun much of the Ottoman Empire at the end of the war, and which argued that Mosul naturally fell not under Turkish rule but under its own mandate for Mesopotamia.

One other diplomatic collision course, among myriad others, lay between Great Britain and France on the one hand and the USA on the other. At this stage Paris and London could have been excused for thinking that the fate of Mosul, and of the former Ottoman Empire in general, was a question that they alone would be able to determine, and that the Americans should have no say in any settlement. The Americans, after all, had never declared war on the Turks and had no troops stationed with their territories. By contrast the two European powers had long had strong political and commercial links with the region, and had invested vast amounts of resources, and lost a lot of men, in defeating the Turks on battlefields as far apart as Gallipoli, the scene of a particularly bloody Allied attack in 1915, and the Hijaz Desert, where Colonel T.E. Lawrence had orchestrated and led the Arab Revolt.

Not only did the British feel they deserved to enjoy the fruits of victory after investing so much, but they also regarded Mesopotamia as a region of vital strategic importance. In a memorandum written at the end of October 1919 the General Staff claimed that it was 'an important link in a chain of contiguous areas under British influence, extending from Egypt to India'. Of course oil added considerably to its value as a strategic asset: 'with a railway and pipeline to the Mediterranean, which is forecasted within the next ten years, the position of England as a naval power in the Mediterranean could be doubly assured and our dependence on the Suez Canal, which is a vulnerable point in our line of communications with the East, would be considerably lessened'.

But by this time London and Paris must have felt that the Americans were as far from getting a stake in the region's oil as they had ever been. After all, American oil companies had been excluded from the Turkish Petroleum Company ever since it had first been established in 1912, and now, after four long years of war, the Americans had just suffered further indignity. For just a few weeks before, the British and French governments had met at San Remo to determine the fate of the vanquished Ottoman Empire and once again the Americans found themselves elbowed aside.

Striking any deal on Mesopotamian oil had never promised to be easy. The challenge of deciding what to do with the vast Ottoman lands after Turkey's military defeat had started to vex Britain and France as early as the spring of 1916, when the governments had looked beyond the immediate horizon of winning the war and struck an initial deal, the Sykes–Picot Agreement, about what to do in the event of an Ottoman surrender: while the French could take Mosul, it was agreed, the British would still have exclusive rights to any oil that was found there.

After the war negotiations between the British oil minister, Walter Long, and his French counterpart, Henry Berenger, had led to a further deal that was signed in Paris in April 1919: if Mesopotamia fell under British rule then the French government would be allowed a minority stake of just 20 per cent in any oil that was discovered there, while the British government would take nearly all of the rest. The British knew that any oil they found in the region would still have to be moved by pipeline to the Mediterranean and would therefore have to cross French-controlled areas, and this meant that offering the French a share in the oil was the best way of winning their cooperation.

But disagreements between the two governments had persisted, and the deal soon fell apart. At San Remo both governments were determined to settle the matter once and for all, and on 25 April a new agreement was signed: as the rulers of Mesopotamia, the British would grant the French a 25 per cent share in a reorganized Turkish Petroleum Company that was soon to be established. But otherwise the British would maintain their iron grip on the area: any petroleum company that operated in the region, the agreement spelt out, 'shall be under permanent British control'.

There was one other reason why London had conceded more ground to France after the end of the First World War. The British knew that if the French were denied the more generous terms they sought, then there was a real prospect that they could look farther afield and join forces with another interested party that was starting to turn its attentions to the Middle East more vigorously than ever before: the USA. So in January 1919 the London cabinet decided that 'His Majesty's Government should at once signify their willingness to cooperate before the French secured American assistance, and before this country was forced by decisions at the Peace Conference to adopt in self-defence and practically under compulsion the policy of cooperation to which it was now invited.'

There were various reasons why the USA was now turning its eye towards the Middle East. On the one hand it had always been a country that was self-sufficient in oil, but there were now growing fears that its own supplies were running short and would soon become exhausted. This was largely because of the immense strain imposed by the war. America may have entered the First World War very late – not until 1917 – but the subsequent effort had nonetheless created a huge surge in demand for oil, and by 1920 some pundits and politicians were darkly predicting that within just two decades the country would be a net oil importer and therefore at the mercy of any exporting country that wanted to hold it to ransom.

In American eyes part of the answer was to stake a claim in those parts of the Middle East that seemed most likely to hold large deposits of undiscovered oil. True, the USA had never declared war on Turkey, whereas vast quantities of both French and British blood had been spilled in the region during four years of war. Nor had the Americans ever negotiated directly with the Turks at any stage of the hostilities. But in Washington politicians felt that this did not give the two colonial powers an exclusive right to a Mesopotamian concession. On the contrary, they felt that because the American war effort had played a vital part in the Allied victory – having contributed more oil than any other participating country – they had as much claim to enjoying the fruits of victory as anyone else: without this effort, ran their argument, Britain and France would not now be in a position to carve up the Ottoman Empire.

In March 1920, having heard some fairly impassioned speeches that spelt out the sheer urgency of the supply situation, the US Senate passed a resolution requesting the State Department to report on measures taken by foreign governments to exclude Americans from oil fields under their control. There were bitter remonstrations against the British government and its insistence that only British nationals were entitled to exploit opportunities within the mandated territories, and calls for Washington to retaliate with harsh economic sanctions, particularly against the Shell Oil Company, which had strong commercial interests in the USA.

Pushing the senators particularly hard in this direction was a well-funded and organized interest group. For seeing the vast profits that Anglo-Persian was reaping from its own oilfields, and feeling sure that Mesopotamia was a hugely promising arena, a number of American oil giants, notably the Standard Oil Company of New Jersey, had started to lobby hard for the right to compete in the region on equal terms with their European counterparts. Even at the time, the precise relationship between the US government and these companies – whether 'the tail wagged the dog' – was impossible to determine, but it is certain that regular conferences were held between representatives of this particular oil company and the Foreign Trade Adviser's Office in the State Department at which the issue was discussed at length and in detail. Before long the Secretary of Commerce, Herbert Hoover, had also invited officials from several other US oil giants to discuss the Middle Eastern issue. These were the Texas Company, Mexican Petroleum, Gulf, Atlantic Refining, Sinclair Consolidated Oil and Standard Oil of New York.

This was not quite the first time that the American giants had eyed up the Middle East. Just before the outbreak of war, Standard Oil of New York – a new company that had just been formed out of the dismembered Standard Oil and made into an independent entity in its own right – had accepted licences to explore for oil in Palestine and northern Anatolia. It had wasted little time in despatching a number of geologists who inspected local seepages and reached a commercial decision to drill for oil at a remote spot near Kurnub, just to the south of Beersheba. At considerable expense, road and buildings were constructed, lorries were brought in and drilling equipment specially ordered from America.

Everything seemed ready for an American oil company to make its first oil discovery in the Middle East until, just as everything was being unloaded at Alexandria, war broke out and the contracts immediately cancelled. After the war, Standard did its best to stake a claim in the region once again and argued that the pre-war licenses it had obtained to explore the Kurnub area of southern Palestine were still valid after 1918. Over the next two years a company representative stayed in the region before leaving without success. No Palestinian oil had been found after all.

It was into this new race, so very different from the one he had left behind in 1913, when his earlier bid for a concession had been thwarted at the last minute, that Admiral Chester strode that summer day in 1920, as he made his way to the State Department and requested governmental backing for his concessionary proposals. Because some of the officials he had then known and dealt with were still working in the same roles as before, and because he in any case cut quite a distinguished figure in his own right, he was given a friendly and sympathetic hearing and went on to make numerous further visits to the State Department over the months that followed.

By this time, almost no one in the State Department, or anywhere else in Washington, appears to have harboured any particular favour towards Chester. Yet this was not to say that the Admiral and his company had nothing to offer Washington. For at this stage the American government had two possible gateways into Mesopotamia, and Chester presented one of them. On the other hand Washington could back its own national oil companies in their bid to win a share of the Turkish Petroleum Company. This approach would have a strong chance of success if Mosul was taken away from Turkish control and then fell under a British mandate before becoming part of an independent state in its own right. For if this happened then Mosul would clearly fall outside the scope of the Chester Concession, which was a narrowly Turkish affair.

But by this time it looked far from certain that the Turks were going to lose control of Mosul. Under the Treaty of Sevres in 1920 the Turks had initially forfeited control over the Kurdish territories, but were now changing their stance altogether and wanting to stake their claim to Mosul. If the Turks succeeded then it looked most unlikely that they would recognize the Turkish Petroleum Company, so closely associated was it with Turkey's arch enemy, Great Britain, and Washington needed to find a way of hedging its bets. It was precisely this opportunity that Admiral Chester and his Ottoman Development Company appeared to offer. Of course there was no reason why the State Department could not do both by supporting the claims of American companies for a slice of Turkish Petroleum as well as Chester's own bid.

In either event, Washington's underlying strategy was to assert that, no matter what happened in the region, America had as much right as anyone else to stake its commercial claim there. This viewpoint was succinctly stated in May 1920 by the American ambassador in London, who wrote a long and detailed letter to the British Foreign Ministry at the instigation of his bosses in Washington. The USA wanted an 'Open Door', ran the argument, through which its citizens and businesses could enter the mandated territories of the Middle East and compete on equal terms with their international rivals. But as things stood, he continued, its citizens were being actively discriminated against in British-controlled areas of the Middle East, notably Mesopotamia and Palestine.

Over the coming months Secretary of State Bainbridge Colby and the American ambassador in London, John W. Davis, spelt out Washington's position in even more detail. As far as Washington was concerned, they argued, the Turkish Petroleum Company had never been granted any rights to explore and exploit Mesopotamian oil. The San Remo agreement, they continued, did not seem to 'be consistent with the principles of equality of treatment understood and accepted during the peace negotiations in Paris', and this blatant unfairness was creating considerable ill-feeling amongst an American public that was increasingly convinced that Britain had 'been preparing quietly for exclusive control of the oil resources' in the region.

News that Washington was pushing hard to gain access to the Middle East deeply alarmed London. In his formal correspondence with Washington, Lord Curzon argued that the USA had no reasonable grounds to complain, since Britain only produced a fraction of the world's oil output whereas the Americans produced more than three quarters. Any suggestion that the Turkish Petroleum Company lacked a legally valid concession was absurd, he continued, and if the Americans wanted to dispute it then the proper place to go was the League of Nations.

But by this time pressure was growing on all parties – on oil companies and their shareholders, on the State Department and on the British government – to make progress and resolve the future of Mesopotamian oil. On 22 June 1922 the chairman of Standard Oil of New Jersey met State Department officials on behalf not just of his own organization but of six other American oil companies to discuss the Middle Eastern question, and as they stepped up the pressure on Washington, so too did the American government raise the diplomatic heat on London. This new bid seemed to make some progress, for on 1 August the American ambassador to London, George Harvey, notified the Secretary of State that the Turkish Petroleum Company had decided to offer the Americans 12 per cent participation in their company. This was clearly a step forward but one that still fell far short of American hopes: 'the seven American companies interested have considered views of State Department and questions concerning American participation and their views are that the percentage you indicated would not be adequate from the point of view of what would be an equitable proportion to allocate to American interests', cabled Anglo-Persian's chairman from Washington.

Still facing heavy pressure from across the Atlantic, the British were forced to give more ground, and by the end of August had increased this proposed share to 20 per cent. Still the Americans were unhappy, prompting Ambassador Harvey to write from London that 'naturally the offer appeared too low to Mr Teagle and there was rupture of official negotiations'.[1] A clash of interests was now clearly looming. At the same time as pushing the case for entry into Turkish Petroleum, Washington also knew that Admiral Chester would offer the American government a good way of hedging its bets in case Mosul fell into Turkish, not British, hands. This was because a renewal of his 1913 concession would, if ratified, grant him a monopoly within Turkey's borders. So at the same time that Washington had been knocking on the Mesopotamian door, demanding its own right of entry, it also quietly watched Admiral Chester pushing his proposed concession further forward.

The principle of Open Door did not necessarily mean singling out any chosen favourites and giving them a helping hand. Admiral Chester, for example, was by this time looked upon favourably but is not known to have been given any preferential treatment: as Secretary Hughes pointed out, Open Door was defined as the policy of according American nationals impartial and appropriate diplomatic support in the assertion of their legal rights without involving the government in any other way, and this prompted the Secretary to conclude that 'at no stage of the negotiations was the American position determined by the so-called Chester Concession'.[2]

Preferential treatment or not, Washington would have warmly received any news that Chester was making considerable and unexpected progress in Constantinople. This news first broke at the end of 1922, when on 5 December the acting US ambassador there reported to the State Department that the Chester group's negotiations were nearing a conclusion and that the Council of Ministers and the Public Works Commission of the National Assembly were being kept closely informed of the outcome. The ambassador felt that Chester's bid had a good chance of success, and it was definitely worth Washington's while to give him full diplomatic backing. Within a few weeks Chester had fulfilled these hopes, winning his concession and on 23 April 1923, in the course of just a single sitting, the Grand National Assembly once again ratified the Chester Concession, granting him the mineral rights in a twelve-mile strip on either side of the new railway in Mesopotamia.

Almost certainly Chester's status as an American citizen had considerably boosted his chances. An American, the Turks may have felt, was unattached by the imperial strings that they feared the French and British would inevitably bring. In the spring of 1923, for example, the Turkish prime minister, Raouf Bey, had argued before parliament that all previous efforts to develop the country with the help of European investment had ended up with respective governments trying to put strong political pressure on Constantinople.[3] Meanwhile Sultan Abdul Hamid is alleged to have urged Admiral Chester to 'take all the public works of Turkey and parcel them out among whatever companies you think ought to have them – only let them all be American'.[4]

But however Chester had managed to win it, news of the concessionary grant caused fury in British government circles because Mesopotamia now fell under its own mandate and was no longer ruled from Constantinople. The Turks had no right to grant anyone permission to work on foreign soil, they argued vehemently, and the Chester Concession seemed to be a blatant and wilful disregard of British authority. The acting British high commissioner in Constantinople was immediately instructed to protest emphatically and to declare that London would not recognize the validity of any such concession.

In Paris, government officials were just as furious. Two days later the French high commissioner in Constantinople, General Pelle, protested to Dr Adnan Bey, vice president of the Turkish National Assembly, about the award, claiming that Chester had been given rights to work in certain regions to which the French had exclusive claim under an agreement dated 21 March 1914. This argument was highly dubious but the French attempted to prove it by pointing to a loan that they had happened to make at the same time, claiming that it was payment for the concession. Paris also lodged an official protest to Washington: if the US government fully approved and supported the concession, the complaint intonated, then 'a diplomatic incident of the first importance might result'.[5]

The Russians also lodged a protest of their own, pointing to yet another deal, one that was signed on 31 March 1900: keen to appease the Russians and furious about the 1899 German deal, they claimed, the Turks had promised to offer Russian companies the first shot whenever railways were to be built in the Black Sea region. This, they continued, was why in 1911 Russia had joined forces with France and assisted French capitalists in obtaining a concession to build a railway from Samsun to Sivas.

Everything would now depend on the political future of Mosul. If it fell into Turkish hands, as Kemal Pasha had been demanding for some months, then the Americans would be able to stake their claim, and Secretary of State Hughes declared that the granting of the Chester Concession marked the triumph of the Open Door policy at the expense of more restrictive deals, such as the Baghdad railway concession, that would keep them out. But since the end of the First World War Mosul had been under a British mandate, and London was now pressing to keep the city under its own grip before incorporating it into the new state of Iraq. Ostensibly at least, Britain's wish to keep Turkish hands off the region had nothing to do with oil: in London Lord Curzon proclaimed that he 'loathed the prominence which was attached to the question of Mosul oil'. But in practice it was widely regarded as such a hugely promising source of petroleum that this consideration could not have been far from British minds.[6]

The British had a lot to lose if Mosul fell into Turkish hands, because the Turks were most unlikely to recognize the validity of the Turkish Petroleum Company's concession. But at the Lausanne Conference British representatives encountered fierce opposition not just from the Turks, who had defeated the Greeks and were therefore in a much stronger military position than for some years, but also from the French. At the end of the First World War there had initially been a united allied front between Britain and France, but strong disagreements had by now begun to emerge. In sharp contrast to the British approach of trying to emasculate post-war Turkey, France wanted to rebuild its power, viewing the country as a possible future ally in the Middle East. So more than at any previous time the British needed American diplomatic backing. Their best hope of getting this was to offer American oil companies the Open Door they demanded, and therefore give Washington a vested interest in keeping Turkish Petroleum afloat.

The question was due to be resolved once and for all at an international conference at Lausanne in Switzerland. The first session had opened in November 1922 and future of Mosul was raised a few weeks later, at the end of January. Right from the start, Washington applied strong pressure on London to accept an Open Door policy that would allow American companies to get involved, and on 15 December representatives of Turkish Petroleum offered their American counterparts a 24 per cent share, equal to that of the three other participants. But in return Washington was expected to renounce any further claims to the region and drop any objections to the validity of Turkish Petroleum's own concession. However, still this did not satisfy the State Department, which was interested in the Open Door as a principle, not as a particular concession for a particular company.

On 24 July 1923 a new treaty was signed at Lausanne that amicably solved the Mosul question. Under this 'friendly agreement', the fate of the Kurds, and of the frontier between Turkey and Iraq, was to be determined by the League of Nations, which would take all the relevant factors – ethnic, linguistic, numeric and racial – into account. But almost everyone apart from the Turks felt that Mosul was certain to be considered as part of Iraq, and that the Kurdish people in general had virtually no affinity at all with Constantinople. Now that Mosul looked set to fall outside the scope of the Chester concession – which would have validity only within a country where no oil was felt to be present – the State Department looked to American participation in Turkish Petroleum as its best chance of winning a stake in Mesopotamia. After years of strenuous effort to win the concession for regional oil, this spelt the end for Admiral Chester.

Quite apart from the outcome of the Lausanne Conference, success would in any case still have been beyond the grasp of the Ottoman–American Development Company. The granting of the 1923 concession created huge internal disagreements between directors, enough for investors to panic and pull out their money. Desperate efforts were made to reassure existing stakeholders and find new ones but to no avail, and on 18 December 1923 the Turkish minister of Public Works cancelled the entire grant of concessions on the grounds that their terms had not been fulfilled. Desperately close though he had come, Admiral Chester was simply not destined to play a starring role in the region.

The Admiral might have had more chance of winning an oil concession if he had turned away from Mesopotamia and looked elsewhere in the Middle East. Even in 1922, large parts of the region had still not been claimed by international oil companies and were politically more inviting than ever before. The dismemberment of the Ottoman empire meant that Constantinople no longer exercised even nominal sovereignty over parts of the Middle East that they had conquered centuries before and subsequently ruled. So would-be oil hunters would no longer have to confront the endless obstinacy and procrastination of Ottoman officials, who had previously made the Mesopotamian concession so elusive. Instead they could now make direct approaches to the rulers of kingdoms such as Bahrain and Kuwait, now free of Ottoman rule both in theory and in practice.

Some parts of the region were also more stable than ever before. Much of the Arabian peninsula, for example, had experienced bitter fighting since the turn of the century but was now quieter than for some time. This trouble had its origins in events of the early eighteenth century, when the emir, Muhammed Ibn Saud, seized large parts of central Arabia before the Ottoman armies swept through the area and restored control. Two hundred years later Abdul Aziz Ibn Saud, a direct descendant of Muhammed, made a determined bid to restore the rule of the Saudi family, and in 1902 succeeded in capturing Nejd, in the very centre of the peninsula. A decade later he had also brought the eastern province of al-Hasa, bordering the Persian Gulf, into his grasp. By the time Admiral Chester was resuming his quest for a Mesopotamian concession, Abdul Aziz had succeeded in bringing many of the peninsula's remaining lands under his control.

In some ways, then, the Middle East seemed to be more inviting than ever before for an ambitious oil hunter. There was only one problem. Almost no one of note thought that, outside Mesopotamia and Persia, the region had any oil reserves left to boast of.

11

Frank Holmes Strides into the Middle East

While the American oil companies and their allies in the State Department were casting an increasingly acquisitive eye on the Middle East, a small local ferry, known simply as a *jalbout*, was quietly pulling into harbour. A few passers-by probably stopped and stared briefly at the Western traveller who stepped onto the quay, rare as such visitors were to this small and largely isolated spot, although most would have carried on with their day-to-day business with barely more than a furtive glance. But none of those who watched could ever have guessed that this new arrival at Manama, on the offshore Gulf island of Bahrain, was now set to play a starring role in the story of both their own island and of the Middle East as a whole.

The man who turned up there on that hot summer afternoon in August 1921 was Frank Holmes, and he hardly looked the part of a great oil hunter. At nearly 50 he was by this time already squat and overweight. Not knowing a word of Arabic, and always dependent on translators from the moment he set foot in the Middle East, many people must have thought him way out of his cultural depth. Relying on a loyal African servant to carry his bags and suitcases, he was not only unfit but also troubled by a serious bladder problem that had already seriously blighted his earlier travels. Yet, as he was now set to prove, he did have extraordinary abilities, not least an adventurous and enterprising spirit, as well as great physical strength and stamina, enough to make him blissfully indifferent to Bahrain's withering summer temperatures. Above all, however, he also had an uncanny feel for finding and exploiting new, untapped sources of oil in places that often were, by any standards, remote, difficult and obscure.

Holmes' astonishing gifts were nurtured in his native New Zealand. He had humble beginnings, growing up on a small farm run by his British-born father, and had left school in Otago at the age of 15 with no qualifications. But his uncle, a mining engineer, gave him the chance to travel widely and acquire new skills, and within a few years the young Holmes had trained as a mining and metallurgical engineer, gaining wide experience of working on a variety of exploration and drilling projects in many different corners of the world, including Africa, Asia, South America and even Russia. Unlike D'Arcy, who was always essentially an investor, he saw such operations more from the perspective of an engineer, judging the likely outcome of exploratory drilling from whatever geological evidence he could draw from the surface.

What drew him to the Middle East, and to oil in particular, were his experiences in the First World War. Although he was already 40 by the time of its outbreak, and a New Zealander by birth and upbringing, he immediately volunteered to serve in the British war effort and was soon commissioned into the Royal Marines, reaching the rank of major. After a year in the thick of action, during which time he saw heavy fighting at Gallipoli and elsewhere, he was ordered to help arrange the delivery of mules from Abyssinia to the British expeditionary army in Mesopotamia, and was despatched to Eastern Africa in late 1915 to help get things under way.[1]

It was at this time, when he was stationed in Somaliland, that Major Holmes first caught the scent of Middle Eastern oil. During a chance encounter with an Arab trader he was intrigued to hear stories of oil seepages along some stretches of the Bahraini coast. In certain places, the trader told him, were concentrations of a dense, black and highly flammable substance that he could easily see for himself. Visiting the area for the first time shortly after, he became interested both in the geology of the Arabian Gulf coast and in what he saw of the Anglo-Persian Oil Company's massive refinery in Abadan. And because he was for a time also attached to the Royal Navy, it was also quite likely that he now had a chance to see the Admiralty's secret maps of the region, which charted the discoveries of Persian oil and marked likely future sources of supply.

After his demobilization in 1918, Holmes, like so many of his contemporaries, appears to have struggled to find any real purpose and direction in his civilian life. As an experienced and qualified mining engineer he could of course have continued along the same path as before the war, perhaps returning to New Zealand to pursue his professional career, or travelling the world in a consultancy role. But by this time his interest in the Middle East appears really to have been set alight, and from his modest London flat he began to look for some opening that would take him to that part of the world.

His chance was to come through a new commercial enterprise that was now being set up in London by long-standing acquaintances. Run by two great names of international commerce, Sir Edmund Davis and Percy Tarbutt, the Eastern and General Syndicate was registered on 6 August 1920 with the object of investigating business opportunities – particularly in the mining sector – throughout the Middle East, and obtaining concessions to exploit them. There was enormous money to be made, reckoned the Syndicate's directorship, in buying concessions before the resources of such a relatively unexplored area were fully uncovered, and then selling on these rights at a later date, when the potential had been conclusively proved and the interest of the outside world set alight: just one successful oil strike could send a concession rocketing up in value, perhaps a thousand-fold, overnight. This was a hugely risky business at the best of times, but all the more so in an area where almost no one thought oil existed in commercial quantities. Yet Holmes leapt upon the chance of involving himself in it, putting himself forward as someone who was familiar both with the intricacies of mining and engineering operations in general, and with this region in particular. By the end of the year he was on his way there as the Syndicate's key Middle Eastern representative.

Holmes' role was essentially to act as a negotiator, introducing himself to the local chiefs and haggling with them to get concessions on the best possible terms. But he had to use his own judgement to decide which of all his many possible venues looked the most promising and offered the largest rewards with the least investment. His first task was to set up a pharmaceutical business in Aden, which soon proved a commercial success. But he also remembered what the Arab had told him in Somaliland years before, and later decided to head off to Bahrain to take a closer look. Twenty miles off the Arabian coast, this British-protected principality consisted of several small and one larger island where His Highness Sheikh Hamad Ibn Isa Al-Khalifa and his elderly father ruled from the capital, Manama.

Doing business in Bahrain, and in all the other Arab principalities in the region, presented any outsider with a dauntingly steep learning curve. For this was a place where commerce was intertwined with the rituals of prayer to a degree that very few Westerners, other than seasoned visitors, could readily comprehend. A member of a prominent business family reflected how 'the *suuqs* [markets] developed themselves around mosques, so that when the men were called for prayer they stopped their shopping or trading and went to pray. Due to the longer time taken in travelling on donkeys, the working hours were shorter and would start much earlier than now – 5 or 5.30 in the morning until praying time at noon.'[2] Nor was it just prayer with which business discussions were mixed, for the *al-gahwa* – or coffee shop – was also the focus of business activity, and it was here, amidst the playing of dominoes and board games and between social chats, that all manner of trade deals were discussed. Making commercial progress also depended on having superb contacts with those who had access to, and could win the sympathy of, local rulers.

But Holmes was undeterred, and as he made his initial survey of the island he soon found a few obvious signs of petroleum deposits. For on the main island, within an area confined by rocky hills, were several small seeps of oil. These were exactly the same seepages he had heard so much about during the war, and about which he had always had such a strong gut feeling. But humble though they were, these signs gave him sufficient encouragement and he decided to press ahead with his plans. He soon managed to arrange a meeting with the sheikh that he hoped would give him enough time at least to try and make a formal request for a concession.

By now he had found several local people who were willing to help him, among them Mohammed Yatim, a member of a distinguished Bahraini family. Yatim spoke reasonable English and offered to act as Holmes' interpreter. But he had much else to offer, because he was also superbly connected throughout much of the region, and was prepared to use his extensive family contacts in Bahrain and beyond to assist the intrepid New Zealander.

Using Yatim as an interpreter throughout the interview at the palace in Manama, Holmes was, however, soon disappointed: the sheikh, it immediately turned out, had no interest at all in oil as a commodity or in granting any rights to find it in his kingdom. This was not just because he was unaware of the enormous importance oil had now acquired in the outside world, but also because, like most of the other Arab rulers, he strongly valued his independence and was extremely wary of allowing any foreigners to get a foothold in his kingdom. Holmes – always known to most of the Arabs simply as 'the Major' – persisted and tried spinning out the meeting, in the hope that he might dissuade the sheikh, but to no avail. For the time being his efforts had been thwarted and he would have to conduct his searches elsewhere in the region.

In late August 1922 he left Bahrain for nearby Arabia, now hoping to introduce himself to Sultan, or King, Abdul Aziz Faisal Ibn Saud, whose court was based further down the Red Sea at the port of Jeddah. His aim was to find out more about the Arabian province of al-Hasa, which Ibn Saud ruled and which lay immediately adjacent to the Bahraini Islands. If oil was in Bahrain, he asked himself, then surely it must also lie in the surrounding region too? But once again, Holmes seemed to be entertaining hopes of finding oil against all the odds, for there were even fewer signs of oil in this kingdom than in Bahrain, and improbable though it may have seemed, al-Hasa was also far more forbidding to explore than the small Bahraini islands. Although it had a few well-watered oases and attractive coastal villages, almost all wholly untouched by Western civilization, it was largely made up of vast expanses of desert that were intimidating even to the small number of nomads and tribesmen who were born and bred there.

But once again the Major was undeterred as he travelled to the kingdom by *jalbout*, arriving in the village port of Ojair after a rough journey, and then wasting no time in introducing himself to the sultan's local representatives. Urged to ride overnight by camel to a nearby settlement in order to catch the sultan, who was just about to leave on a journey of his own, Holmes was now able to discuss his exploration plans in person and hand over a very basic draft concession for the king and his advisers to take a close look at over the coming weeks.

In his daily diaries, Ameen Rihani, an American citizen of Lebanese extraction who had become a close royal confidant, often noted the extraordinary impression that Holmes made on local Arabs, and how he was himself immediately taken aback by the sheer oddness of the visitor's appearance. For Holmes often sported a thick loose-fitting tweed jacket and corduroy trousers that would have looked wholly out of place anywhere in the Middle East: 'He wore over his conventional European clothes a thin *aba* [veil] which concealed nothing; and over his cork helmet, a red kerchief and *ighal* [headware] which made his head appear colossal', Rihani wrote. This, he continued, made the Major appear somewhat ridiculous, since 'in this attempt to combine good Arab form with comfort and hygiene, he certainly looked funny'.[3] Other contemporaries were also taken aback by what they saw. Colonel H.R.P. Dickson, at one time the British government's Political Agent (local authority) in Bahrain and later Kuwait, found Holmes 'amazingly amusing', not least because 'he carried a large white umbrella lined green, wore a white helmet as issued to French troops in Africa, and over his face and helmet a green gauze veil – quite like pictures one has seen of the tourists about to visit the Pyramids'.[4]

The impression he made was probably all the more extraordinary because of his habit of travelling throughout the region with, of all things, a butterfly net, which he often tried to make as visible as possible whenever there were other Westerners around. The reason he did so was simple, even if it was also utterly unconvincing. Not wanting to arouse the interest of rival oil companies, particularly the formidable Anglo-Persian Oil Company whose representatives and agents were dotted all over the region, he posed as a butterfly collector who was researching the obscure varieties found in the Middle East.

Not many people were taken in by this, particularly on an island where word travelled fast. When staying with Colonel Dickson's family in Bahrain, he once explained to an intrigued Mrs Dickson that he was 'a butterfly collector, and I have been told that a wonderful black variety, known nowhere else in the world, is to be found in the Qatif oasis. I have already called it the Black Admiral of Qatif and am out to get a specimen. Then my name will be famous.' His interlocutor was not convinced, however, particularly after hearing so many rumours about both her intriguing guest and the presence of oil in the kingdom: 'Major Holmes', she replied, 'this is the first time I've heard of an oil seepage being called by the name of a butterfly'.[5] The Major's reply was dramatic, as he rushed round the table and shook her by the hand: 'My God you are a wonderful woman!', he exclaimed, 'I shall telegraph today to the curator of the Zoological Gardens in London and ask that you be made a Fellow of the Zoo!' It was not long afterwards that Mrs Dickson received a letter from the Gardens announcing that she had, indeed, been elected a fellow.

Holmes had another favourite excuse to explain his presence in the region. In his diaries, Ameen Rihani mentioned how in 1922 he had once been travelling on board the SS *Bajora*, leaving the port of Basrah en route to Bahrain only to find himself in the company of only one other passenger, a Westerner who he felt was 'too effusive for an Englishman'. 'There was no ice to break: we had to speak', he recorded, and when the two men had tea together later that day the Westerner told him 'that he was travelling in those parts for his health'. Rihani had his doubts about this story, particularly when it turned out that Holmes seemed a bit too well connected, and a bit too familiar with the region, than one would expect of a casual tourist visiting for health reasons. 'Later I saw my fellow-passenger speaking with Saiyed Hashem [a senior Arabian official] and I was surprised that he knew him. But there were more surprises for me in our second conversation, which I opened with a commonplace remark about the heat in Iraq.'

Rihani records the conversation that then followed.

'It is worse in Asir because of the dampness', remarked Holmes.

'And you have travelled in Asir?'

'I have visited the Saiyed Idrisi in Jaizan.'

'And you lived in that fort – the guesthouse?'

'Two weeks.'

'Then you know Dr Fadl 'ud-Din in Hudaidah?'

'Very well. I lived with him in that big house there.'

Rihani now felt somewhat irritated. 'Something of annoyance was working itself into my surprise that this man, who does not even speak Arabic, should have been to those places before me!' Later, when Rihani discovered Holmes' true purpose, he exclaimed simply 'Ha! So the Major is travelling for his health … he was no longer a mystery to me.'[6]

Some of the Major's mannerisms and habits also raised eyebrows. A chain smoker who always travelled with large supplies of tobacco at his side, Holmes had a distinctive habit of smoking a cigarette at the same time as he talked, a difficult task for anyone to perform but one that, as his contemporaries noted, he was highly adept at undertaking. Nearly everyone who met him for the first time commented on the cigarette that always seemed to hang from the corner of his mouth, bobbing up and down in precise rhythm to the speed of his speech, and of which he even seemed to be wholly unaware as he chatted away in his characteristically loquacious way.

Yet although Holmes may in some ways have seemed ludicrous to native Arabs and fellow Westerners alike, his presence, personality and demeanour appear to have immediately made their mark. For if his excuses were not always convincing, Holmes appears to have made a charming guest. 'His anecdotes were legion', as Dickson recalled, 'and he exuded charm', always keeping his hosts amused and entertained over their evening meals and the drinks that followed. Invariably talkative, humorous and friendly by nature, harbouring no inhibitions of any kind, and of impressive stature, Holmes was generally much liked by Arabs, a good number of whom seem to have gone out of their way to help him along. And wherever he went, he always remembered the importance in Arab culture of being generous with gifts. Dickson recalled that, on first meeting the sultan, the New Zealander arrived with 'an amazing number of presents ... over fifty cases, leather bags, boxes and guns'.[7]

Other Westerners, such as two American visitors who paid a visit to Bahrain, noticed his quick and easy affinity with the locals. 'You would probably be interested in our impression of Major Holmes from the few days we have been with him', they wrote back home. 'He is a rather stout man about 55 years of age and rather bald ... From what we have seen and heard, he appears to be on extremely friendly terms with the influential Arabs and we believe he could go farther toward obtaining concessions from them both in Arabia and Iraq than any other European or American here.'[8]

Besides his winning manner with the local people, Holmes seems to have been blessed with an uncanny sense of timing. During his first foray into Arabia, he was unaware that, just weeks later, Ojair was to host a regional treaty conference to determine exactly where the borders between Kuwait, Saudi Arabia and Iraq would lie. Britain would be chairing this meeting, trying hard to negotiate a compromise in an area in which it had so much influence, and the Anglo-Persian Oil Company was poised to take full advantage of the conference and Whitehall's role in order to establish closer ties with the kingdom and perhaps make its own bid for a Saudi oil concession. And it turned out that Anglo-Persian's chief representative in the region had even written to the sultan shortly before to arrange discussions on this and some other matters.

Holmes went to Arabia not to attend the conference but instead personally to deliver a draft of his concession proposal to Ibn Saud. Soon after his arrival he came across Ameen Rihani, whom he had met on board the SS *Barjora* a few months previously. Crucially, Rihani had the ear of the king and now appears to have done whatever he could to help the New Zealander's own bid to win royal favour. Rihani advised Holmes that his best chance of meeting Ibn Saud was to proceed to al-Hasa as soon as possible for 'if he rode all night he would get there on the following day and have an interview with the sultan before he started for Ojair'. In the meantime he would get to work on Holmes' document, suggesting amendments and improvements to the Arabic draft. Holmes was 'much pleased' by this advice, recorded Rihani, 'and bestrode a mare with a sore shank and caving haunch ... and slowly moved off towards the Nufoud, followed by three white donkeys carrying his interpreter, his Somali and the baggage'.[9]

Rihani's liking for the eccentric former army officer became clear from his diary entry: 'later in the evening, I regretted his going, for I certainly should have enjoyed the Major more than his document, on the twenty pages of which were his twenty signatures in full. Of what interest to me, in truth, is a concession to drill for oil and minerals and salt in the province of al-Hasa?' Rihani's willingness to help him win royal favour now becomes clear: 'for the sake of the sultan, however, I read the document and appalling Arabic translation, clause by clause, and summoning from the past my long neglected business sense, I was able, I think, without hurting the prospects of Major Holmes and his Company to make a few suggestions.'[10] Whether Holmes managed to meet the sultan before his departure we do not know, but in the course of his journey he found out about the looming Ojair Conference and began making his own way there, knowing that this was his best chance to push his case for the concession.

The setting for the great conference was certainly impressive. Ibn Saud, wrote one witness, had a large camp of 'white tents of every size and description, about half a mile to the west of the old fort and customs buildings'. At the very centre of his encampment was one particularly large tent that was used as both a conference hall and a dining room, while the king also had two separate tents of his own, one of which was used for sleeping, the other for rest. In the immediate vicinity were the king's entourage of leading courtiers, and a bodyguard made up of around 300 handpicked men.

Soon after arriving on 21 November, the various sides began negotiations to determine their borders. 'There was no give and take whatever', as Colonel Dickson recorded, 'both sides making ridiculous demands all the time.' Dickson recalled the opening exchanges between the contestants, each of which immediately revealed the highly traditional – and to a Westerner extremely peculiar – perspective from which they all viewed their disagreements. The Iraqi spokesman, Sabih Beg, got to his feet and argued that 'since God created the world and history began to be written, Iraq's boundary extends south to within twelve miles of Ibn Saud's capital. Riyadh ... As God is my witness, this and only this is the true boundary and cannot be disputed.' This then prompted Ibn Saud immediately to leap up and roar his reply: 'I know that from the days of Abraham, my great-grandparent, the territories of Najd and the Badawin world have extended as far north as Aleppo and the river Orontes in north Syria.' It was 'from this sort of beginning', Dickson wrote, that 'the arguments went on for five whole days, with many similar incidents all through, sometimes pianissimo and sometimes fortissimo.'[11]

When Holmes, now on his second trip to Arabia, had turned up at Ojair, he was initially unaware of what was going on. Although caught by surprise, he was in characteristic style completely undaunted by all the comings and goings and wasted no time in introducing himself to those present, brandishing a letter of introduction from Abdul Aziz Al Qusaibi, Ibn Saud's trade representative in Bahrain. In his diaries Ameen Rihani described how Holmes 'loomed up on the horizon unexpectedly as usual, and incorporated himself into the Ojair Conference' before he 'pitched his tent between the two camps, not far from our side, however; and he frequented the tents of both the sultan and the High Commissioner'.[12] But while he enjoyed the company of his fellow Westerners, Holmes nonetheless also kept himself apart, eating 'with his own people although he does not share their confidence'.[13]

Yet, although he mixed happily with other English speakers, Holmes knew that his bid for the concession would immediately encounter very strong opposition from Anglo-Persian, which would view the Syndicate as a threat to its overwhelming commercial hegemony in the region. Prompted by Rihani, Ibn Saud had raised the question of the oil concession at the very end of the Ojair conference, and asked the British representative, Sir Percy Cox, if London would have any objection if it was awarded to the Syndicate. Holmes was willing to visit the province of al-Hasa and make an initial search for oil, Ibn Saud informed Cox, and was keen to get hold of a concession. Sir Percy replied that London would accept this. 'Go ahead', came his reply, 'but I warn you that the Eastern and General Syndicate is not an oil company and will probably sell the concession to others.'[14] Now that Cox had nodded his approval, Holmes was invited into the royal tent to argue his case and try to persuade the sultan to proceed with the project. Dickson, the only other person now present, described Holmes' presentation:

> He mentioned the further possibility of finding copper, then pointed out on the map the extent of the concession he was after, which was roughly a long rectangle bounded on the north by the new Kuwait Neutral Zone, on the south by Salwa, which is on the hinterland of Qatar, and on the west by a straight line sixty miles from the sea and parallel to it, so as to include the Wadi al Miyah and the Dhila'at al Kibrit in the Jauf area, some twenty-five miles south-west of the Kuwait Neutral Zone.[15]

Quite why Cox had not blocked Holmes' move at this early stage remains unclear, but Dickson yields a clue. He points out that Cox always harboured a certain personal dislike for Holmes, and obviously regarded him as a threat to the interests of both Anglo-Persian and the British government, but judged that he could not safely condemn him in the particular circumstances of the moment: 'being personally very fond of Ibn Saud, and not wanting to antagonise him after the boundary affair, he pacified him by leading him to believe that His Majesty's Government was out to help him develop his country and gain him revenue'. In other words Holmes had 'got in by the back door' and had been extraordinarily lucky not to find Cox blocking his way:[16] feelings had started to run high during the Ojair Conference, and the British government, having organized and chaired the proceedings, was taking a lot of the blame when some participants failed to get what they wanted. Had Holmes arrived in the kingdom a few weeks earlier to try his luck, then he would not have been nearly so lucky.

But the competition between Holmes and the British was far from over, for Cox now came under renewed pressure from London to dissuade the sultan from granting the al-Hasa concession until the British government had had a chance to make a firm offer of its own. Cox was so insistent that he even drafted a royal letter for the Saudi king to sign and send to Holmes, informing the New Zealander that the king was not free to make a decision without first consulting London. Of course, such strong diplomatic pressure caused both indignation and alarm in royal circles, and Rihani recorded in his diary that three times the sultan refused the request made by Cox, who three times reissued it. Cox also made a direct approach to his rival, warning him to keep his distance: 'the time is not ripe for it', as he told Holmes, adding that 'the British government cannot afford your company any protection'.[17]

Over the coming months, Holmes waited impatiently for a firm decision from the sultan. Would he grant a concession to the British after all? Or perhaps refuse it to anyone, either because he would buckle to pressure from London or else just be too wary of making any decision? By early spring there was still no word from the royal court and, although not one to give up easily, Holmes was ready to accept that his mission to both Arabia and Bahrain had failed. He prepared to sail home.

Rihani, however, was quick to dissuade him. He knew that the sultan still felt bitter about the outcome of the Ojair Conference, and would probably still be more sympathetic to Holmes' bid than to the British. So he did his best to sound upbeat: 'I told the Major to change his mind and go back to al-Hasa', recorded Rihani, because 'the sultan will soon be there'. Rihani went further. I will give you a letter to him', he told Holmes, 'and I'm certain you'll get the concession. Never mind what Sir Percy Cox says.' Rihani, it turned out, had strongly advised Ibn Saud to favour Holmes' bid at the expense of the British. A deal with the Syndicate, he had told the sultan, would come with far fewer political strings attached than with Anglo-Persian, so closely affiliated with the British government had it by this time become.

It was not long before Rihani was proved right, and on 6 May 1923 the sultan finally made up his mind to ignore Cox's advice and instead grant the Eastern and General Syndicate a concession to explore for oil in al-Hasa. In return for an annual rent, which according to one witness was worth an advance payment of a relatively meagre £2,000, Holmes now won the exclusive right to search for oil over an area of 36,000 square miles along Saudi's east coast. If any oil was discovered, ran Clause 17 of the deal, then the sultan 'shall have the right to have allotted to him, as fully paid shares, twenty per cent of all and every class of shares issued by any company which the concession may form or float for the exploitation of the concession'. A year later, the sultan went further still, also granting the Syndicate an option for an oil concession in the 'Neutral Zone'. This had been established at the Ojair Conference, and covered an area of around 2,500 square miles adjoining the southern boundary of Kuwait, and bordering the Gulf coast to the east and Saudi Arabia to the west and south. It was 'neutral' because it was divided between the two states.

One reason why Holmes managed to win the concession was simply that he was more determined to do so than the British government, which felt much less sure that the region harboured any real petroleum deposits. The strong pressure that Cox put on the sultan to keep Holmes out did not reflect any conviction that Arabia was worth exploring but a straightforward desire to frustrate any foreign competition in the Gulf. In 1923, one APOC official who was keeping a careful watch on events wrote that 'I personally cannot believe that oil will be found in his [Ibn Saud's] country. As far as I know, there are no superficial oil-shows, and the geological formation does not appear to be particularly favourable from what little we know of it'. He continued by saying that 'in any case no company can afford to put down wells into a formation in these parts (however favourable) unless there is some superficial indication of oil'.[18] The British were instead concerned simply to keep others out of a region they regarded as their own natural sphere of influence, adjacent as it was to the transit routes to British India and to the vastly productive Persian oilfields. Charles Greenway, chairman of Anglo-Persian, stated in a management meeting in 1924 that 'although the geological information we possess at present does not indicate there is much hope of finding oil in Bahrain or Kuwait we are, I take it, all agreed that even if the chance is 100 to 1 we should pursue it, rather than let others come into the Persian Gulf and cause difficulties of one kind and another for is'.[19]

But the central reason why Holmes had gained the edge over his competitor was that Anglo-Persian had such strong connections with the British government. This counted heavily against it in two different ways. On the one hand the Saudis, like the Bahrainis, were robustly independent and extremely wary about selling out their kingdom to any foreign government. But they always knew how close the ties between Anglo-Persian and Whitehall were, and it was significant that a strict term of Holmes' al-Hasa concession was that 'the Syndicate shall not sell to the Anglo-Persian Oil Company Ltd either as to the whole or part thereof, any oil or mineral concession or concessions that may be granted by Your Highness to the Eastern and General Syndicate Ltd'.

Anglo-Persian's close ties with the British government had also counted against it because of Ibn Saud's displeasure about the legacy of the Ojair Conference. Its outcome was, reckoned Dickson, 'a serious error', because it imposed an 'arbitrary boundary of Western type between Iraq and Najd' that forced the Saudi leader, 'almost for the first time in history', to restrict the customary movements of some of his tribes. Feeling 'outwitted' by Sir Percy Cox, Ibn Saud had probably vented his anger and frustration by awarding the concession to the chief rivals of those who had organized and chaired the conference throughout.[20]

Holmes may have been virtually alone in thinking that this region had any petroleum deposits to boast of, but alone or not he was absolutely determined to press ahead and look elsewhere in the Gulf to find more concessions. He now travelled not only to the Farsan Islands in the Red Sea, where some very promising oil seepages had reputedly been found, but also turned once again to Bahrain and to the nearby principality of Kuwait.

12

Holmes Bids for Kuwait and Bahrain

As if inspired by his spectacular successes, Holmes wasted barely a minute in winning some more. On 9 May 1923, just three days after Ibn Saud had granted concessions for al-Hasa and the Neutral Zone, he sent a telegram from Bahrain to the ruler of Kuwait, Sheikh Ahmad. The telegram ran:

> I have most important letters from Ameen Rihani who has made enquiries concerning myself and Company advising Your Excellency not to grant oil concessions to any other Company without first seeing the terms offered by my Company. My representative will bring by next steamer the letters and terms to present Your Excellency. Am pleased to inform you that I have secured the approval of His Highness Ibn Saud of my Company and secured the concessions against all other Companies who negotiated with His Highness.
>
> Major H.

Far from firing a shot in the dark, Holmes was taking careful aim. His moves were tightly planned and well choreographed. Playing a vital role was his interpreter and assistant, Mohammed Yatin, who happened to have superb contacts in the kingdom, chief among them being the secretary of the council of state, one Mullah Saleh, who worked right at the sheikh's side. Urged by Holmes to make the most of these contacts, Yatim despatched his own telegram to Saleh, sending it so that it would arrive at just the same time as the Major's. It ran:

> I have today posted to you an important letter. I hope to arrive in Kuwait one week later to discuss important matters dealing with oil concessions. Strongly urged that you advise His Excellency the sheikh to see the liberal terms offered by the Company which has been successful with His Highness Ibn Saud before giving any oil concessions to other companies. I bring an offer on the same liberal terms for his Excellency's consideration. I consider this question most important and vital for your country.

Before leaving for the principality, Holmes was also able to persuade some leading families in Bahrain to write for him some compelling letters of introduction to help him on his way. He also knew that the sheikh would be much impressed by his success in winning the al-Hasa concession, a success that had of course dramatically boosted his status as a key player in the region. As he arrived in Kuwait in mid-May, and was introduced to Saleh by Yatim later the same day, the Major knew that his search for a Kuwaiti oil concession could hardly have got off to a better start.

Something deep down told Holmes that the principality was well worth exploring for oil, and although he was not altogether alone in this assessment, he did feel more upbeat than almost anyone else. In March 1913 Sheikh Ahmad's father had given the British authorities permission to undertake a detailed oil survey whose subsequent findings were far from discouraging. Concluding that the principality's prospects were 'not unfavourable', its authors rated the area around Burgan to be the most promising place to undertake test drilling, pointing out that 'there is no reason to believe the nature of the beds beneath Burgan should be different from that of the Fars in Persia, and they may be looked upon therefore as sufficiently porous to retain oil in workable quantities'. But the author also emphasized that there was no firm evidence that oil was present, and that any exploration work would be fraught with risk. 'This locality', ran his report, 'is not on the line of strike of the rich oil deposits now being worked above Ahwaz, and is, in fact, over 170 miles to the south west of this line. This does not necessarily mean that oil in commercial quantity does not occur below Burgan, but it adds a decidedly speculative element to any operations.'

Cautious though this report was, the lure of Kuwaiti oil had prompted Admiral Slade of the Royal Navy to pay the kingdom a formal visit in 1913, while London also pressed Sheikh Mubarak to give the British government priority if he were ever to grant any future concession. In October 1913, the sheikh penned a letter, addressed to the British Political Resident at Bushire, that gave London what it wanted: 'if there seems hope of obtaining oil', it ran, then 'we shall never give a concession in this matter to any one except a person appointed from the British government'.

If Kuwaiti oil ever was discovered, then London certainly had a strong claim to exploit it, for the principality had historically enjoyed strong ties with the British government. Although for many years Kuwait had been under the nominal suzerainty of the Ottoman Empire, it had in practice always enjoyed a high degree of independence, and in 1899 the Turks had been unable to stop the Kuwait leader from striking an alliance with Great Britain. This deal, which was signed on behalf of the British government by its Political Resident in the Persian port of Bushire, included one particularly important term: the sheikh, his heirs and successors, it ran, must not 'cede, sell, lease, mortgage or give for occupation or for any other purpose any portion of his territory to the Government or subjects of any other power' unless Whitehall specifically agreed.

These ties became closer still in the years that followed. British planners recognized the kingdom's strategic importance and reckoned that its ports could provide a safe anchorage for their warships, a convenient coaling station and a potential base to use in the event of any clash with the Germans, who had a very strong presence in nearby Khadima. They also knew that a base in Kuwait could help them prevent arms flowing from the Persian Gulf into Afghanistan and then eventually reaching the North-West Frontier province of British India, conceivably setting the whole continent alight. Approaches to the Kuwaiti ruling circle were made, and in 1907 Sheikh Mubarak had leased an area of land, west of Kuwait city, to a British government that saw its new entitlement as an effective way of counteracting another threat: Germany's plans to build a railway between Berlin and Baghdad.

By the time Holmes arrived in the Middle East, London had other reasons to build up an alliance with Kuwait. By 1922 it was concerned about Ibn Saud's growing power, knowing that the Saudi king was a rival or even an enemy of Britain's protégés in Syria and Iraq. Some influential voices in Whitehall argued that Kuwait could act as a buffer against Saudi pretensions and that strong relations with Sheikh Ahmad, who had assumed the reins of power in early 1921 at the age of 36, were vital.

For all these different reasons, the British government was deeply alarmed to hear of Holmes' arrival in Kuwait that May afternoon in 1923. If the Syndicate won the concession there, then Whitehall officials were well aware that it would not have the financial clout to explore for oil, let alone extract it. It would instead soon sell its rights to a third party, one that could very well be associated with a rival, or even an enemy, foreign government. The Anglo-Persian directors were equally alarmed, knowing that Kuwaiti oil, if it were ever found, not only potentially offered huge profits but that its overproduction could depress prices in the region and hammer the company's own profits from Persian oil. A battle to win the Kuwaiti oil concession would have to be fought, and it was now under way.

Hearing the news about Holmes, Anglo-Persian's first move was to despatch an urgent telegram to Sir Arnold Wilson, who was based in the Persian Gulf port of Abadan. Wilson had gone a long way since undertaking the arduous task of guarding Reynolds' drilling team in Persia, back in 1907. His stamina, ability and enthusiasm had so impressed APOC's officials that they had quickly promoted him, offering him a senior managerial role at Abadan. The telegram, which reached Wilson in Abadan on 17 May, just days after Holmes' arrival, instructed him to pull out all the stops to get Anglo-Persian's draft concession finished and signed. With customary speed and efficiency, Wilson left hurriedly for Kuwait and wasted no time in negotiating with the sheikh, giving him a gentle reminder that he was obliged, under the terms of the 1899 deal, to get London's permission before granting any foreign concessions at all.

In the meantime, Holmes was probably too busy taking in his new surroundings to give much thought to Anglo-Persian's rivalry. His first sight of the kingdom would have been from the mailboat as it moved from the open seas into Kuwait

Bay, a huge crescent that stretched about 20 miles from east to west. As the boat moved steadily through blue-green pellucid waters, passing by numerous fishing vessels that were returning to harbour with their day's catch of sole, mullet, tunny, sea trout and pomfret, it would have approached the bay's southern shores, and Kuwait town would gradually have come into view.

Set in a flat and sandy plain, and surrounded by limitless stretches of desert sand, this rapidly growing town was then home to around 100,000 people. In its midst were numerous mosques – over forty of them in total – markets and bazaars, through which the town's many lanes, streets and alleys wound their way. In between were numerous ordinary houses, most of which were simple ground floor structures, although their high parapet walls, which enclosed part of the roof, would have made them seem bigger. Holmes may also have got a glimpse of the ancient wall that centuries before had been built around the town to guard its people against the attacks of marauding Bedouin tribes, or perhaps seen something of an imposing array of buildings which stretched from the seafront towards the very centre of the town. This was the sheikh's principal palace, which among the locals was known simply as Dasman, 'the Place of Bounty'.

Imposing though it may have been, Dasman was not particularly impressive. Coloured dull grey, and the product of a curious mishmash of architectural styles, it had windowless outer walls and a random, box-like construction that was far from pleasing to the eye. Most mornings the sheikh would move from these living quarters to the *serai* – the building's administrative quarter – overlooking the seafront, and then start his daily business in the company of his personal bodyguard and administrative staff.

It was here, to Dasman, that Holmes would have to go to meet the sheikh and win his favour. In one sense at least, this was not too daunting a task, for most Europeans had found that Sheikh Ahmad was a congenial personality as well as an impressive figure. He was, wrote Colonel Dickson, 'a strong, good-looking and pleasant man of the same type as his father', an individual who was easy to talk to, amiable, good-humoured and who, far from prevaricating, had an ability to make decisions with lightning speed, bespeaking enormous confidence in his own judgement.

There was one other thing, besides the sheikh's affability, that promised to make Holmes' task of winning the concession easier. For although the Kuwaiti leader, like nearly all the other heads of state that Holmes had met along the way, was a devout Muslim who enforced *sharia* – strict Islamic law – with an unbending rigour, he was also a Europhile, and one who was particularly well disposed towards the British. Some of his rooms in Dasman palace were furnished like a European home, and he had built up an extensive collection of Western rifles, cameras and numerous other inventions, all of which he was highly adept, even expert, at using.

The sheikh did, of course, have his faults, chief among them being that, 'like every Arab of pure stock, he was a man of immense pride; while he could not endure a discourtesy or forget an injury and, if taken the wrong away, was at times very awkward to handle'.[1] Such a thin skin partly reflected the simple fact that he was unused to anyone disagreeing with him. As Colonel Dickson wrote, 'it had always been the custom for sheikhs of Kuwait to rule personally and autocratically to avoid all delegation of authority'. On his accession to power local people had demanded more representation than ever before, and a council of twelve members was set up to consult him and the people he ruled. But it met only rarely, and in practice things carried on largely as before.

Using Mullah Saleh's influence, Holmes wasted little time in introducing himself to the sheikh, who had been well briefed about his new acquaintance and was doubtless intrigued by the man who stood before him. Using Mohammed Yatim as his interpreter, the Major explained his situation, telling Ahmad what he had come in search of and what he had to offer. A preliminary round of talks between the three men proved to be a good humoured and friendly affair, and Holmes was soon able to strike up a good rapport with his host. But he could not afford to spend too much time here. He would have to leave his ideas for the sheikh to deliberate upon, while heading back to Bahrain to continue with his hunt for Middle Eastern oil. If he could win a concession there, then he knew he would have a far greater chance of doing the same in Kuwait and elsewhere: he was well aware of the rivalry between the different leaders, each of whom tended to be jealous of all the others.

Holmes knew only too well that investing any time or money into the search for Bahraini oil was reckoned by almost every expert to be even more unwise than looking in Kuwait. In June 1905 a British geologist, Guy Pilgrim, had taken a close look at the Bahraini islands but failed to find the clues for oil that he had hoped to find: 'I cannot recommend that any serious thought be given to possible mining operations in the sea North of Halul', he wrote, 'at all events not until mining operations of a less expensive nature in other localities in the Gulf shall have given us a reasonable hope that an exploitable reserve of petroleum exists anywhere in the Gulf, and shall have proved that such local indications are something more than mere surface manifestations connected with a deep-seated and fitful volcanic activity.'[2]

Other oil experts had shown a bit more interest in Bahrain's prospects, although not much more. In 1913 S. Lister James, who acted as Anglo-Persian's chief geologist, made a tour of the Middle East and noted in his subsequent report that 'in view of the definite occurrence of asphalt and the ideal nature of the structure [in Bahrain], it appears inadvisable to ignore the area before testing with a fairly deep well'.

So it was hardly surprising that the Anglo-Persian Oil Company had never really had much interest in searching for oil in Bahrain, or indeed in Kuwait. Its senior directors were really interested only in keeping out their competitors who might, on the off chance, defy all the odds and strike lucky. As Charles Greenway, Anglo-Persian's head, argued in September 1924: 'Although the geological information we possess at present does not indicate that there is much hope of finding oil in Bahrain or Kuwait, we are, I take it, all agreed that even if the chance be 100 to 1 we should pursue it, rather than let others come into the Persian Gulf and cause difficulties of one kind and another for us.'[3]

It was in the same spirit that in May 1918 the APOC chairman also wrote to the Foreign Office. This letter formally asked for government assistance to win a regional oil concession that would not only 'cover all oil deposits which may be contained in such part or parts of Mesopotomia' but 'also cover the territories of the Sultan of Kuweit in which we have already carried out a considerable amount of geological investigation in anticipation of obtaining the concession'. It was the same concern – to keep others out of the region – that prompted him to make this request.

But Holmes had no interest in what any of these 'experts' may have thought. He had supreme confidence in his own judgement, which was doubtless swayed by the various rumours and stories he and others had heard over the preceding years. One such story was told by an American visitor to the island, J. Calcott Gaskin, who was later appointed as the Assistant Political Agent in Bahrain. He recorded how

> at the end of March, when some of the headmen of the Dawasir Arabs came to pay me a friendly visit, amongst other things in their conversation they mentioned that on the conclusion of the pearling season in September 1902, a diving boat owned by a friend of theirs was beating up the Gulf from one of the southern pearlbeds. At about ten to fifteen miles north of Ha'lul island, the attention of the people aboard was attracted by an agitation of the surface confined within a circle of some yards in diameter … [as] liquid bitumen was being thrown upwards to the surface which smeared both sides of the boat as they passed through it. If these statements are true it would appear that a natural spring of liquid bitumen or crude petroleum which occasionally is found in eruption, exists somewhere in the locality indicated and may be worth exploiting.[4]

Holmes' big chance came in the late autumn and winter of 1924, when much of the Persian Gulf was badly hit by heavy storms that seriously affected the water supply of some of the offshore islands. This was because Bahrain had almost no inland wells of its own, and instead relied for its freshwater supply on divers who filled goatskins from freshwater springs deep under the sea and brought them to the surface. Such operations were of course always dangerous but during violent storms were quite impossible to undertake, and this meant that the kingdom, like many other parts of the Gulf, was now affected by a serious water shortage.

The Bahraini people did have a few other sources of water. Further inland there were some springs from which fresh water was often brought to market, but once again they hardly offered much of a solution. There were only a handful of these wells, and getting anything out of them was extremely laborious and time-consuming. Some of them were said to be 20 fathoms deep, and to draw out water a goatskin bucket had slowly to be lowered down via a pulley and then pulled back up again by donkeys or camels. After this the water would still have to be transported over long distances, and when it did eventually come to market it was, not surprisingly, very expensive. Most people relied on the natural springs that lay near their homes and which could be used for washing and cleaning but only rarely for drinking. Otherwise, quite simply, they had little choice but to drink filthy water and hope for the best.

Holmes knew that a severe drought was not far off, one that could easily cause everyone extreme hardship as well as provoke riots and demonstrations that could badly damage the sheikh's authority. He also knew that the kingdom was largely dependent for its income on pearling. Even at the very best of times, this was not a particularly rewarding occupation, for diving deep underwater to find pearls demanded a lot of skill, endurance and courage on the part of the diver, who never earned very much to compensate for the high risk of drowning.

These diving operations started when large caged baskets were lowered by rope to the sea bed from a small sailing ship anchored over a carefully chosen spot. A diver would then plunge overboard while holding a large stone that quickly dragged him below the surface before putting all the oysters he could find into the basket. These divers not only had to be supremely well practised at holding their breath but also needed to use a knife, strapped to their sides, to fend off any sharks, or the even more feared barracudas, that lurked in the waters. Then, with his lungs bursting, the diver gave the signal that the sailors above had been waiting for, tugging the rope that was wrapped around his waist before being pulled straight to the surface.

By the early 1920s these pearling techniques were no different from those used thousands of years before. Perhaps because the seas were becoming over-exploited, however, local divers were by this time finding it harder than ever to find pearls in sufficient quantity to keep their own pockets lined and the kingdom's coffers filled. The sheikh, in other words, was highly susceptible to suggestions that he needed an extra source of income. The Major was now quick to see the opportunity this presented. As an experienced engineer who had already taken a careful look at the island's geology, he knew that there were several underground springs that he could tap into. So why not haggle with Sheikh Hamad, in truly

Arab fashion, and offer to find and open up some inland wells on the clear condition that, in return, he was offered a concession to explore for oil?

He moved fast. With the assistance of Mohammed Yatim, who had agreed to split his time between Kuwait and Bahrain, Holmes put his proposals to Sheikh Hamad, who leapt on the offer to drill for water but, unwilling to let outsiders into his kingdom unless he really had to, balked at the catch. But the Major persisted, threatening to rescind the deal unless his demands were met in full, and the sheikh, desperate to solve the island's water crisis, eventually gave way, granting him exclusive permission to drill between twelve and sixteen water wells and to search for oil if water was found. If he found nothing, ran the deal, then he would earn nothing: 'the price being naught if he should meet with failure but $150,000 per well and consideration of his application for an oil concession if he should succeed'.[5]

Hearing the news back in London, the Syndicate's directors now pulled out all the stops to find Bahraini water, commissioning a top expert, T. George Madgwick, an engineering professor at Birmingham University, to undertake a detailed survey of the island. At the same time they despatched the specialized drilling equipment that would be needed for the operations and, with the help of one Captain Albert H. Farley, a director of Phoenix Oil and Transport Company, also headhunted two highly experienced drillers. None of this was easy to organize. Inevitably delays ensued, first for the completion of the survey, and then for the various pieces of equipment to arrive. In May, plans went even more awry when the engine broke down, forcing Madgwick to leave the island and sail for Port Said, picking up the spare parts that had to be specially shipped in from the Iraqi city of Basrah. But eventually, after long delays, work got going and by the autumn of 1925 the hunt for Bahraini water was well and truly under way.

This was by any standards a demanding task, for not much of the land on these islands was particularly pleasant or hospitable. Most of it was just low-lying desert that was 'sprinkled here and there', as one Western visitor put it, 'with fertile spots encircling small villages. These fertile regions are irrigated from springs and wells, and grow dates, melons and a few vegetables.'[6] But most of the area was arid, barren and, even in autumn, uncomfortably hot.

It was not long, just four weeks, before the Syndicate's directors back in London heard the news they had been waiting months for: a message from Holmes that a strong flow of water had been struck, at a depth of 142 feet, and was gushing from one well at the rate of 110 tons every day, and from another at a rate of 140. News spread like wildfire across the island, and local Arabs immediately hailed Holmes and his team as heroes. The sheikh and his deputies and chief advisors were equally jubilant, the former declaring himself immensely pleased that a guaranteed supply of fresh water had been found, especially one that was very conveniently located.

The sheikh now wasted no time in offering the oil concession that Holmes had bargained so hard for. On 2 December 1925, acting on behalf of his elderly father, he offered the Syndicate exclusive rights to drill for oil over a two-year period, together with an option to renew for a further two, in return for an annual payment of 10,000 rupees. A catch, however, was that the rights could not be transferred to anyone else unless the sheikh, acting on the advice of his British advisers, specifically agreed.

Holmes had always known that the British government enjoyed just as strong a position in Bahrain as it did in Kuwait. In 1861 Britain and Bahrain had signed a Treaty of Perpetual Peace and Friendship that encompassed issues such as maritime aggression, commerce and slavery, and this deal had enabled the British to establish an extensive regional network of diplomats and administrators that was based in the kingdom. It was always unthinkable that the British would ever allow the Bahrainis to determine a matter as important as finding and exploiting oil without prior approval from the local Political Agent, or else directly from Whitehall.

The immediate problem for Holmes and the Syndicate was to find an oil company that would now make a generous bid for their hard-earned concessions in both Saudi and Bahrain. The Syndicate simply did not have the vast resources and infrastructure that were needed to conduct a proper search: it had been financially stretched even by the task of finding water, but locating oil, which required much deeper and more protracted drilling, was technically and financially far more demanding. But whom could they now sell these rights to, recouping their expenses and making the profit they wanted?

The search for a suitable buyer certainly did not start well. Soon after signing the al-Hasa concession, the Syndicate had arranged for a team of Swiss geologists to visit the islands and make a detailed report on the prospects for finding oil there. Holmes waited for them to arrive and then watched them get to work, hoping desperately that they would strike lucky and find the crucial pieces of evidence he needed. But after spending the winter of 1923 there, the team returned to Europe empty-handed, wholly without the positive results Holmes and the London directorate had wanted. The leader of the group, Dr Heim, admitted that Bahrain was situated on a type of rock formation that was potentially oil bearing, since it formed 'a large and very gentle anticlinal dome', but felt that this was not in itself particularly important. He continued by saying that 'there is no reason to suppose such an oil horizon at the depth below Dj.Dukhan. It is true that the Cretaceous and Eocene Formations of Persia and of Syria and Palestine sow numerous scattered oil seepages and asphalt outcrops in the limestones, as is the case on Bahrain, but none yet has proved to produce oil in paying quantities. To drill on the dome of Dj.Dukhan not only would be extremely expensive, but also a pure gamble.' In the meantime the Syndicate was still trying hard to lure international oil companies but, without any hard scientific facts to go on, continued to find their job extremely tough going.

The case for caution must have seemed a compelling one. By 1926 the only Middle Eastern country producing commercial quantities of oil was Persia, and there were no known oil seepages of any real note anywhere in the whole Arabian peninsula other than at a remote spot near the Qatif oasis in al-Hasa and amongst some sand dunes in the vicinity of Burgan in Kuwait. Many investors steered well clear of the region as a whole, regarding any exposure as a large and unnecessary risk. The question of who would now get involved in the venture, buy out the concession and save the Eastern and General Syndicate from financial disaster must have weighed heavily on the minds of both Holmes and Madgwick as they sailed back to Britain at the end of 1925. Years of hard, patient work on Holmes' part would be wasted if the concessions failed to arouse any commercial interest. The Syndicate's strongest card was probably Professor Madgwick, who felt that the islands' geological formation was particularly favourable to the accumulation of large quantities of oil, and who now urged the Syndicate to raise the necessary funds to try to develop Bahrain itself.

But finding the Syndicate's directorship distinctly unenthusiastic and much keener on selling the concession to a third party, Madgwick and Holmes now approached a number of possible buyers to gauge their interest. Cory Brothers & Co, which had made a fortune exploring and drilling British coalfields, was initially tempted by the idea but was unhappy about the contract terms and refused to commit itself. Numerous other independent investors barely even raised their eyebrows, being much more interested in funding search operations in more familiar African fields than in taking enormous commercial risks in a region as unknown as the Middle East. Others in the industry were aware that the governments of Persia and Iraq were lobbying hard to increase the oil production from their own oilfields, since the proceeds of the oil's sale would give them more foreign exchange. If this happened then there would be a global oil glut that would allow prices to fall and make it much harder for any investor to recoup the huge expenses of searching for oil – even if oil was ever found, of course.

There were still the big players of the oil business to approach, however. Yet Royal Dutch Shell and Anglo-Persian were far too involved in sorting out the complicated international wrangle about who owned what in Iraq, a country that was felt to offer much more promise. The directors of Anglo-Persian were also sure that that if no British company took up the Syndicate's offer, then nor would any of their international rivals: each, it was felt, tended to follow suit. Both companies turned Holmes' offer down flat, probably regarding him as little more than an adventurer, gambler and, above all, an amateur. The Major continued to tour the dining clubs and offices where he thought the right type of investor might lurk, and was said to have become 'an interminable bore' as his efforts became increasingly persistent, even if they were no more successful.

One reason why the British were relatively complacent about transatlantic competition from the fast-growing American oil companies was their conviction that the USA, after a post-war hitch, was once again self-sufficient in oil and would remain so for some time to come. By the mid-1920s vast American oilfields, such as Huntingdon Beach, had flooded the domestic market with what seemed to everyone to be a limitless supply of good quality fuel, causing prices to fall drastically. The panic of just a few years before, when America suddenly seemed highly dependent on oil imports, seemed like a distant memory. Many US companies suddenly began to relax their previously frantic efforts to secure new sources of supply, while their European rivals saw more reason to develop existing supplies. They preferred to stick to established sources such as Persia, Iraq and the East Indies rather than take big commercial risks elsewhere.

Such complacency about the future of oil made the task of selling the concessions for al-Hasa infinitely harder, and finding no real interest from anyone, the Syndicate's directors discontinued exploration operations, defaulted on their annual payments and watched helplessly as Sheikh Hamad looked ready to cancel the Bahraini deal. By the midsummer of 1926, after four years of hard work and effort on everyone's part, financial disaster seemed to be looming for the Eastern and General Syndicate. To make matters worse, Holmes had been so busy working in Bahrain that he had barely had the time or opportunity to notice what was going on elsewhere in the region. He did not realize, for example, that he had a very determined and able enemy, who was trying his utmost to stop him from getting the Kuwaiti concession.

13

The Incredible Haji

Preoccupied with his search for oil in Bahrain, Arabia and the Neutral Zone, Holmes had been unaware just how much controversy his proposed concession had been stirring up among Kuwait's high and mighty, many of whom regarded it as a dangerous foreign threat to their kingdom's independence. Nor did the Major at this stage know that this ill-feeling was now being orchestrated by the efforts of an enemy who was determined, clever, resourceful and, even by Holmes' own remarkable standards, wholly intriguing and supremely mysterious.

His name was Haji Abdullah Fadhil Williamson, and he had been sent to Kuwait by the Anglo-Persian Oil Company to rally the growing opposition to Holmes' concession. With Haji's help, Holmes' various enemies in London had felt sure that they could now step in to block the Major's way and, at the very least, make his life much more difficult. Williamson seemed just the right man to come to their assistance. In sharp contrast to Holmes, who was a relative newcomer to the region and never made any effort to learn its language or wear local clothes, Haji had lived and worked in the Middle East for more than 40 years, spoke flawless Arabic, invariably dressed in local garb and was a devout and committed Muslim. He knew the people, their land, mentality and ways as well as anyone else alive, and had by this time acquired a formidable, almost legendary, reputation amongst the local people. But although in every sense a committed Arabist, he was also a patriot with strong ties to his native land, Great Britain, whose government was glad to lend him its full support.

All this, of course, was remarkable, but then everything about Haji Williamson's life was stranger than fiction. Born William Richard Williamson in Bristol in 1872, he had run away from an unhappy family life by joining the merchant navy at the age of thirteen, heading for Australia. Conditions on board were harsh even for the most experienced seafarer, particularly when the ship encountered violent storms in the notorious Bay of Biscay, but the vulnerable young William also had to endure all manner of brutal treatment: on one occasion he suffered one of the harshest punishments that any sailor could receive – being ordered to climb the ship's tall masthead to act as a lookout. Even in the most clement conditions this was a very unpleasant task, but in the rough seas and bitter cold that Williamson was forced to endure (because of some trivial wrongdoing he was said to have committed) it was almost tantamount to torture. But although he was always of quite small, slim stature, he had immense physical strength and almost fanatical powers of determination and concentration that enabled him to pull through such horrendous ordeals.

Surviving this journey, and then stowing on board a ship bound for California, proved to be only the beginning of his many adventures. Over the next few years he worked as a whaler in the Arctic Seas before heading for the Barbary Coast of South America, where he was held by the Spanish authorities who wrongly suspected him of assisting local rebels in their armed struggle for independence. Thrown into prison and forced to join a chain gang, he managed to escape back to North America, where he joined the Gold Rush, prospecting for both gold and oil, while also working illicitly as a cattle-hustler. Even by this time he was still only nineteen.

It was during the next leg of his extraordinary travels, however, that his life and fortunes were to change dramatically. From America Williamson took a ship bound for British India, where he intended to start a new life, and stopped off en route in Arabia. Though he intended to stay only for a few days before resuming his journey, he was immediately overwhelmed by everything that he saw, heard and felt. The whole area somehow seemed to be beckoning him. He overheard the conversations of local people and, feeling captivated by their mysterious cadences and harsh guttural sounds, felt a deep longing to learn their native tongue, and as saw them kneel down to pray, he felt an irrepressible need to convert to Islam. He wasted little time in finding work in Arabia, joining the local police force in the British-run principality of Aden and ditching his plans to head for India.

Williamson's immersion in Arabian culture had not gone unnoticed by the British authorities. They were taken aback to hear, for example, not only that he had now changed his name but also that his commitment to the Islamic faith was so deep that he had, quite voluntarily, undergone ritual circumcision (amongst people for whom anaesthetics were quite unknown) to follow the example of local men. Fearing that he was now set to travel into parts of Arabia that were Turkish controlled, where he might perhaps easily stir up trouble, the British authorities became nervous, and decided to expel the maverick twenty-year-old from Aden. Haji was put on board a ship bound for India, but such measures were of little use against one so determined, and it was not long before he was able to escape back to the land that had left him spellbound. Dressed in Arab garb – the white *kiffieh* headdress and flowing robes – and sporting a strong suntan, he must have seemed little different from all the Arabs who boarded SS *Bancoora* in Bombay. He passed the checkpoints unchallenged and then headed back to the Gulf, stepping off not at Aden, where he thought the authorities might be on the lookout for him, but in Kuwait, which he now saw for the first time.

By the time of the outbreak of the First World War in 1914, Haji had a vast knowledge of much of the Middle East. He was also well connected and spoke perfect Arabic. But he still retained some loyalty to the land of his birth, even if by this time he had not visited its shores for some 30 years, and he was quick to offer his services to the British authorities, who were busy fighting Turkish soldiers throughout the Middle East and beyond. Haji's detailed knowledge of the area proved an immense asset to the Intelligence Corps, which he now joined as a civilian member, and so too was his willingness and ability to insinuate himself behind Turkish lines. From his home near Basrah he would travel far to undertake detailed reconnaissance of Turkish positions, evading capture by melting into the local crowds or, if his enemies were really hot on his heels, disappearing into the vast marshlands that lay between the Tigris and Euphrates rivers, and where he knew that his enemies would not dare follow him.

On one occasion he managed to track down two Turkish officers, regarded by the British authorities as key sources of information, leading to their capture. The two men, Williamson ascertained, were being sheltered by one of the local tribes. Being so familiar with local customs, he knew that the tribal leaders would not surrender the Turks: the officers were their *faifh* (guests) and were therefore *dakhile* (inviolate), and the tribesmen were obliged by an ancient code of honour not to break their promise. The tribes would fight to the death, explained their leaders, to defend their guests. Haji tried to reason with the tribal leaders and the Turks. The British army, he argued, would not respect their oaths and would simply fight their way past them to capture the men: if the officers simply surrendered or were handed over peacefully then everyone could avoid a lot of unnecessary bloodshed. Eventually the Turks agreed to surrender themselves to the British, but after they had left the tribal camp Haji decided to release them: if they were honourable enough to sacrifice their own freedom for the sake of their Arab hosts, as he later argued before horrified British officers, then so should he be honourable enough to release them.

In the course of his war career, Haji had happened to meet with a senior and very well connected British army officer, who was astonished by the extraordinary gifts of such a remarkable man. The officer's name was Lieutenant Colonel Arnold Wilson, who was not long returned from the oilfields of Persia and who plays a central part in the story of the search for Middle Eastern oil. After the war the two men resumed contact and Wilson, then based in Abadan for the Anglo-Persian Oil Company and acting for Whitehall as a regional Civil Commissioner and Political Resident, wasted little time in offering him a job with Anglo-Persian. In 1924 Haji accepted this post and began his work as a regional Inspector of Gulf Agencies on the company's behalf.

Part of Haji's role was to find and organize a chain of supply bases in and around parts of the Persian Gulf that Anglo-Persian needed to keep its exports flowing. Often this involved locating suitable places for depots and warehouses, finding and recruiting local labourers to carry out the work and then supervising their work. But his involvement went much further than that. He also advised the senior management about every aspect of the region, often passing judgement on their plans, liaising with local tribal chiefs on Anglo-Persian's behalf, and escorting some company employees on their more adventurous journeys. He also undertook his own surveys of Halul, Das and other islands in the Gulf that were thought to have some oil-bearing potential, and sometimes travelled to places that were considered too wild and dangerous to invest in. In other words, he had, in effect, become one of the oil hunters of the Middle East.

For Anglo-Persian's employees, who were at this time touring so many corners of the region in search of new markets and oilfields, Williamson's grasp of local dialects and customs certainly came in handy. On one occasion he escorted an APOC official in the Qatar peninsula to meet a local leader, who insisted on holding a special banquet in honour of his new guests. In the evening whole carcasses of roasted sheep had been placed before every one of them, and it was etiquette for a guest to punch his fist into the dead creature's head, fish out its eyes and then devour them, quite raw, in front of everyone. The young visitor turned green as his turn came to try this dish, considered locally to be a great luxury, and he managed to slip the sheep's eye down his shirt without anyone noticing. But there were still more sheep eyes on the menu, and Williamson, seeing the man's discomfort, told the tribal chief that his guest's gratitude for this particular dish was so great that he wanted to eat them later, before retiring to bed, rather than rush them during the meal. To the visitor's enormous relief, the chief smiled at the compliment and nodded his assent.

On another occasion, the oil explorers of the Anglo-Persian Oil Company had a very near miss as they sailed along the coasts of Dhofar, an area they thought might be worth exploring for some hidden petroleum deposits. Waiting for them, however, was a flotilla of boats full to the brim with bloodthirsty Shihu tribesmen, brandishing guns and spears as they made a beeline for the unfortunate visitors. These tribes had a terrible reputation, for in the preceding months they had claimed the lives of several other European travellers. But as the pirate boats approached and the heavily outnumbered explorers braced themselves to be slaughtered, Haji stood up and shouted to them, using his fluency in the Shihu dialect to the full. Knowing that the region was dependent for its income on finding and selling underground pearls, he tried desperately to pull the right strings. The party had heard that pearling conditions were poor, he shouted, and had come to them with scientific knowledge that would help them find more pearls than ever before: so their rulers would regard it as a very serious matter indeed, he continued, if anyone touched him or his crew. The pirates now realized that this was Haji Williamson they had inadvertently come across and, knowing his legendary reputation, backed off.

Being so familiar with the terrain, Williamson was also approached by his employers to find areas of land that might make suitable landing strips for their aircraft. The company had always used airstrips in Persia, but its ruler, Reza Shah, had recently decided to renegotiate the leases, regarding their original terms as too generous and thinking that there was nowhere else outside Persia where the planes could go. He was proved wrong, however, when Haji suggested some places that would be ideal for runways, and where they could be built at relatively meagre cost. It was not long before construction on the new landing strips was started and Reza lost out heavily by forfeiting the leases. Soon afterwards, Haji was warned that he could never again make his way to Persia since a furious shah was blaming him for the failure to renew the leases, and had sworn to exact a bloody personal vengeance against him.

Now, in 1924, Haji received a new set of instructions from Abadan. His task was to stop Frank Holmes getting a Kuwaiti oil concession, and to use all his personal influence to persuade as many leading figures in Kuwait as he could find to join his cause. Williamson's loyalty to Britain was immense, and he would have been worried that if Holmes won the Kuwaiti oil concession, he could easily sell it on to one of Britain's international rivals. He had as yet never met Holmes, but would doubtless have regarded the New Zealander as nothing more than a bumptious upstart who was taking the liberty of meddling in a region he had no real knowledge or understanding of, and no true feeling for. So he left his Basrah home for Kuwait, harbouring a very personal motive, not merely a professional one, for stopping Holmes.

Williamson's first ports of call in Kuwait were the homes of the powerful Sabah and Al Ghanim families, whose leading members he had known for many years and in whom he had immense trust. These were two of Kuwait's most distinguished and successful families, ones that had made their money from commerce and had subsequently acquired enormous political influence over the sheikh, who often conferred with family members on all manner of issues. Haji felt sure that he could win them over to his side and that they would then try to dissuade the sheikh from doing any deal with Holmes.

Once he was in Kuwait, it was not long before Haji found another reason to want to stop Holmes from making any progress. Once again, this was the most personal of motives. On his arrival in Kuwait, Haji was introduced to Mohammed Yatim, Holmes' trusted adviser and translator who had been acting as his agent in Kuwait during Holmes' long periods of absence. Haji formed a very strong personal dislike of Yatim, although it was one that he never really explained or accounted for. Part of the trouble, perhaps, was Yatim's enthusiasm for forms of entertainment that Williamson, notoriously devout and severe, frowned upon: for example the correspondence of one of Anglo-Persian's representatives had recorded in March 1925 how Yatim 'has engaged a band and some dancers and is giving private invitations to the Sheikh and to different leading people nearly every night at his house'. No matter what the cost, Haji felt, he must try to stop such a man from getting the concession.

Sending Williamson to Kuwait to rally opposition to the granting of the concession was just one card that Anglo-Persian was playing against Holmes and his Syndicate. In London its directors also lobbied Whitehall to lean as hard as possible on the Kuwaiti leader. These efforts seemed to bear fruit when on 6 September 1923 the British government stepped into the tussle and put its huge weight behind Anglo-Persian. Acting with the support of the highest levels of authority, the Colonial Office despatched a long letter to the Political Resident in Bushire that pitched long and detailed arguments against Holmes' bid for a concession. In particular, the letter pointed to the terms of the 1899 agreement and its nationality clause, and stated that the New Zealander was 'avowedly, and probably actually' violating this deal because he did not have London's prior approval. The letter also emphasized that the East and General Syndicate simply did not have the same proven expertise in the discovery and exploitation of oil as the Anglo-Persian Oil Company, which had by now been working the wells at Masjid-i Suleiman and elsewhere in Persia for fifteen years.

Anglo-Persian's aims were the same as before: trying to keep its competitors out of an arena that it had never had any real interest in developing itself. Its directors had always been highly sceptical about the prospects for finding oil there in any commercial quantities, and these doubts were reinforced in 1924, when Dr Heim had published his discouraging report on the region as a whole and when, shortly afterwards, APOC's own independent team of surveyors and geologists had reached similarly disappointing conclusions. But the company was still very concerned that Holmes' Syndicate could easily sell any concessionary rights to an American oil giant, such as Standard Oil, that could fund extensive exploration efforts. And it was just possible, they felt, that a really well funded and organized exploration operation would eventually defy all the odds and somehow and somewhere find large petroleum deposits.

Sheikh Ahmad felt trapped between these competing interests. On the one hand he could not simply disregard the terms of the 1899 agreement with the British government and lose favour with a country that was still at the height of its imperial power. Yet at the same time he liked Holmes enormously, and was smarting with indignation about his treatment at the Ojair Conference, when he felt the British had failed to do enough to protect his interests: the British, it seemed, had failed to placate both sides at the conference, since the Saudis were equally indignant about their own treatment.[1]

But although the odds stacked against him were formidable, Holmes' persistence was at this stage reaping some rewards. In the course of his second visit to the kingdom, on 31 March 1924, the Major pushed his case for a concession in the Neutral Zone and was now surprised to find that the British government's Political Representative in Kuwait was not standing in his way: King Ibn Saud had already granted Holmes permission to explore his half of the Zone, reasoned Whitehall, and Sheikh Ahmad would feel a strong sense of injustice if he was not allowed to grant permission for exploration of the Kuwaiti sector. On 17 May 1924 the Syndicate was formally awarded an option on the Neutral Zone, a concession that considerably heightened its status not just in Kuwait but throughout the region as a whole.

But Holmes was still making no progress in his battle to get hold of the Kuwaiti concession. He knew that this was partly because Anglo-Persia was still straining to win the sheikh's favour, inviting him to visit its showpieces – the Persian oilfields and the vast refinery it had built at Abadan – that could not fail to impress. By now word had also reached him of Williamson's determined efforts to stir up the hostility and enmity of those who could whisper in their leader's ear. But whatever the reason, his attempts to win the concession he so badly wanted were plainly not working. By the spring of 1926, the Major decided to try another approach. If he had won the favour of the Bahraini leader by drilling for water, he reasoned, then why could he not try the same tactic in Kuwait? With Sheikh Ahmad's permission Holmes began his search for underground water wells, hoping that he would find not only good favour but in the process also discover really compelling evidence of oil. He did not have much of an opportunity because under the agreement he was allowed to dig only four such wells, but in the course of the next twelve months worked hard to uncover the seepages that he longed to find.

It was at this point, just as his hopes were fading, that Holmes made a breakthrough: one of the wells showed slight traces of oil. Working at this site with only a handful of local men, he was able to keep this discovery to himself, refusing to tell anyone on the island just in case any of Anglo-Persian's many local agents and sympathizers got wind of what had happened. He wanted to keep this his own closely guarded secret, knowing that it might easily be the crucial piece of information that could finally tempt a foreign company to buy out his concessions.

Holmes had by now done all he could to tempt foreign buyers to back the Syndicate's bid for a Kuwaiti oil concession, and also to interest them in buying its rights to explore Bahrain, al-Hasa and the Neutral Zone. But now the task of selling these interests was made easier by another development. For during his trip to Bahrain, Professor Madgwick had noticed a rock structure that he called 'a perfect dome' – perfect, that is, for bearing oil. Never before, he was prepared to say, had he ever come across an oil structure as striking as the one he had seen in Bahrain, and this, he felt sure, had huge potential that no oil company could afford to ignore. Shortly afterwards, on 23 September 1926, he reported his findings in more detail, arguing that Bahrain's rock structure 'is so striking that in conjunction with the asphalt – which is regarded as a desert seepage – there can be no hesitation in saying that test drilling is called for ... Bahrain and the adjacent coast must stand on its own merits and may not be regarded as a possible extension of the fields in Persia ... in my opinion, any oil geologist gifted with reasonable optimism would advise as I do, that a deep test is warranted.'[2]

Here lay the Syndicate's greatest source of hope as its directors now continued with their search to find a buyer of their existing concessions in Bahrain, al-Hasa and the Neutral Zone, and who might help them persuade the Kuwaiti leader to grant his own concession. But it was a bolt from the blue when a telegram arrived from New York that immediately raised their flagging spirits. Although neither Holmes nor the Syndicate's directors had ever been in touch with with any of the top American oil companies, Professor Madgwick had over the preceding weeks been corresponding with a well-placed New Yorker about two issues. One such issue was very much Madgwick's own personal business: a possible job opening for him to work as a petroleum consultant to the Canadian Dominion government in Alberta. The other, however, was the Bahrain concession, and the telegram explained that Madgwick's description of oil prospects in the principality was of great interest and could very well find American buyers, whom he was now willing to approach with the recommendation that they take things further forward.

The name of this New Yorker, set to play a crucial role in the search for Middle Eastern oil, was the president of the Oilfield Equipment Company, Thomas E. Ward. He had seen and heard much about Madgwick's upbeat report regarding Bahraini oil prospects, and he was extremely keen to learn more. Winning Ward's interest and sympathy proved to be an invaluable asset, for he was superbly well connected with a good number of other individuals who he felt sure would have some interest in backing the project. Over the coming weeks Holmes and Ward arranged a hectic itinerary of interviews with potential backers, some of whom dismissed their proposals out of hand, while others raised their eyebrows and asked if they could send their own surveying team to the region to take a closer look.

Ward's interest, and Holmes' own hopes, had doubtless been raised considerably by the dramatic news that suddenly surged in from Iraq. For on 15 October 1927 at Baba Gurgur, a few miles north of the predominantly Kurdish city of Kirkuk, a drilling team suddenly struck oil at a depth of 1,500 feet. This had been no ordinary discovery. For as the drill bit hit the underground seam, a vast torrent of oil exploded to the surface, jumping more than 50 feet above the derrick and flooding the surrounding area, even swamping whole villages for miles around. Hundreds of miles away, even in neighbouring Persia, villagers heard the distant roar of the torrent as it flowed and felt the ground beneath them shudder.

Meanwhile, after a lot of surveying work on the ground and extensive bargaining in the offices and hotels of the USA, Canada and England, deals were finally struck. On 30 November Thomas Ward signed a contract on the Syndicate's behalf that granted the American corporate giant, Gulf Oil, an exclusive option to acquire its Bahrain concession, and signed up Holmes to act on Gulf's behalf in his present role. In a separate deal Gulf also secured a similar option on the Syndicate's concessions to explore for oil in al-Hasa and the Neutral Zone. The Syndicate's directors had been under huge financial pressure far too long, and could at least breathe a long sigh of relief.

Anxious to keep careful tabs on the moves of its international rivals, the British government had all this time been closely monitoring Holmes' own movements, as well as the activities of the Syndicate as a whole. Anglo-Persian's informers would certainly have known straightaway when he had left the Middle East, and the company may have felt renewed concern that competitors were hovering. When Holmes returned to Bahrain in spring 1927, he appears to have been well aware of how closely he was being watched, and commented that: 'Since I have made the road to the seepage and built the huts there, the APOC geologists have been three times to Bahrain port. On two of these visits they have visited the oil seepage and taken away samples of the bitumen and oil sands ... I hear that the geologists have already reported that Bahrain is well worth boring ... the work at the seepage has exposed some interesting things, among them a larger showing of oil bitumen.'[3]

But he felt reasonably sure that the British were unaware of exactly who he had struck his new deal with, and his hunch was confirmed when he returned to Bahrain alongside a team of Gulf Oil geologists. On 19 February 1928 he wrote that:

> It should not be supposed that we are not being watched and our competitors have begun a campaign to annoy us ... they have guessed wrongly and are quite convinced that your men came from the Standard Oil Company. The Chief Political Agent of the Gulf is coming to Bahrain next week with the avowed intention out from what we are doing and what our connections are. I think I can hold my own with him, but we shall see. All this questioning and agitation will die down in a little while, but we want to keep it under control until our campaign had been brought to a successful issue.[4]

The American team quickly made positive findings, concluding that 'a test well favourably located on the Bahrain anticline may reasonably be expected to encounter oil', and emphasizing that the principality's location, supply of cheap local labour and political stability made it an ideal investment. This is exactly what Anglo-Persian and the British government were afraid of, and shortly afterwards the British Political Resident, Colonel Haworth, told Holmes sharply that APOC was 'dreadfully annoyed' that the Syndicate had found such strong foreign backing.

But the British government was fast preparing to make its own countermove. Remembering its historic diplomatic ties with Bahrain, the Colonial Office wrote to the Syndicate, pointing out that it would insist on a new clause being put at the heart of the company's contract with the kingdom's ruler. This clause would affirm that 'the Syndicate shall at all times be and remain a British Company' and could not in way be 'directly or indirectly controlled or managed by a foreigner or foreigners or by any foreign corporation or corporations'. Gulf Oil was at this time selling its stake in Bahrain to Standard Oil of California, while retaining strong links with Holmes and the Syndicate, and the British government continued strongly to push its case. This did not intimidate the Syndicate directors, who fired back that the lease would not be conveyed to a third party 'without the consent of the sheikh' and that 'such consent shall not be unreasonably withheld'. Open conflict between them clearly looming.

But despite running into such obstacles over Bahrain, Holmes was now in a position to continue his quest to win the Kuwaiti concession, a quest that had by now already been going on fruitlessly for five years. At the end of April 1928 he made a further visit to the kingdom, this time en route to Bahrain, and was warmly received by Sheikh Ahmad and his advisers. This was a good start to his journey, for just a few hours earlier that same day Ahmad had been approached by Anglo-Persian's local representative and had refused to grant him an audience. Holmes felt his confidence surge, and on 6 May penned a letter to the Gulf Oil Company explaining in detail why, after his meeting with Ahmad, he felt that he now had the upper hand over his British rivals. To begin with, he explained, the sheikh had started off their meeting by commenting 'that I have proved a friend of the Arabs and would be more likely to help them than any other party, and that I had no political aspirations, being purely commercial as had been proved in Bahrain'. This remark, the Major pointed out, was a clear reference to the British government and its strong links with Anglo-Persian. Not only that, he continued, but the Syndicate's success in Saudi was helping their Kuwaiti cause, for 'the sheikh has been in constant communication with Ibn Saud during the past two months, and I feel sure that Ibn Saud has told him to ask plenty for his territory'.

There was one other reason, however, why Holmes was now feeling so positive about winning the Kuwaiti concession: the growing American interest in the project, and the powerful reaction this elicited from Ahmad. In his letter the Major wrote that 'it is interesting to observe the greedy attitude the sheikh exhibited when I hinted to him that the company I was representing had an American tang about it. The Arab rulers certainly suspect every move of the British, this suspicion is largely removed when American money is suggested.' By winning the interest of Gulf Oil in Kuwait, Holmes had in fact drastically increased the Syndicate's bargaining power. For the first time it was as commercially strong as the mighty Anglo-Persian Oil Company, since it now had the financial clout of the Gulf Oil Company to win new concessions and exploit existing ones to the full.

But high though Holmes' hopes were lifted, the concession was still proving surprisingly elusive. In June 1928 he presented a copy of his draft concession and details of the extra payments he was offering to make, but still the sheikh refused to make any firm commitments. He did seem well disposed to Holmes personally, however, and to the Syndicate's cause, but it was still not quite possible, he added, to take things any further forward.

Back in New York, Gulf Oil officials were as surprised as Holmes at just how protracted the foot-dragging was turning out to be. It defied all the rules of the oil game, as one of them put it, to turn such an offer down while the going was good: 'one of the tenets of the religion of the oil people is to take what is obtainable as and when it can be had, because experience had taught that the future is always uncertain, particularly when political questions or viewpoints become involved'. But Holmes sensed what was going on behind his back, and in July wrote back to New York saying that 'opposition have been most virulent and are still very active; their attitude has been more to prevent the signing of our draft rather than endeavouring to secure concession at this moment for themselves'. Later, in a letter written on 1 November 1931, he noted that 'the APOC's agents have been very active and are still so, both with their money and propaganda. The APOC subscribed liberally to the hospital and schools and managed to secure the help of some of the leading merchants'.[5]

Holmes was right, for there was a lot of domestic opposition to the granting of an oil concession to any foreign entity. For all this time, wholly unknown to him, Haji Williamson had been hard at work, rallying Holmes' existing enemies and busily making him new ones, while also trying hard to win sympathy in the royal palace for the British cause. His efforts seemed to pay off when in August 1928 the sheikh and his council decisively rejected the Major's draft terms, demanding both larger royalties and a provision that any concession should only be granted to Holmes personally and not transferred to any third party. One of Williamson's key allies was Yusuf Ahmad Al Ghanim, the eldest son of the family that he had long been so well connected with, and whose support he had always counted on. By this time Yusuf had also become an official in Anglo-Persian's regional network, and his support was now greatly to assist British efforts in keeping Holmes at bay. To make matters even worse for Holmes, the British Political Agent in Kuwait was now demanding the insertion of a British 'Nationality Clause', similar to the one that was still obstructing any Bahraini deal, into any agreement that the sheikh might want to strike for Kuwait.

But despite the strength of this resistance, there were two things that had nonetheless now started to work in Holmes' favour. One was the kingdom's growing financial crisis. Kuwait's economy was highly dependent on its sale of pearls, but the pearling seasons of the past few years had been very disappointing. To make matters much worse, the Saudis had blocked a lot of Kuwaiti trade with their own kingdom, while the economic crash that affected so much of the world economy after 1929 was also starting to bite.

Confronted by a dire economic situation at home, Sheikh Ahmad now began to see Holmes' approaches in a new light. He wrote that 'I am anxious that oil resources should be developed with as little delay as possible. It was a stab to my heart when I observed the oil work at Bahrain and nothing here.' But crucially Anglo-Persian still didn't seem interested in exploring for oil, only in keeping everyone else out, and the New Zealander began to look like the kingdom's economic saviour. Although Holmes feared that the British had got wind of the oil seepages he had found earlier, whilst searching for water, Anglo-Persian was paying far more attention to another very disappointing geological report it had received from a highly respected expert: 'it is very improbable that, in the total absence of direct geological evidence, a convincing case could ever be made out by this means for exploring the unknown depths of Koweit [sic] territory with the drill … the unfavourable view of prospects in Koweit that is deducible from Professor de Bockh's synthesis of all previous work cannot be gainsaid'. The surveyor concluded bluntly that 'the absence of geological structure suitable for the accumulation of oil in commercial quantity shows that there is no justification for drilling anywhere in Kuwait'.

For Holmes and his supporters, however, the catch was the Nationality Clause that meant that, without London's permission, no one was likely to get anywhere. But the British government's commitment to this clause was fast coming under pressure from a very powerful source: the American government. Keen to lobby on behalf of its oil companies and promote the cause of an 'Open Door' in the Middle East that would allow them to compete on equal terms with its rivals, Washington put strong political pressure on the British government to lift the condition in Bahrain. Its efforts paid off and on 30 May 1929, after weeks of legal, political and diplomatic wrangles, London agreed in principle to allow Gulf to buy the Bahraini concession.

By this time the American oil giants had made big strides into the Middle East. For on 31 July 1928, nine months after the massive discovery at Baba Gurgur, more than three years after the Iraqi government had granted the Turkish Petroleum Company a 75-year oil concession and after years of wrangling, the future of the Mesopotamian oilfields had at last been settled. Under the deal, the three European players – Royal Dutch Shell, Anglo-Persian and the French Compagnie Francaise des Petroles (CFP) – each took 23.75 per cent stakes in the TPC while the rest was assigned to an American joint venture, the Near East Development Company, that was formed out of the constituent parts of various American corporations, including the company that Frank Holmes was working on behalf of, Gulf Oil.

This development now raised Holmes' hopes of striking a deal over Kuwait. On 4 August 1930 he arrived back in Kuwait and dined with the sheikh, who Holmes said was 'friendly and quite willing to give us the Concession'. On 6 August, however, the Political Agent in Kuwait told Holmes that London was still insisting on a Nationality clause if a concession was offered, prompting the Major to send an urgent cable back to the Syndicate's London office telling the directors of the bad news.

14

The Great Philanthropist

In the deserts that straddle the border between Kuwait and Saudi Arabia, not far from where Holmes and Williamson were busily vying for influence over Sheikh Ahmad, a handful of Americans travellers were continuing their journey. They had set out from Basrah some days before and then headed southwards, determined to make the most of their two new Chevrolets to explore as much of these vast oases as they could over the coming weeks.

Close to the border, as their cars moved over a slight sand knoll, the travellers saw in the distance what seemed to be a large group of camel-bound Bedouin tribesmen, about 150-strong. When they approached from a length of about 300 yards, the travellers were intrigued to see that these nomads bore highly distinctive white turbans, and they decided to take an even closer look. It was only as they got much nearer that the Americans realized their mistake. For these were not random desert tribes they had stumbled on but something much more dangerous and sinister: these were members of the Ikhwan, 'the brothers'.

The Ikhwan were hardly to be trifled with, for ever since their emergence in the Arabian desert a decade or so earlier, they had championed a brand of Islam that, even by the harsh local standards, was considered radical, even fanatical. Inspired by the teachings of the eighteenth-century thinker Muhammed Ibn Abdul Wahhab, they sought to follow the example of the Prophet Muhammed in all things, and always imposed a severe puritanical austerity on any individual or community that fell under their sway. Over the previous decade or so they had conquered and captured a considerable part of the Arabian peninsula, since their armed militias had worked to support Abdul Aziz Ibn Saud, helping him and his followers to push back the forces loyal to his great political rival, the Hashemite family. Since then thousands of ordinary Arabians had been forced to live according to the rigid standards that were subsequently forced upon them.

By 1928 the Ikhwan had acquired a fearsome reputation not only for their fighting prowess but also for their hatred of the infidel. In their eyes, there was no greater threat to their puritanical ideal, and no greater insult to Islam, than the presence of non-Muslims in their homeland, particularly in such close proximity to Mecca and Medina. The sight of a motor car approaching them in the distance, and of white faces on the front seats, would immediately have made them furious, and their immediate reaction would have been to reach for their rifles and open fire.

Sure enough, the shooting soon started. The chauffeurs managed to swerve the two cars round and speed off, while the Ikhwan rallied their camels and gave chase, continuing to fire wildly. 'The chances are that, had they dropped off their mounts to get a firm aim, we should all have long since been cut to pieces', as one survivor subsequently wrote.[1] The cars soon outpaced the camels and the travellers got out of their enemy's sight and then, at last, out of their range altogether. They should, after all, have heeded the warnings of the tribesmen and shepherds they had met earlier and who had urged them to turn back while the going was good. But as the travellers made their escape, they realized that one of their number, an American missionary named Henry Bilkert, had not been so lucky. He had been caught by a stray bullet and by now had started to bleed profusely. They tried desperately to make their way to the nearest doctor but soon realized they had left it too late. Bilkert died a few hours later.

This was certainly not the first of Charles Richard Crane's adventures in the Middle East, although it was certainly his most dangerous. But he was undaunted by the experience, even if most people of his age would not have been quite so resilient. For he was by this time nearly 71 and often struck people as somewhat frail: 'I see old Crane walking in, his head and goatee forward, his protruding blue eyes twinkling and his legs shaky so he totters as he comes forward and says "Salaam, Salaam"', as someone described him in the course of his last decade.

But frail though he may have been, Charles Crane remained as determined as ever to continue both his journey in the area and his long love affair with the Middle East as a whole, a love affair which had lasted more than a decade. He had made his first visit there in 1919 when specially chosen by President Woodrow Wilson to act as an American envoy. Wilson had wanted Crane and Henry C. King, an American academic, to study public opinion in the territories of the Ottoman Empire. This was considered to be a vitally important matter because the president had vowed to respect the principle of 'self-determination' in these areas and declared that 'the wishes of these communities must be a principal consideration in the selection of the Mandatory'. So in the weeks ahead Crane and King went on to visit numerous towns and villages, heard thousands of delegations and read even more petitions in order to gauge popular feeling.

There was one simple reason why Wilson had offered Crane this prestigious appointment, and that reason was gratitude. Crane had donated generous sums of money to Wilson's election campaign in 1916, and Wilson, who went on to win the race by a narrow margin, was anxious to return the favour. To have had Charles Crane's financial backing would have been enough to make any presidential candidate jump for joy, for by the outbreak of the First World War in 1914 he was one of America's richest men. The family business had pioneered new bathroom and sanitary fittings – notably the flushing toilet and sprinkling showers – that had sold in vast quantities the world over and soon earned him millions while making his Chicago-based Crane Bathroom Equipment Company one of the most famous enterprises in the world.

For Charles Crane, however, making money had never really been an end in itself. He was always deeply concerned about the state of both American society and of the wider world, and felt it was his duty to play his part in making things better. By the time war broke out in 1914 he had already sponsored an astonishing array of good causes overseas: in 1905, for example, he gave the staggering sum of $100,000 'towards relieving misery among the Albanians' and set up new schools in Constantinople for the underprivileged. He also badly wanted to contribute to the political campaign of Woodrow Wilson, a man of 'sterling qualities' who he felt could change the state not just of America but much of the rest of the world.

Like other travellers before him, such as Haji Williamson, Crane's first foray into the Middle East was to change his life forever. He quickly became smitten with its every aspect, fascinated by the people, language, religion and culture. Here, he felt, was a region that appeared barely to have changed since the time of Muhammed, Moses and Jesus, and which was untarnished by the selfish decadence of his homeland. It was all the more fascinating because large parts of it were known to only a small number of Americans. Crane wrote openly of his fascination: 'The peninsula of Arabia is the home and natural habitat of prophets, and I wanted to get as near as possible to the conditions of life out of which appears every now and then a great prophet. Naturally one does not expect a prophet to grow out of the complicated machinery of the modern state.'[2] But although Crane was above all a romantic traditionalist, he also wondered, paradoxically, if he could somehow use his fabulous wealth to help improve local people's living standards while at the same time preserving their traditions and customs.

Over the next few years, he made several approaches to local rulers, offering to meet them to explain exactly what he could offer. Nearly everyone he approached harboured considerable suspicion about his ultimate motives, thinking it was simply too good to be true that this wealthy American would want to invest time and money to help them unless he too was going to reap considerable rewards. There was one ruler, however, who did want to know more: Imam Yahia of the Yemen.

This kingdom was probably the most backward, underdeveloped and impoverished region of the entire Arabian peninsula. Only two American citizens had ever previously visited the capital, Sana'a, by the time Crane arrived there in the winter of 1926 to explain what he had to offer. He would pay for experienced geologists, he told Imam, to survey the region and locate any possible sources of fresh water or, more ambitiously, of precious stones. The Yemeni leader was interested, for he had heard reports that some tribesmen had tried digging to find such resources, and he now tentatively agreed to take things one stage further: if Crane wanted to send a geologist to his kingdom, at his own expense, then that was fine.

Charles Crane now decided to head for home, starting the long journey by taking a steamship that moved southwards down the Red Sea and stopping briefly at Aden. During this brief sojourn, he had a chance to meet the local American vice consul, John Loder Park, and told him about his new plans. This turned out to be a stroke of luck, because by chance Loder Park happened to know someone ideally suited to undertaking just such a task: an American geologist called Karl Twitchell, who had a lot of experience in undertaking remarkably similar projects in Abyssinia and who would himself shortly be on his way back to New York.

Within just a few months, Charles Crane and Karl Twitchell had met in New York and got on extremely well. Crane offered to handsomely reward his new acquaintance in return for undertaking a detailed survey mission of Yemen, and for advising its ruler how his backward kingdom could be brought closer to the modern age. In the autumn of 1927, Karl Twitchell arrived at the Yemeni port of Al Hudaydah, accompanied by his assistant engineer Lowe Whiting. He wasted no time in getting to work, looking closely at places that could make suitable mines, oil drilling sites, roads, gardens and crop sites. He also showed local officials how the latest farming instruments and machinery worked and how pumps, engines and windmills could be used to generate electricity and water supplies. With his expert knowledge he supervised the construction of a steel highway bridge, and gave local farmers advice on agricultural techniques that would greatly improve their crop yields. All of this was financed by the wealthy and philanthropic hand of a great American businessman who professed, with the utmost sincerity, that he had no wish other than simply to improve the lot of people who he was very fond of.

By the time Crane made his next visit to the Middle East, in 1930, news of Twitchell's operations in Yemen had travelled far, and one individual who was aware of developments there was Crane's host in Cairo, Sheikh Fawzan al Sabik. Fawzan, who was an Arabian by birth, acted as an official representative to King Abdul Aziz, and had invited Crane to his Cairo home in order to discuss the sale of a particular breed of Arabian horse that his American visitor hoped to introduce to his own homeland. In a gesture of supreme generosity, Abdul Aziz instructed Fawzan to offer his new visitor two pedigree horses as a gift: Crane was clearly a generous man himself, the king felt, and deserved generosity in return. A delighted Charles Crane was taken aback by the gesture, and wanted to know how he could return the favour. Could he perhaps offer to fund operations in Arabia similar to those that were proving so successful in Yemen? Would the king allow him, he asked, to despatch a survey team to take a close look at the land?

Fawzan was surprised by the suggestion, since he was well aware that all his fellow Arabians were deeply suspicious of any foreign involvement, particular on the part of non-Muslims, in their homeland. To make matters worse, Saudi was still in a very volatile political state, since just shortly before the Ikhwan had instigated a bloody rebellion that was only put down with considerable difficulty. But he agreed to take things one stage further, and sent a cable to Jeddah to put Crane's request before the king.

The reply from Jeddah came far quicker than Fawzan had expected. Within hours he had received a cable back, saying that Crane and his surveyors would be most welcome to visit the kingdom and undertake the work they proposed. The king, it turned out, had heard about Twitchell's progress in Yemen and was keen to make the most of similar expertise if he had the chance. Now, more than at any earlier time, he desperately needed this support, for in recent months his kingdom had begun to sink into an economic malaise.

The Saudi economy had always been highly dependent on the proceeds of *haj*, the Islamic pilgrimage to Mecca. For the Muslims who made their way from every corner of the world to this holy city not only had to pay for special visas to undertake their trip but also brought quite considerable sums of money with them to spend along the way. Since 1929, however, the number of pilgrims had fallen sharply as the worldwide global recession began to bite. Throughout the 1920s the average number of visitors to Mecca each year had always been around 125,000 – enough to provide the king with a very substantial annual income of around £1 million. But these numbers had now started to fall sharply, plunging to just 40,000 by 1932. In particular the kingdom had always been able to rely on a regular influx of tens of thousands of Indian Muslims, but their number had suddenly dropped when the price of crops and agricultural produce had dramatically crashed in the world market, leaving many of them virtually destitute.

By the time Crane was making his approach, the Saudi king had started to become increasingly concerned. One member of his close itinerary recorded how he suddenly lost his composure during a car journey, grabbing the arm of one of his companions and exclaiming how 'if anyone could offer me a million pounds now, I would give him all the concessions he wanted'.[3] For the king to make such sudden outbursts was almost unheard of. It was into this dire, even desperate, situation that Charles Crane strode when, on 25 February 1931, he arrived at Jeddah. He stepped off a small steamer that always pulled into harbour at the same time, 10.30 in the morning, every other week and brought post, groceries, newspapers and a handful of visitors before it sailed on further south. He had come at the invitation of King Abdul Aziz, who wanted him to spend a week in the town to discuss his offer in more detail and reach a firm agreement about how to proceed. With his trusted guide and adviser, George Antonius, at his side the great philanthropist was greeted at the quay by local notables and several ferocious looking warriors and then taken to a huge house, which belonged to Sheikh Mohammed Nasif, a leading and learned citizen of the town. Then he got ready to meet the king.

Seeing Jeddah for the first time would have been a powerful experience. Other Western visitors of the time were taken aback by its natural splendour. 'The sea is a marvellous blue; inside the lagoons it becomes turquoise in the shallow water threaded by streaks of purple caused by seaweed', as one traveller described its harbour. Viewed from afar it looked even more impressive, surrounded as it was by golden desert and then, further away in the distance, the Arabian mountains, which climbed several thousand feet high. The town itself was 'white and brown … giving the idea of a fortress, as it is enclosed on three sides by a high wall, its minarets stand out against the sky, its quaint carved wooden windows bulge over the narrow streets'.[4]

And as he made his way through its streets and bazaars, lined by rows of palm trees that gave some welcome shade, Charles Crane would have been overcome by 'the acrid pungent smell of the east, a compound of spices, coffee, camels, penetrating and alluring'.

But while this was in some ways a town that had barely changed for thousands of years, there were a few discernible signs of modernity creeping in. The main such change was the arrival of the motor car. Just five years before, in 1926, there had been no more than a handful of cars – maybe a dozen at most – in the country as a whole. But by the time Crane arrived there this number had increased to more than a thousand, most of which were owned by officials in government and major companies, and all of which were made by Ford, the giant American manufacturer that had been granted exclusive access to the Saudi market. Otherwise there would have been little to remind him of home: the town's expatriate population was tiny, not least because most Westerners had heard about its reputation for unbearable summer humidity and did their best to avoid it.

Crane had much to do in the course of his short visit, and had only a few hours' rest before he was taken to the royal palace, a two-storey building on the edge of town, to meet the king. He had heard much about the 50-year-old Abdul Aziz, but would nonetheless have been taken aback by his enormous height; he stood well over six feet tall and was, in the words of another Western visitor, 'a very giant of a man'.[5] Perhaps he was also surprised by the bashfulness of his manner: 'an essentially shy person', recorded the new visitor in his diaries, as he described how the king gave him a very lengthy first handshake, dropping his eyes and looking at the floor as he muttered his initial greeting.[6]

But such self-consciousness was perhaps understandable: the Saudi king had only very rarely met Westerners and was slightly overwhelmed by the experience. He was keen to celebrate the occasion and had arranged for special festivities to take place in honour of his new guests. Later that evening, in front of the king, his family and two very impressed Americans guests, local Bedouin tribesmen performed a version of a traditional war dance, known as the *ardha*, that culminated in truly deafening style as the tribesmen pointed their rifles to the skies and opened fire.

Over the next few days, Crane and Abdul Aziz began to discuss their propositions in more detail. The king's shyness had by this time worn off, and he made a powerful impression on his visitor. 'When at rest his face is immobile and usually overcast as though with some permanent sadness', wrote Crane, 'but all of a sudden the subject moves him, or a secretary glides in with some whispered message, and his features light up with excitement or curiosity.'[7] Ibn Saud now explained that his kingdom stood in desperate need of piped water, without which agriculture, industry and basic living standards were all doomed to languish. Finding a source of supply, and helping to pump it into the main cities would, he explained, be the greatest service that Crane could offer him. Crane, of course, knew just the man for the task, someone who was familiar not just with this type of work but also with the region, its conditions and, above all, its people. He could despatch Karl Twitchell, he explained, to take a close look at the country and hopefully find the water supplies that the Saudis needed. With Crane offering to arrange all this at his own expense, King Abdul Aziz was hardly in a position to refuse. He immediately nodded his assent.

Twitchell was still in Yemen, heavily involved in the complex task of building a highway bridge over the Wadi Laa river, when on 30 March a cable unexpectedly arrived from Charles Crane, who had by now sailed back to New York. This new Saudi challenge much appealed to him, and he left his number two, an American engineer named Ballard, to stand in for him before taking a local ferry to Jeddah, arriving there on 15 April. Within hours of his arrival, the young American engineer was carefully inspecting Jeddah and its surroundings, looking for signs of underground wells and getting a better idea of the town's infrastructure. This part of his work was the easy bit, especially as Crane had already made special arrangements to send some of the materials he would need. These included a sixteen-foot-high windmill, based on the latest American design, that raised around 40 gallons of water every minute and was now to make a significant difference to the town's water supply.

Accompanied by Khalid al Qarqani, a North African by birth and at this time one of the king's leading economic advisers, he then made his way into the surrounding deserts, firstly visiting Wadi Fatima, a short distance outside the town along the road to Mecca, and subsequently travelling further up the Red

Sea coast to look for signs of underground water. This gave him an initial taste
of the much more demanding journey that he was subsequently to make, for the
king asked him to visit al-Hasa province and compile a report on his findings.
The trouble was that al-Hasa was more than 1,000 miles away, and to get there
he would have to cross whole stretches of desert that no American had ever seen
before.

Nearly a month later, Karl Twitchell had finished most of his work and had
finally made his way back to Jeddah. It would soon be time for him to return to
Yemen, but before he did so he would have to give the Saudi authorities some
idea of what his findings were. It was to this end that, on his return from al-Hasa,
the finance minister, Sheikh Abdullah Suleiman Al Hamdan, invited him to his
home at Nazla just outside Jeddah, and waited anxiously to hear what his visitor
had to say. Twitchell knew just how keen the sheikh would be to hear an upbeat
report, for he was well aware that the kingdom was fast sinking into a financial
mess. 'Political conditions in Saudi Arabia were by this period relatively stable,
the king's authority unquestioned', as he later wrote. 'But the territory was
economically at its lowest ebb. Never self-supporting in food, without minerals
or industry or any other resources, the Arabian population had long lived at the
barest level of subsistence.'[8] During their meal, the finance minister admitted
just how dire the kingdom's financial situation had become, and explained that
Twitchell and his New York sponsor held the vital key to a much more prosperous
future.

But Twitchell's findings were not set to give the sheikh much of an uplift.
Finding water would not, he admitted, be an easy task, and he had discovered no
obvious inland source that could provide basic irrigation and help turn deserts
into oases. But he had seen some mines and excavations at the village of Umm
Garayat, near the town of Wejh, that suggested the possible presence of some
minerals of real value, as well as a few seeps of oil near Duba and Muwailih. So
it would be worthwhile hiring some other engineers and geologists, each with
a more specialized knowledge than he had, to take a further look in this area, if
the king would agree to it.

There was one snag, however, which was that by now even the vastly affluent
Charles Crane was starting to feel the pinch of economic recession, and it was
only with some difficulty that he was able to continue the surveying operations.
A few weeks later, after returning to Yemen for a short while, Twitchell finally
received new instructions from New York to go ahead with his proposal to
undertake more detailed surveying: Crane would give him £700 to cover his
initial expenses while also sending out a survey team to join him in Jeddah.

Twitchell was by now getting a far better idea of where to concentrate his
efforts. In the course of his travels he decided that there were particular areas
around Taif and Jeddah where it would be worth his while drilling for water and

minerals, and accompanied by a very able engineer called Henry Mosley, and Ahmad Fakhry, a trusted Arab, he organized drilling operations in these areas. Starting in July, the work could continue for six months before Crane's funding ran out, and the three explorers, together with the local men they hired, worked feverishly to make progress.

In the end, however, they produced only disappointing results, and managed to find gold in only very limited quantities. In Jeddah, the king was as disappointed and exasperated as the Americans, feeling that months of hard work, and a very substantial amount of money, had been thrown away. Clutching at straws, he asked Twitchell if he had seen any sign of oil, and if there were any funds left to justify a brief expedition to areas where there were known seepages. The young American had just enough time and money to make a brief excursion into the Hijaz desert, and on New Year's Eve 1931, with no time to waste, he led a party made up of two Ford cars, two trucks, 30 men, tents, tyres, petrol supplies and spare parts into the desert oases. Led part of the way by an extraordinary Englishman – heavily bearded but remarkably resilient and a brilliant Arabic speaker – Twitchell and his men began their long and arduous journey, heading firstly to Riyadh and Al Hufuf, and then moving northwards to Dhahran.

Twitchell was taken aback by the sheer severity of the land around him. Only a fraction of it was farmed, and even camels sometimes struggled to survive, managing to find just a little poor pasture in the desert soil. He was able to bring some relief to one carefully chosen place, however, sinking a small artesian well on the edge of the foothills and allowing the immediate vicinity suddenly to bloom with burseem and, before very long, with corn. By now, however, there was little time to look for underground springs. He needed quickly to find signs of oil, and this spot in the hills of Dhahran, where several seepages were rumoured to have been found, seemed the most promising. Looking carefully at the hills, some lava flows and the local rock formations, he felt able to draw up some basic conclusions.

Once again he was disappointed. He badly wanted to reward his patrons' generosity and give them good news but could find absolutely no signs of oil. What he did notice, however, was that the geological formations were the same as those just a short distance away at Bahrain, where he knew that engineers and geologists maintained high hopes of finding oil. This was the most encouraging thing he could tell his patrons when he reached Jeddah to deliver his findings. The evening before he left the kingdom, Twitchell dined with Sheikh Abdullah Suleiman and Sheikh Yusuf Yassin, two very senior Saudi officials who both advised the king. He had seen some signs of both oil and minerals that were worth pursuing, the American explained, and some places where much-needed roads and bridges could be built. But he knew that, back home, Charles Crane was out of pocket and in no position to take things any further.

Exasperated, the two Saudis asked their visitor if he could help them find any foreign backers who could fund the search for oil and gold. Twitchell nodded his assent and agreed to ask for Crane's help as soon as he arrived back in New York. Not only would he hate to see his own hard work squandered, but he had by this time also developed a deep fondness for the local people and wanted to do all he could to help them improve their lot. On his arrival back home, Twitchell got the answer he had expected. Crane, a natural philanthropist, was pleased to help Saudi in any way he could, and was quite happy for some other party to use Twitchell's findings as long as it was ultimately to the benefit of the Arabs.

Twitchell now concentrated his efforts on arousing the interest of America's leading oil companies. At the very least, he reckoned, he could find some sponsorship to undertake a further survey, one that would hopefully yield conclusive proof of large quantities of Saudi oil. Armed with his geological reports, he introduced himself to some of the top names in the trade. First came Terry Duce of the Texas Company; then it was Stuart Morgan of the Near East Development Company, together with his chief geologist Norval Baker. But in each case the response was the same. Times were hard, they sighed, and it was impossible to justify such a high capital outlay unless there were clear signs of oil in the kingdom. It was just such signs, however, that Twitchell conspicuously lacked.

Of course while both Morgan and Baker were only too well aware just how much oil had been found in Iraq, they also knew that in the past few years so many other Middle Eastern oil ventures had gone badly wrong. Only shortly before, Shell had followed the advice of its chief geologists and signed a deal to drill for oil in the Farsan Islands, buying a concession that had been on offer for some years. In January 1927 it registered the Red Sea Petroleum Company on the London Stock Exchange as a subsidiary of Anglo-Egyptian Oilfields and then dispatched a drilling team to the region, establishing a test well at Zifuf. The drillers worked hard and bore deep into the ground but found nothing except huge quantities of salt. So if a market leader like Shell could come so badly unstuck, wasting a large fortune on a project that its best scientists had strongly endorsed, could not the same thing happen to its American competitors?

Dispirited but undeterred, he made his way to the offices of the Gulf Oil Company in Pittsburgh, where he was introduced to Guy Stevens, its commercial director. Stevens was interested in his proposals and felt that they had promise. The trouble for his company, however, was that it could not proceed with any operation without first getting the assent of some other international oil giants, some of whom he knew would be quick to deny it. This was because Saudi fell within the ambit of an agreement struck in July 1928 by all the various participants – American, French, Dutch and British – in the Turkish Petroleum Company. More than at any previous time, each of these participants recognized and acknowledged that their activities in the Middle East and beyond were interlinked: overproduction in one place would depress the price of oil in another, thereby affecting the income and profits of each and every oil company. They therefore agreed to work together and not to develop oil anywhere within the region without the active participation of the others. This agreement applied to the whole area that Calouste Gulbenkian determined by picking up a thick red pencil and boldly, almost haphazardly, drawing a line along the boundaries of the former Ottoman Empire: this was the 'Red Line Agreement', and any place that fell within the ambit of the red line was subject to the deal.

But Twitchell still had one last card to play, for he had yet to approach the other key player in the oil game, Standard Oil of California, known ubiquitously as 'Socal'. This company had already brought the Bahraini concession, and Twitchell was aware that its directors might well be looking for new ventures in the Middle East. When he met the company's New York representative, A.S. Corriell, his hopes were suddenly raised much higher. Twitchell's research immediately grabbed Corriell's interest, and shortly afterwards he was invited to meet the company's chief geologist, H.J. Hawley and then, a few days later, its chief directors, Mr Loomis and Mr Lombardi. But even if Twitchell did manage to interest an oil company in a Saudi concession, getting a foothold in the kingdom would be no easy task, for there were obvious barriers to be crossed – political as well as linguistic – before the drilling could even start. What was needed was an intermediary, someone who was familiar with every aspect of this land but who also had access to and influence in the corridors of Saudi power.

15

The Battle for Kuwait

From the moment in 1932 when he stepped into the Kuwaiti negotiations, Archibald Hugh Tennant Chisholm always struck observers as an archetypal Englishman abroad. Fair-haired, tall, thin and always impeccably dressed, the Oxford-educated aristocrat invariably cut a fine and distinguished figure that could hardly fail to impress those who met him. Sometimes sporting a monocle, in the true spirit of P.G. Wodehouse, and harbouring a particular fondness for whiskey and soda, he was often caricatured by the American press as a quintessential upper-class English gentleman.

This, indeed, is a very fitting description of the young Chisholm when, at the raw age of 30, he arrived in Kuwait to negotiate with the sheikh on behalf of the Anglo-Persian Oil Company. After all, he came from a very distinguished British family that could trace its origins back thousands of years and whose ancestors had been closely associated with both the Tudor monarchs and, it seems, figures as eminent as Oliver Cromwell and Lord Byron. As chairman of London's most exclusive dining club, the Athenaeum, and editor of *The Times* from 1902, on and off, until 1920, his late father had enjoyed considerable influence among Britain's governing elite.

Archibald had followed closely in his father's footsteps, making his way from Westminster public school – where William Knox D'Arcy had also once been a pupil – to his father's old Oxford college, Christ Church. Academically at least, his Oxford career was dismal, and he graduated in 1925 with the lowest honours degree – a Third Class – in Classics. This, however, was not much impediment to his professional career, and soon after graduating he made a brief foray into the world of journalism, working for the *Wall Street Journal*, before moving into business and joining the Anglo-Persian Oil Company, whose chairman, Sir John Cadman, was a family friend. By the time he was despatched to Kuwait to lead the negotiations for a concession, he had spent more than five years at Anglo-Persian's regional base at Abadan and at its offices in Tehran.

Chisholm had been carefully briefed about both the man and the methods he would have to confront. He knew that in Major Holmes he could scarcely have found anyone more different than himself. This was most pronounced in his appearance because Holmes, in sharp contrast, was stout and not tall. But

there were also clear differences in their manner and style. For while Chisholm
was well known for his refined manners, the Major could be coarse, direct and
even brutal in his ways, sometimes preferring to speak his mind without much
thought for the consequences or anyone's feelings.

But very different though they plainly were, the Englishman certainly did
not underestimate his rival. He was well aware that Holmes, by sheer force of
personality and a certain charm, had a way of rubbing along with the locals and
establishing a good rapport with, and gaining the trust of, most of those he met
and dealt with. He played bridge with numerous Arab friends over long evenings,
and even felt generous enough towards one of them, Mohammed Yatim, to send
his son to school in England. It was not long before Chisholm became aware that
'the sheikh is very impressed by Holmes, and especially by the fact that he was
offering good money down for a concession document expressly stipulating that
he would immediately set to work'. He also commented that 'Holmes is in fact
vis-à-vis the sheikh in a very strong position, what with his success in Bahrain,
his free way with money, and his apparent faith in Kuwaiti oil'.

Chisholm rented a house that was about half a mile to the southwest of the
town centre, just inside the confines of the ancient town wall and slightly further
out from Holmes' seafront home. After his arrival he had just a day or two to
settle in before he would be taken to the royal palace, formally introduced to the
sheikh and then get down to begin the negotiating process. He was under huge
pressure from his employers to outbid Holmes and win the concession, and on
30 May 1932 the company's London office cabled Abadan saying simply that they
'consider it essential to use all methods in our power to prevent Sheikh Ahmad
giving concession to Syndicate'. The rivalry between Chisholm and Holmes now
began in earnest.

Winning the sheikh's favour, Chisholm knew, would be not just about offering
him the right concession. It would also be about winning his trust and goodwill.
Well aware that this was Holmes' strength, Chisholm now tried to beat him at his
own game. One after the other, for months on end, the two men made successive
visits to the palace to outbid the other not just in concessionary payments but
also with gifts and presents. When Holmes put on a huge feast for the sheikh,
Chisholm put on an even better one a few days later. When Chisholm gave the
sheikh a radio set as a present, Holmes turned up soon after with an even more
sophisticated one. The sheikh once said that his car needed headlights, and within
a short time two lots had arrived, one from the New Zealander and the other
from Chisholm, who had specially ordered a pair from Anglo-Persian's Abadan
office. When his Gulf employees became frustrated by the slow rate of progress,
Holmes was authorized to present the sheikh with a brand new Sunbeam car,
costing £905, or more than $4,300, only to find that Chisholm had soon ordered
one as well.

This rivalry was not unpleasant, in contrast to the acrimonious vein of Williamson's dislike for Yatim. 'Holmes and I were at daggers drawn for a year', the Englishman later wrote, 'month after month we lived as neighbours, meeting with invariable courtesy and no rancour, each making our calls on the sheikh, each in turn suggesting some new clause and knowing that the other would act accordingly. Each Sunday we met in church.' While Holmes had no problem in winning the sheikh's favour, he knew that his bid faced a much more serious obstacle. Under the terms of the long-standing treaty between the two countries, the Kuwaiti leader could not offer any foreign company or individual any business in his kingdom without the prior approval of the British government. Now it was clear that London was intending to use every asset at its disposal to keep its rivals at bay and would not hesitate for a minute to exercise its veto against Holmes and his American sponsors.

In November 1931 Holmes decided that he needed his sponsors to find ways of putting much more pressure on London over the issue. 'I personally consider that we have been patient and considerate to a fault', he cabled, 'and that we are now justified in making use of every weapon, diplomatic or otherwise, which we possess.'[1] The only way forward would be to get assistance at the highest level, and this could only mean directly approaching the American government in order to pressure London into giving way over the matter. Holmes knew that the British government's veto was at this time affecting not just Kuwait but also the Bahraini concession, which Gulf Oil, and then Standard Oil of California, were theoretically blocked from taking up. This meant that he had an even better chance of finding support in Washington.

On 30 November Gulf Oil opened up discussions with State Department officials, admitting that, without their assistance, the battle for the concessions was looking lost. 'We feel now that our efforts have been exhausted and unless we have the prompt assistance of the US government, the combined pressure of the British government upon the sheikh and activities of the APOC in Kuwait may shortly result in completely destroying any opportunity for us to obtain the Kuwait concession.' Reports coming in from Kuwait were also suggesting that they were starting to lose ground and would have to act fast. Holmes told them that Chisholm, Williamson and their agents were stepping up their activities to try and thwart the Major's bid to win the concession, targeting the sheikh's family and ruling circle, as well as the kingdom's most influential merchants. At the same time Anglo-Persian had sent a new team of geologists to undertake a preliminary survey and a test-drilling programme, and were also trying to put great pressure on the sheikh to come to a firm decision.

Soon, however, it had become clear that their pleadings to the State Department had yielded results. On 3 December State officials cabled the US Embassy in London and instructed them to take up the matter with Whitehall, making clear

Washington's interest in having an open door to the whole of the Middle East, not just Iraq. The American ambassador, General Dawes, then held a series of meetings with the British foreign minister, Sir John Simon, and was soon pressing for a firm decision about what exactly the London government was going to do about the situation. As weeks became months, it became clear that the Foreign Office had no particular interest in changing the status quo and was hoping that the matter would quietly disappear. Washington had not hitherto made any specific request for a formal change of policy, but on 26 March the US Embassy was instructed by Washington to take this course of action, and four days later wrote to the Foreign Office to make an official request for an 'Open Door' to Kuwait. Reluctant to cross swords with its immensely powerful transatlantic ally, the British government stood down. In early April 1932 the new ambassador, Andrew Mellon, informed Washington that he had heard a favourable reply and just over a week later received a letter from Simon, agreeing to drop the nationality condition and allowing foreign competitors equal and fair access to the Kuwaiti market.

It was now a straight fight between the two competitors, but although Holmes had won this particular battle, not everything was going his way. On 3 May, not long after he had travelled back to Kuwait, he had a serious row with Sheikh Ahmad, who accused him of exploiting a private letter he had written by using this private correspondence in a bid to get the US government on his side. For ten whole days the sheikh refused to grant him an audience, and this was the only time that, during their nine-year acquaintance, the two men ever appear to have fallen out. When Holmes eventually managed to patch things up, on 14 May, he had acted just in time, because it was then that the Anglo-Persian management took everyone by surprise by formally offering the sheikh, for the very first time, a concession.

In this contest, Chisholm felt that he was doing rather well, and his spirits were not dampened by the British government's retreat over the nationality issue. The sheikh, he felt, was still basically pro-British, and 'has informed the Political Resident that, other things being equal, he would rather see the Concession go to a British concern in view of his relations with Britain'. He also felt sure that Sheikh Ahmad would make a deal soon, since he 'needs money badly as his finances are in a very bad way; he is being hard pressed by what *vox populi* there is in Kuwait to raise money from oil, or at least from people who want to look for it'. He had become all the more desperate, Chisholm felt, because he was aware that there was a world glut of oil, and that most international companies had neither the spare cash to search for more supplies, nor any pressing need to do so.

Meanwhile, at Socal's main headquarters at San Francisco, on the other side of the world, preparations were being made to exploit the Bahraini concession to the full in the hope of finally striking oil on the islands. In March 1930, after weeks of preparation, two of the company's most trusted employees, William Taylor and Fred A. Davies, were asked to travel to Bahrain to take a closer look. Taylor, as a logistics officer, was tasked with assessing the island's infrastructure to see where and how a drilling team could later follow them, while Davies, widely considered to be the company's leading geologist, was to locate the best place for the drillers to start work, using his own judgement as well as the findings made two years before by Gulf Oil geologists who had visited the kingdom.

The two men began their epic journey at the beginning of April, setting sail from New York on the SS *Ile de France* and heading for London. After the transatlantic crossing they took trains first to Paris and Vienna and then finally arrived in Constantinople, on 18 April, after more than three weeks of travelling. Still they had much further to go. Their next task was to cross the Bosporus, long seen as the boundary between Europe and Asia, and then stop off at Haydarpasa. After that came another long train journey, one that would take them through the Taurus mountains of southern Turkey to the ancient Roman city of Aleppo along the Syrian–Turkish border, finally stopping in Nisibin. Here they had arranged to be picked up by car and to be taken, in a special convoy, to the Iraqi cities of Mosul, Nineveh and Kirkuk. Finally on 30 April they got to Baghdad, staying at its high-class Carlton Hotel, where Taylor wrote a letter to his head office informing them of their progress: 'we had good dirt roads all the way. Yesterday am we left Mosul for Kirkuk and it rained on us all day, with the result that instead of five hours it took us eleven, but the train waited on us at Kirkuk so we got here this am at 6 o'clock … we were met at the train by the East and Gen Syndicate man, who informs us that Maj. Holmes will be along in a few days and will communicate with us. Weather very nice.'[2]

Bahrain was not very far off now, and both men were getting a taste of the conditions they would encounter there: 'temperature here 109F yesterday, and we are promised some *warm* weather as we proceed towards Bahrain', as Davies wrote. After two days recuperation at the Carlton, both men were off again to complete the last leg of their journey. Leaving by train they now travelled past Babylon and Ur and then finally arrived at Basrah, where they boarded a steamer and began an 80-hour voyage that would take them to Mohammerah, Kuwait, Bushire and then, at last, Bahrain.

With their ship anchored a few miles offshore, they were met by Holmes, who hired a motor launch to pick them up and taxi them ashore. Resting for a few days in their new home, the two Americans had a chance to get to know their host, whom they had heard so much about. They took an immediate liking to him, while also being taken aback by his sheer depth of knowledge about the region as a whole and the contacts he seemed to have there. This prompted Davies to write that: 'when we left Baghdad we had no idea that Major Holmes was familiar with conditions in Iraq or was paying much attention to them, but on talking with him we discovered that he is very much interested, has been following it closely and is well acquainted and has considerable influence with the Government officials'.[3]

After their brief recuperation, they were taken out to see the oil seepages that Holmes and the Gulf Oil men had found some time before. Even a brief look at them was enough to give Davies an insight into the geological structures beneath, and he wrote soon afterwards that 'we drove out to the old seepage one morning and while we were there only a very short time, I believe there is faulting present at that point.' Before long these and other indications had helped him pinpoint the best place to start drilling. The site, he argued on 31 May, should 'fall close to the southeast corner of the mountain Jebel Dukhan (440 feet high, so not much of a mountain) … in an entirely new country where nothing is known concerning the behaviour of the structures, I presume the best shot is right up close to the top.' This was because 'the only surface evidence of oil and gas on Bahrain is the bitumen deposit which lies about 3 miles south and a little east of Jebel Dukhan. All the asphalt at present exposed is in the edges of one pit 15 to 18 feet deep and is all in a local accumulation of surface sand … there is no liquid petroleum in evidence anywhere but in the walls of the pit, the saturation is such that the rock is rubbery under the hammer and freshly broken surfaces present the black, glistening appearance of semi-fluid asphalt.'[4] But Davies was still doing little more than guessing when he now pinpointed a suitable spot for the drillers to start work, marking it clearly by building a cairn of rocks that he then topped with a flag.

A few months later a drilling team arrived on the island and got ready to start work at the spot that Davies had marked. This was no minor operation they were conducting. It was, on the contrary, a large-scale, highly organized and, by the standards of the day, very sophisticated venture that was being carried out by a team of dedicated and highly skilled engineers.

At 6 am on 1 June 1932, at a depth of just over 2,000 feet, 'the drill pierced a layer of blue shale. The men smelled oil and heard an ominous rumbling. Very cautiously they drilled another eight feet' and oil flowed. 'It was', continues the archive of the Bahrain Petroleum Company, 'a driller's dream.'[5] Taylor, it turned out, had showed exceptional judgement when pinpointing the best place to drill, and had come within just 50 feet of locating the tip of the underground rock formation that bore oil.

News of the oil strike in Bahrain caused something of a frenzy in the boardrooms and on the stock markets of the watching world, while also galvanizing the negotiations for a concession in Kuwait. If there was oil in Bahrain, everyone seemed to be saying, then why not Kuwait? The need to win the concession there suddenly seemed all the more pressing, even if everyone now knew that Holmes was personally in a stronger position than ever: after all, he had been almost alone in arguing that Bahrain was well worth exploring, defying the views of numerous scientific experts by doing so, and now that he had been proved right so conclusively, his reputation and standing before Sheikh Ahmad and others soared sky high.

Chisholm and Anglo-Persian knew that they had a real fight on their hands, and upped their offer to Sheikh Ahmad from 20,000 rupees to 25,000. But the sheikh was a canny negotiator and knew that, in the light of events in Bahrain, he could afford to ask for considerably more. He flatly rejected the British offer and instead demanded a new concession, one that was long-term and guaranteed him regular payments throughout. Telling Holmes that he was still awaiting his counter-offer, he saw the strength of his position and commented simply that 'I now have two bidders and from the point of view of a seller that is all to the good'.[6]

Still the negotiations went on. Chisholm urgently consulted with his seniors in Abadan, and arrived back in Kuwait on 14 August 1932 bearing a new draft concession document that he felt sure the sheikh would be impressed by. Ahmad courteously received him, and the two men now held a series of meetings, but despite giving an upbeat response he would still not firmly commit himself. Exasperated, Chisholm recognized that Ahmad was really just playing for time and only wanted to see how much more he could extract from both sides.

The Englishman also knew that Holmes, with such strong American backing, could at any minute outbid him to win the concession, and that Kuwaiti resentment at earlier British attempts to interfere in his kingdom's affairs had caused a certain amount of ill feeling. 'There is no doubt that Holmes will now make more play than ever with his pro-American and anti-British argument, and at this particular juncture such an argument unfortunately must have some appeal to the sheikh', as Chisholm wrote to London. He made more effort than ever to win Ahmad's favour with lavish hospitality, throwing parties that could not fail to impress: 'APOC is feeding all and sundry', as Holmes wrote to his American patrons, asking for more funding that would help him counter these efforts.[7]

Each side now continued to try to outbid the other. In early March 1933 the senior director of Anglo-Persian, Sir John Cadman, visited the sheikh in person and offered him an initial upfront fee of 200,000 rupees. Holmes' chief spy at the court, Mullah Saleh, was close at hand, however, and he soon learned of the agreement and its terms from this source. Within hours he had sent a cable to Gulf Oil headquarters, where senior directors authorized him to make an immediate counteroffer of 250,000 rupees, while he also sought to win the sheikh's favour by offering him and his family free supplies of petrol and kerosene.

It was not just these promises that helped his cause. For it was at this time that Holmes' personal reputation – already high because of events in Bahrain – soared even further, because King Ibn Saud had declared an initial interest in granting his own concession to Standard Oil of California. Yet some months before the Major had been almost alone in predicting that the American company would win the deal, and he had been sure enough of his judgement to tell Ahmad what he thought was going to happen. Standard had not yet won the Saudi deal but had a head start, and once again Holmes' predictions looked set to be uncannily accurate; the Kuwaiti leader could hardly fail to be impressed.

But Chisholm was not one to be easily outdone, and a few weeks later he flew over to Kuwait from Abadan in a new plane that Anglo-Persian had specially chartered and invited the sheikh to take a ride. This was his first ever flight, and as the plane soared over his kingdom and parts of Iraq could be seen far below, Ahmed was thrilled and astonished by the experience. When they touched down he was quick to return the invitation, and he now asked Chisholm to accompany him on a voyage around Bahraini waters on his personal yacht.

But Holmes and Chisholm, and their superiors, all knew that matters could not go on like this indefinitely. Holmes had by now been trying to win the Kuwaiti concession for more than a decade, and it was plain that his rivalry with Anglo-Persian was merely playing into the hands of the Kuwaiti leader, who was doing all he could to extract more and more from his international suitors. The only way forward was for the two competitors to strike up some sort of deal, and on 14 December 1933, after intense and secret rounds of negotiations, the Anglo-Persian Oil Company and Gulf Oil signed two initial agreements that formed the basis of a new partnership. This joint venture would henceforth be known simply as the Kuwait Oil Company.

Both Holmes and Chisholm were relieved that the years of rivalry between them were over. Neither harboured any personal animosity towards the other, and both were keen to move forward to new challenges. When in February 1934 Holmes arrived back in the kingdom after a journey to London, he was amazed to find Chisholm waiting for him at the landing strip, ready to whisk him back home. The long professional antagonism between the two men had come to an end, and now at last they could work together. They began to attend the sheikh's functions together, and agreed to keep each other immediately informed of any developments. The thawing of relations even extended to Haji Williamson and Mohammed Yatim, whose animosity many people were well aware of: on one occasion Sheikh Ahmad invited both men to dine with him, as if making a bid to bring them together so that the new oil venture, in which they were both involved, would not be torn apart by personal dislike and mistrust.

Negotiations were now under way between the newly formed Kuwait Oil Company and Sheikh Ahmad to sign and seal a concessionary agreement. But although it never occurred to Chisholm that the new joint venture could fail, Holmes was not so sure. In May 1934, as the negotiations continued, he seemed to sense that another company was involved in the bidding, even though he could have had no way of knowing it. Holmes himself was about to leave the kingdom for a few weeks, heading back to London once again, and was concerned that a rival might see his absence as an opportunity. Working on his intuition, he urged a puzzled Chisholm not to leave Kuwait in case a third party stepped into the negotiations and stole their prize just when it seemed to be in the palm of their hand. He was so concerned that he even wrote to Gulf Oil's London representative, saying quite simply that 'the risk of bringing in outside applicants is very great'.

Holmes clearly had something of a sixth sense, for time and again his judgement had been proved correct, even though it was largely based only on gut feeling. He had already been proved right over the presence of oil in Bahrain, and now his fears of third-party involvement were also realized. For although almost no one else knew about it, there had by this time been a series of secret meetings between the sheikh and just such a potential competitor. This was the London-registered Traders Ltd, what Holmes termed a '100 per cent British company', and during his absence from the scene this competitor had stepped into the void. Making enquiries among his best contacts and associates in Kuwait Holmes learned, to his astonishment, that his intuition was correct and that during his absence the sheikh had indeed been holding several meetings with a mysterious 'Mr Gabriel' from 'Trade Arts Company Ltd'. Chisholm was equally amazed by the accuracy of his insight, and wrote that 'some sixth sense, resulting from his eleven years close acquaintance with Kuwaiti affairs and Sheikh Ahmad's personality, must have prompted him that there was danger in the air'.[8]

Holmes and Chisholm pulled out all the stops to make sure that they did not lose their concessionary prize, and on 23 December 1934, after more than twelve years of negotiation, the agreement was at last formally signed in Kuwait by the sheikh, Holmes and Chisholm. Under its terms the Kuwait Oil Company also agreed to give the sheikh more than 25,000 rupees for a trip to London that he planned to make, and offered him a series of annual cash payments in lieu of free petrol supplies. With the agreement signed and sealed, the two men left the kingdom for the last time, flying out from Basrah four days later.

Less than three years later, the newly formed Kuwait Oil Company was also ready to start work. Its engineers had decided to start their first well at Bahra in northern Kuwait and began detailed surveying of the site on 16 March 1935. The Company's administrative and technical staff, as well as its heavy equipment, began to arrive in the kingdom a few months later and the first drilling started in May the following year. After months of strenuous effort, and boring down to the then unprecedented depth of 8,000 feet, the engineers changed tack and opened up a new site at Burgan, further south, where years before Dr Heim and others had undertaken a survey but considered the spot to be without real promise. It was not long before this proved an inspired choice, however, for during the night of 23 February 1938 the first well there struck oil in huge quantities at a depth of 3,672 feet.

Philby jumped at the chance, resigning from the civil service and heading straight for Jeddah. Within hours of his arrival, at the end of November 1925, he had renewed his acquaintance with Abdul Aziz, whom he had not seen for eight years. The men talked for hours before Philby raised the issues that had prompted him to make his trip. The Arabian leader mulled over the outline of the concessionary proposals before replying that he would consider them further, in due course, before reaching any firm decision.

Abdul Aziz was keen to establish a good rapport with his English visitor, recognizing how useful he could be. Speaking excellent Arabic, Philby could act on the king's behalf as an intermediary in any dealings with the various Western businesses – not least the giant American car manufacturer Ford – that were trying to establish a foothold in the kingdom; and speaking fluent French, he could also liaise with the Egyptians, with whom the Arabian leader was hoping to open up a new diplomatic dialogue. So Abdul Aziz knew that he would be able to make good use of Philby in this capacity as an intermediary, and wanted him to stay there to work on his behalf.

Philby was anxious to stay. For, like Williamson before him, he 'had fallen in love with Arabia'.[2] He now based himself in Jeddah, buying a house at Bait Baghdadi, a spot close to the town centre that gave him easy access to the king and his officials. His home, he wrote, was 'a huge, ramshackle and rather picturesque building, about a century old and built in piles of land reclaimed from the sea', and one of the largest and finest buildings in Jeddah, built out of local stone and teak coloured wood imported from Java.[3] His many visitors were always particular impressed by the roof garden, where he carefully cultivated flowers that were very rarely seen elsewhere in the Arabian peninsula.

Among the two dozen or so other Westerners in the town, Philby made a powerful impression. This was not always a flattering one since he had always been well known for his irascibility, arrogance and conceit, but his hospitality was always generous and his conversation usually fascinating. The Winchester and Cambridge-educated intellectual also had some wide-ranging interests, including a strong affection for his pet baboons, which lived in some large cages in his home and which were often seen walking through the town at the side of, and usually hand-in-hand with, an eccentric Englishman who seemed to enjoy rebelling against established conventions. 'I was an iconoclast with marked leanings to the left and was generally regarded in Jeddah society as something of a Bolshevik', as he later wrote in his memoirs.[4]

Over the next four years, Philby established a close working relationship with the royal court, gaining the king's trust and good favour. But he was still something of an outsider, not just because he was by birth an Englishman but above all because he was an infidel. In August 1930, however, mainly for career reasons but perhaps also as a gesture of defiance towards his own homeland,

16

Philby of Arabia

Three months after Karl Twitchell's findings had first aroused so much interest on the other side of the Atlantic, a middle-aged Englishman made his way to what was one of London's most prestigious restaurants. His venue was Simpsons in The Strand, situated in a fine Edwardian building with a highly traditional interior, and which was renowned both for its outstanding cuisine and its high prices.

The staff at Simpsons were used to seeing all manner of highly distinguished guests from every walk of life, but even they might have given their new visitor a second glance. For in the summer of 1932, 47-year-old Harry St John Philby was something of a celebrity in Britain, a figure of great repute who was the subject of numerous newspaper stories and radio broadcasts. For a time people everywhere seemed to talk about his amazing exploits. It is no exaggeration to say that he was, for this brief period, something of a household name.

It was as an explorer that Philby had made his reputation. He was thought to have been the first person – or at least the first Westerner – to have crossed a vast desert area of the Arabian peninsula that was uninhabited and uninhabitable.[1] To get across Ar Rub al Khali, 'the Empty Quarter', and survive was by any standards an extraordinary feat, one that even local tribesmen had watched with awe, reverence and astonishment. For this was a vast area that was almost entirely barren and where a complete dearth of fresh water would make even camels collapse. If his provisions ran out too soon, as could so easily happen on any expedition, then a traveller faced a long, agonizing death of thirst or hunger.

Philby was, however, a man of astonishing physical stamina and truly remarkable determination. Exploring Ar Rub al Khali had long been one of his ultimate ambitions, and he had pulled out all the stops to arrange it. 'I shall never want anything more from the Arabs', as he wrote to his wife back in London. For more than two years he lobbied the Saudi king for permission to make the journey and eventually, in December 1931, was given the go-ahead. He wanted to move as fast as possible to make his way to his starting-point at Al Hufuf, meeting up along the way with an American geologist by the name of Karl Twitchell and escorting him for part of the journey. He arrived there on Christmas Day and hurriedly hired the camels, guides and provisions that he would have to take with him. Finally, on 7 January, he felt ready to set off, and his caravan – made up of 14 Arabs, 32 camels and three months of supplies – left Al Hufuf in thick fog. For the first few miles the journey would be easy enough, but thereafter, as they faded into the desert sands, he knew that the challenge of crossing over 400 miles of desert would begin in earnest.

If Philby was daunted by the sheer arduousness of the task before him, he did not let it show. 'I was gloriously conscious of physical well-being and spiritual contentment', he later wrote, 'as I marched through the desert in a climate that was as nearly perfect as possible.' Collecting all sorts of fossils, insects and rocks along the way, and carefully charting his course, he felt in his element and gave constant encouragement to the native Arabs at his side, nearly all of whom were soon physically exhausted, demoralized and very frightened by the dire predicament they had willingly put themselves into.

News of Philby's venture had already spread far and wide. It was the talk of the Saudi royal court and the local Arab population but had also proliferated much further, making the columns of British newspapers and the airwaves of its radio broadcasts. But as Philby's caravan disappeared into the deserts – and days became weeks and, eventually, months – many people began to fear the worst. It was only towards the end of March, as the party reached the small town of Bisha, that word broke out that 'Philby had been seen'. The great Englishman had survived his ordeal and appeared to have broken a new record. Within hours, news of his achievement made headlines in the world press.

On his arrival back in London a few weeks later, Philby enjoyed something of a hero's welcome. He was commissioned by *The Times* to write a series of articles and by a number of eminent institutions, notably the Royal Geographical Society, to give lectures about his experiences. A leading publisher of the day signed him up to write a book, while the BBC pressed him for interviews. Philby, it seemed, was a true British hero in the same legendary mould as Lawrence, Burton, Speke and Livingstone. Philby had assumed that he had been invited to Simpsons restaurant on that July day to discuss his travelling experiences. For shortly before he had received a letter from a senior American diplomat in London, Albert Halstead, that suggested introducing him to a particularly important visitor from the USA. 'Please permit me to introduce to you the Honourable Francis B. Loomis, formerly Under Secretary of State of the United States, and a gentleman whom I have known for many years', the letter ran. 'Mr Loomis has been impressed with your work in Arabia, and would like to meet you. I am quite certain that the meeting would be mutually agreeable.' Loomis was in London for a mere three days in the second week of July, and had just enough time to see Philby on the same day as his departure back to the USA.

In the course of their meal, it soon became apparent that the American businessman had rather more on his mind than hearing about Philby's great exploits. His real interest was to win a concession to find Saudi oil, and he wanted

to probe the Englishman's interest in working on Socal's behalf. Just a few wee before, on 31 May, his drillers had struck vast quantities of oil in nearby Bahra he told Philby, and the geologists felt sure that Saudi Arabia shared the sai geological fault lines. If Philby could help Socal win the contract then he wou be amply rewarded. Loomis knew that the discovery of Bahraini oil would p Socal's competitors hot on his heels. Twitchell had toured the office of America leading oil companies just a few months before and found almost no intere Now all that was set to change. Saudi Arabia had suddenly become very h property indeed.

The Standard Oil chief also knew that if any one individual was well placed t help him, then it was surely Harry St John Philby. This was not because he ha undertaken such remarkable travels through whole stretches of Saudi, and wa also revered by many of the local people as a result; nor was it simply because b this time the Englishman had more or less become one of the Arabs himself. I was essentially because he had the remarkable privilege of having direct acces to the king. It was hardly surprising that, compared to Philby, Frank Holmes wa yesterday's man, by now a largely forgotten individual who had no influence at all in the closely knit world of Saudi politics.

For any outsiders to have so much influence in the affairs of a notoriously xenophobic country was of course extremely unusual, but Philby was in his own way just as remarkable as the other great Englishman who exerted similar powers, Haji Williamson. Philby's own association with the Middle East had started years before, when at the height of the First World War he had been sent to the region to serve as a British diplomat. A visit to the Arabian Peninsula followed soon after, in 1917, when he formed part of a British legation that was led by Sir Percy Cox, Civil Commissioner of Mesopotamia. One of the mission's chief aims was to meet and win the support of Abdul Aziz Ibn Saud, then the ruler of the Najd and al-Hasa provinces in Arabia. Formidably talented, Philby worked hard to learn the Arabic language, and by the end of the war not only spoke several loca dialects but also had acquired a close familiarity with much of the region.

After the war Philby joined the Indian Civil Service, but quickly becam disenchanted and eventually began to look for new challenges. His chance car during a stay in London in the summer of 1924, when he happened to mee city businessman, Remy Fischer, who seemed to have much to offer. Fischer l high ambitions to move into the Middle East and was aware of Philby's c familiarity with the region. Would Philby be interested to work in Arabia or behalf, he asked? There were a number of business deals in Arabia that he interested in getting hold of, and he could offer Philby a generous commi if he would help broker them. He was particularly interested, he adde winning concessions to conduct the flow of pilgrimage traffic to and from to open and run a state bank and, finally, to search for minerals.

Philby converted to Islam. In his memoirs he presented this in rather more idealistic terms, claiming that 'ever since my early days in India I had been greatly attracted by Islam and its highly simplified emphasis on what seemed to me the eternal verities of life and philosophy. I had long ceased to be a Christian [but] it was not till I went to Arabia that I came into contact with what seemed to me undeniably a pure form of Islam, deriving exclusively from the original sources of its inspiration, the Koran and the Traditions of the Prophet.'[5] But whatever the exact reasons may have been, Philby was now a Muslim and was given the new name of Abdullah, or 'The Slave of God'.

From the moment of his conversion, Philby's professional career in the Middle East took a huge step forward, for now that he was a fellow Muslim the king felt that he could trust him far more closely than ever before. Philby also knew that he at last had a real chance of fulfilling a long-cherished ambition. He had long been pressing the king for permission to cross Ar Rub al Khali, but the king had always flatly turned his request down, reluctant to let any infidel cross his kingdom's holy soil. But Philby's patience was finally rewarded, for within a few months of his conversion the king gave his assent. He also began to give the Englishman – by now a long-standing acquaintance – closer access than ever before to the very heart of his government. By 1931 Philby had in effect become a close and trusted adviser to the Saudi king, nearly always standing at his side or within very close proximity, travelling with a handful of other very senior officials who had also won royal trust. It was hardly surprising that foreign businessmen like Francis Loomis were only too keen to get to know this remarkable man and get him on their side.

In the refined atmosphere of Simpsons restaurant, the world of Saudi politics must have seemed far away when, that summer day of 1932, Philby met with his American visitor. Philby's reaction to Loomis' proposal was mixed. The American, it was true, was offering to pay him generously in return for his support but, on the other hand, he felt sure he would have more to gain if Socal had more competition on its heels: at that time the American giant was the only candidate for a Saudi oil concession, and it could therefore afford to keep its financial offer relatively low.

Keen to keep the Americans on their toes, Philby quickly tipped off a contact, Dr G. Martin Lees, in the Anglo-Persian Oil Company. 'I can pass on for your private ear', he wrote to Lees, 'a piece of information about a territory in which I understood from you that your folk might be interested. I have been approached by an American concern to apply to the Government for a concession of the exploration and exploitation rights in the Hasa province. I am not in any way committed to serve the interests of said company; but I am generally disposed to help anyone practically interested in such matters … my main object is to get the concession going in the interests of the Government.' Emphasizing that 'financial stringency is beginning to open the doors of Arabia to industrial exploitation', he asked Lees directly if Anglo-Persian would also be interested to meet the challenge and throw down the gauntlet.[6] He knew that the Red Line Agreement blocked Anglo-Persian's path but thought that the largely British-owned Turkish Petroleum Company – now renamed the Iraq Petroleum Company – would still be able to proceed.[7]

By the time Philby made his way back to Arabia, towards the end of the year, the race for the Saudi oil concession was well and truly under way. At Jeddah representatives of the two contestants had arrived and were getting ready to fight it out. Socal's representatives were Lloyd Hamilton, a 40-year-old New York lawyer who could negotiate his way through the technicalities of the agreement, and Karl Twitchell, whom Socal had hired as a consultant geologist. Pitched against them was the representative of the Iraq Petroleum Company, one Stephen Longrigg. He did not promise to be a pushover, since he was a brilliant speaker of Arabic and also had the full support of the British government's diplomatic representative to the kingdom, Sir Andrew Ryan.

Ryan had only just arrived in the kingdom and was slowly getting used not just to its climate and people but also to the antics of Harry Philby, who seemed to harbour a strong aversion to his former colleagues in the civil service and was always quick to find an excuse to bait them. Ryan had first reached the harbour on board HMS *Clematis* and one night, as he was half-asleep, was surprised to hear someone singing. It was pitch dark but he looked down from the deck onto the water below and, to his astonishment, could make out the figure of a drunken Philby, sitting on board a small rowing boat. The eccentric Englishman, it turned out, had composed a poem of welcome whose every line rhymed with 'Ryan', and had then rowed the boat out from the quay in order to give the bewildered diplomat a special recital.

But the rivalry between the two camps was nonetheless always good spirited, and in such a small expatriate community both were grateful for the others' company. The Americans stayed at the best hotel in town, the Egyptian Hotel – 'not exactly a first-class establishment', as Philby put it, 'but the best we had to offer in those days' – while Longrigg lodged at the British Legation.[8] The handful of Western travellers who passed through the kingdom at this time noted the good rapport between them: 'the rivalry does not appear to spoil the friendly relations existing between all parties, even when Mr Longrigg discovers broken glass in his coffee cup!', wrote one British traveller who dined with them in Jeddah one evening. 'After dinner we played bridge and on breaking up the party at midnight, the moon looked so enticing that several of us went for a drive in the desert to the creek and had a bathe.'[9] This was because there were so few Westerners in town, she continued, that 'everyone seems determined to make the best of life, though entertaining is somewhat difficult, as with the exception of meat all foodstuff are imported from Egypt and have a heavy duty to pay, while alcoholic drinks of every description are strictly forbidden'.[10]

Philby spoke at length and in detail with the king about how best to proceed. He felt that the discovery of Bahraini oil gave them the clear upper hand in negotiations, and he persuaded the king to insist on a payment of £100,000 in return for the concession. The Americans were awash with cash, he emphasized, and could easily afford such a fee now that their appetites for oil had been whetted. Philby was wrong, however, to suppose that events had been working in his favour. On the contrary, the stringent Saudi demands seemed all the more unreasonable because they contrasted so unfavourably with the very generous terms of the Iraqi oil concession. By early 1933 the Anglo-Persian Oil Company was also too embroiled in disputes with the Persian leader, Shah Reza Pahlavi, to start making active bids anywhere. Philby recognized these pressures, and on 16 January wrote a letter to Loomis saying that 'I quite understand that the speculative nature of the Hasa terrain deters your friends from immediate acceptance of the Government's conditions … the lavish arrangements made with the Iraq Government by the Iraq Petroleum Company have rather queered the pitch for concession hunters in this part of the world, while the action of the Persian Government in respect of the D'Arcy Concession has not been without its effect'. He was adamant, however, that none of this should put the Americans off the Saudi trail. 'But the main point is that Ibn Saud's government owes a good deal of money, and has had to default on its payments to its creditors.'[11]

The negotiating process between the two companies now threatened to drag on for some considerable while, but Abdullah Philby knew that he could capitalize on these long delays if he was hired by one of them and was paid regularly. He knew that Socal had far more money at its disposal than the IPC and in April struck a deal to work on the Americans' behalf in return for generous payment. Under the terms of the deal he would receive $1,000 per month, which would be backdated to January, and a further $10,000 fee if Socal went on to win the concession. This was not all, for there would be a further $25,000 sum if oil were found in commercial quantities plus an additional 50 cents for every ton of exported oil. Even with all of his children at Britain's most expensive boarding schools, Philby could afford to smile.

Philby was ultimately out to line his own pockets, although his fellow British would have needed to offer him considerable sums of extra money to sway him away from their rivals. In his writings he leaves no doubt as to his real loyalties. Although claiming that 'in view of my relationship with King and his Government, I could not decently agree to help any party to the competition in the event of both parties being willing to go all the way', he also admitted that 'in so far as my advice might be of any avail with the Government, I should, for purely political reasons, have been inclined to favour the Americans, whose record at that time was entirely free of any imperialistic implications'. But in the final analysis he was playing a numbers game: 'otherwise', he concluded, 'I should favour the highest bidder, for the advantage of the government'.[12]

To begin with, he kept secret the news of his deal with Socal, hoping to win the trust and good favour of the British delegation. His acting skills proved effective, prompting Ryan to inform London that he was 'sure Philby was uncommitted'.[13] Eventually, however, word of Philby's new affiliations broke, and Longrigg and Ryan must have realized that they had lost a powerful potential ally to the other side. If the confidence of the British was dented, however, they did not let it show. 'I am sorry that you have decided definitely to throw in your lot with the other camp', wrote Martin Lees to Philby, 'I hope, and expect, that events will prove that you have backed the wrong horse, and that it may be possible for you to change over later.' Ryan, in particular, kept a stiff upper lip, and 'always seemed confident that the outcome of the negotiations would be in accordance with his desires'.[14]

As the negotiations got under way, the American team gained an early clear lead. They had far more financial clout at their disposal and were determined to outbid anything their rivals could offer. As the different contestants sat around an enormous table and put their bids in, the Americans spoke in terms of thousands while Longrigg was authorized only to talk in hundreds. The Saudis also feared that the British bid might come with political strings attached. One Saudi official present, Muhammed al Mana, recalled how 'we all felt that the British were still tainted by colonialism. If they came for our oil, we could never be sure to what extent they would come to influence our government as well. The Americans on the other hand would simply be after the money, a motive which the Arabs as born traders could readily appreciate and approve.'[15]

For a brief moment, towards the end of March, Hamilton and Twitchell did become genuinely afraid of just one individual who suddenly stepped into the Saudi scene. His name was Frank Holmes and, never one to give up easily, he had come bouncing back into the world of oil negotiations. Socal officials were mindful of the remarkable reputation he had acquired throughout the Middle East, and they felt concerned enough to monitor his movements and keep their Saudi representatives fully informed. On 26 March a cable was sent from Socal's office in Bahrain stating that Holmes had left the island bound for Saudi while two weeks later, on 10 April, the great man duly arrived at Jeddah on the steamer SS *Taif*.

Word spread fast about the new arrival. Philby was pleased to introduce himself to the New Zealander, who struck him as 'a man of considerable personal charm, with a bluff, breezy, blustering buccaneering way about him ... in the best sense of these epithets'.[16] But despite his remarkable personal qualities, Holmes was not much of a contender for the Saudi concession. Proposing to divide the kingdom between the three main competitors, he balked at the amount of cash he would have to fork out for his own share. Not only that but he had very limited credibility with the Saudi leader, since he had won the al-Hasa oil concession nearly a decade before but had been unable to find a buyer and then run short of cash. Philby later wrote that 'the gallant Major undoubtedly had the faculty of impressing people; and he certainly had achieved some striking successes. But I never thought that he had a chance of securing the Hasa concession for the second time, and for a song.'[17] Holmes, not surprisingly, did not last long and soon after his arrival Lloyd Hamilton wrote to Philby saying that he had been forced to postpone a meeting 'as I am busy getting the Major off on the *Taif* this morning'.

What really now clinched the deal for the Americans, however, was not Philby's own influence so much as the complete reluctance of the British negotiators to offer the Saudi king what he really wanted: gold. For Abdul Aziz gold was the best form of hard currency in a part of the world where prices were apt to shoot up with alarming rapidity, and Longrigg, Ryan and their bosses, completely failing to grasp just how important it was for the king, offered him only rupees to clinch the deal. As Longrigg himself later admitted, 'the IPC directors were slow and cautious in their offers and would speak only of rupees when gold was demanded. Their negotiator could do little, and agreement was reached without difficulty between Hamilton and Sheikh Abdullah.'[18]

Now that they were the only runners in the race, Hamilton felt free to cut the Saudi demands down to size. The king had initially asked for £100,000 but the Americans offered a relatively meagre £50,000 and refused to budge. The king may have been disappointed by the huge reduction but Philby advised him to lower his demands and strike a deal on similar terms. So on 8 May Abdullah Suleiman and the king nodded their assent to Socal's offer for a concession that covered al-Hasa province: the Americans would make an initial payment of £35,000 in gold sovereigns, but subsequent payments would bring this figure up to £60,000 after two years. If oil was discovered 'in commercial quantities' then Socal would pay 'the sum of £50,000 gold, with a further sum of £50,000 gold a year later'.

There were a lot more details for Hamilton and the king's lawyers to work through, but within two weeks draft contracts had been drawn up, and the long negotiating process finally culminated at the king's Kazam palace in Nazla, a suburb of Jeddah, on 29 May. King Abdul Aziz put his own signature to the concession while Najib Salaha, an official of the Saudi government who was acting as interpreter, passed the elaborate fountain pen to Lloyd Hamilton and whispered to tell him where he should sign. Within weeks, Standard Oil had made special arrangements to ship to the kingdom £30,000-worth of gold sovereigns, each and every one of which was specially counted out at the Jeddah branch of the Netherlands Trading Society Ltd, witnessed and watched by handpicked representatives of both sides on 25 August.

For the moment at least, Philby's work as an intermediary was done, and he could afford to take some leave. Just before he set sail for England, however, he made a point of calling on Ryan, ostensibly to inform him of the new deal, struck in secret between the king and Socal, but really just to gloat. 'I suppose you have heard that the Americans have got the concession', he told the British diplomat quietly, feigning a slight sympathy. 'He was thunderstruck', recorded Philby, 'and his face darkened with anger and disappointment. He had made certain that his influence behind the scenes, unobtrusive as it certainly was, would have turned the scales in favour of the British competitor. But it was not to be: even he had not appreciated the fundamental issue at stake, the size of the initial loan, of which Ibn Saud's government stood in urgent need.'[19] Philby also thought that Ryan had made the mistake of overestimating the reputation of the British government among the Arabs, and had wrongly supposed that the king's 'love of Britain would make him oblivious of the charms of others'. But Ryan had failed to realize, in Philby's opinion, that 'true love must be reciprocal' and that the Saudis did not feel that London had always done its best for them.[20]

The way was now open for the newly formed California Arabian Standard Oil Company, or 'Casoc', to begin its search in earnest. On 23 September two of their leading geologists, R.P. 'Bert' Miller and S.B. 'Krug' Henry, landed on the eastern coast of Arabia alongside Karl Twitchell, who had driven across Arabia from Jeddah to meet them. They wasted little time in getting straight to work, hiring a number of camels and lodging overnight with their Saudi agents before moving straight on to Jabal Dhahran, five miles inland from the coastal village of Dammam. After that they made a long journey to the oasis around Al Hufuf, where they began their detailed geological surveillance in earnest. To begin with this work was done on the ground, as they carefully inspected local rocks and searched for signs of oil seepages, but the following spring they also hired a light aircraft, using new aerial reconnaissance techniques to search for the right rock structures.

After several months' work, the Casoc team earmarked a site near to Jabal Dhahran that they deemed suitable for drilling, and in 1934 began to set up a permanent camp where the drilling team could be based. Things had of course changed rather dramatically since the days of Reynolds and Rosenplaenter. The engineers had found a spring under the sea that gave them fresh water and built a road that linked the camp with the coast, making it much easier to move the constant flow of materials and manpower to and from the site. These drillers also had all the same modern amenities as their contemporaries back home – bars, restaurants, air conditioning units, swimming pools, saunas and tennis courts – and could at least withstand the ferocious summer heat in relative luxury.

Drilling work at Well No. 1 got under way on 30 April 1935, and a year later it had reached a depth of 3,200 feet, while a second well had been dug down to a depth of 1,700 feet. By the spring of 1938 a total of six wells had been dug and nearly all of them had borne some fruit. The trouble was that none were yielding oil in anything like the quantities that any of the geologists had hoped for. Well No. 1 produced a mere 100 barrels a day, while No. 2 poured out barely 4,000 before suddenly starting to run dry. The other four yielded far less, even though each had been bored down to a considerable depth of 2,000 feet.

The explorers redoubled their efforts, tantalized by the knowledge that oil was close at hand but still hard to unearth. Desperate to find some clues, they spent days looking inside caves, often crawling on their hands and knees in search of fossils embedded in rocks, molluscs and seashells that would allow them to date the various geological formation they came across. Finally, in early 1938, the Americans pinpointed what seemed to be the most promising location, and decided to deepen the particular well, No. 7, that was closest. On 16 March Well No. 7 started to gush out more than 2,000 barrels a day and showed no signs of running dry. Saudi oil had now started to flow properly.

Ryan, Longrigg and the senior officials in the Iraq Petroleum Company must have watched the Americans strike black gold with the greatest envy, but all the more so as their own bid to find Saudi oil had in the meantime proved doubly disappointing. For, having lost the concessionary rights elsewhere, the IPC had in early 1936 decided to apply for permission to drill in the Hijaz province on the east coast of the Red Sea. This was a largely volcanic region, but it was bordered seawards by a thin strip of sedimentary rock that several geologists felt was worth exploring, and their optimism prompted the IPC to form Petroleum Development (Western Arabia) Ltd in return for initial payment of 35,000 gold sovereigns. Starting in 1937, the company's geologists spent more than two years exploring the region and drilling in carefully selected places, concentrating their work on an area on the Farsan Islands which seemed to offer particular promise. But, despite drilling seventeen wells over eight of the islands, no trace of oil was ever found, and the operation was abandoned.

The IPC did have a bit more luck elsewhere in the region. In the course of the Saudi negotiations, their geologists had also become interested in the flat and arid peninsula of Qatar that lay across shallow seas to the east of Bahrain. This promised to be an even more desolate place to work than Saudi, for its only real settlement was the village capital, Doha, while the land was barely cultivated and had no water supply. It was made up of only a few thousand people, some of whom were desert nomads while others subsisted simply from fishing.

The explorers were undeterred, however, and in June 1930 a British official, acting on behalf of the IPC, visited the Qatar capital of Doha and visited the elderly Sheikh Abdullah al Jasim al Thani to take things a stage further. The sheikh gave him permission to explore the kingdom over the next two years, and after this initial surveying was finished, in early 1933, the IPC was keen to push for a full concession. In May 1935 the sheikh yielded to British pressure and assigned Anglo-Persian the exclusive rights to drill for oil in return for an initial payment of 400,000 rupees, an annual rental of 150,000 rupees and a share of royalties if oil was discovered. Anglo-Persian immediately transferred its rights to the Iraq Petroleum Company, and work got under way.

The Qatar concession did bear some fruit, although it took some time to do so. Being such a remote and backward region, it took the IPC considerable time to build up the necessary infrastructure and establish a link with the outside world: a jetty at the port Zakrit was built at considerable expense, telephone networks and a water supply established, and while materials and a workforce, made up of Arab and Indian labourers, were specially shipped in. But when drilling began in October 1938 it quickly became apparent that the underground rocks were far more resilient than expected. Eventually, however, after boring down to the very considerable depth of 5,500 feet, oil was discovered in commercial quantities: an initial survey assessed the well's likely output to be around 5,000 barrels per day, and by the outbreak of the Second World War, in September 1939, Qatar's future as an oil producer seemed secure.

The centuries-old rumours, it had turned out, were true after all. The Middle East was awash with oil.

The Legacy of the Oil Explorers

On a cold February morning in 1947, an enormous wreath of flowers was delivered to a tiny rural church deep in the Essex countryside, where a simple funeral service was about to take place. Sheikh Ahmad, the ruler of Kuwait, had sent flowers to commemorate the death of Major Frank Holmes, who had died quietly at his farm near Chelmsford at the age of 72. The wreath was a last tribute to a man who had not only played a lead part in his kingdom's story but who for some time had been a close and trusted oil hunter, adviser, acquaintance and friend.

After the Kuwaiti concession was signed, Holmes had returned to Britain to take up farming, rearing prize cattle and living quietly with his wife. He could not quite put the Middle East behind him, however, for shortly after his arrival he received a letter from Kuwait offering him the chance to act as the sheikh's personal representative in London and he jumped at the chance. Over the next few years he made frequent trips to London in this capacity, sending regular letters and cables to Kuwait in order to keep his contacts there closely informed about events and developments and, on one brief occasion in 1935, the sheikh had even paid him a brief visit during a short stay in Britain. At his home memorabilia of his years in the Middle East abounded, and he was always glad to tell his extraordinary and amusing stories to visitors, locals or indeed to anyone who was interested to drop by and hear them. He also soon acquired a reputation as a hospitable and generous host, one who loved to chat and reminisce over large cups of his favourite drink, coffee, although he always insisted that 'only the best coffee is good enough'.

The service was a quiet and simple affair, but the Major had the distinction of having a prominent and complimentary obituary in the national press. In his piece in *The Times* on 5 February, Archibald Chisholm described how Holmes was undoubtedly an 'outstanding British personality in the Middle East' who was 'uniquely responsible for discovering the vast petroleum resources of Arabia'. He was, continued Chisholm, 'a formidable personality', an individual who 'had those qualities of generosity, friendliness and frankness which Arabia most admires', and who had considerable achievements to his name.

Like Frank Holmes, a few of the other oil hunters also retired quietly after playing their own distinctive part in the opening chapter of the long and colourful story of Middle Eastern oil. Following Reynolds' discovery at Masjid-i Suleiman, William Knox D'Arcy soon lost ownership of the Anglo-Persian Oil Company and, although he had acquired a personal fortune from the venture, he had played no further role in the story by the time of his death in 1917. Charles Crane died in Palm Springs in 1939, followed seven years later by Admiral Chester, who was buried in Arlington National Cemetery. Haji Williamson, already quite elderly by the time he tried to thwart Holmes' bid for Kuwaiti oil, retired on a full APOC pension and died peacefully near Basrah in 1958, followed three years later by that other maverick British Arab, Harry St John Philby, who had not lived quite long enough to see his son become one of Britain's most infamous traitors. Archibald Chisholm passed away in 1992, less than two years after the first Gulf War, in which dictator Saddam Hussein quarrelled with the Kuwaitis over oil and invaded their kingdom in order to seize control of its vast reserves.

But some of the other individuals who feature in the same story subsequently went on to achieve much more. George Reynolds, although he was already not far off 50 by the time he started his hunt for Persian oil, subsequently moved to Latin America and played an important part in the discovery of Venezuelan oil in the early-to-mid-1920s. Archibald Chisholm left the employment of Anglo-Persian and later became the editor of the *Financial Times*, and subsequently a colonel in Britain's wartime armed forces. Dr Young, who had made such a vital contribution to the work of Reynolds' team at Masjid-i Suleiman and provided them with medical support in extremely arduous conditions, enjoyed a distinguished professional career after retiring from Anglo-Persian in 1936. He went on to join St Mary's Hospital in central London, where he helped develop a number of vaccines and worked closely with Sir Alexander Fleming to produce penicillin: on his death in 1952 a bronze plaque was dedicated to his memory and personally unveiled by Fleming.

The story of at least one of the oil hunters, however, was marred by a sense of tragedy. After coming to Reynolds' rescue in 1907, Arnold Wilson had risen high in the ranks of the Anglo-Persian Oil Company, fulfilling all the ambitions he had always cherished. But on the outbreak of the Second World War in 1939, he was desperate to play a part in Britain's war effort, even though he was 56 years of age by this time. He joined the volunteer reserve of the Royal Air Force to train as an air gunner. Never one to flinch from duty, Wilson was killed in action on 31 May 1940, shot to pieces by a German plane during the early stages of the Battle of Britain.

Many of the oil hunters were soon forgotten after their brief moments of glory in the Middle East, the only exception being Holmes, who for some time was revered as *Abu Naft*, 'the father of oil'. Their legacy is nonetheless plain to see today. Ever since Reynolds first struck oil at Masjid, the Middle East has been the world's primary source of petroleum, and the region looks set to continue playing

Philby of Arabia

Three months after Karl Twitchell's findings had first aroused so much interest on the other side of the Atlantic, a middle-aged Englishman made his way to what was one of London's most prestigious restaurants. His venue was Simpsons in The Strand, situated in a fine Edwardian building with a highly traditional interior, and which was renowned both for its outstanding cuisine and its high prices.

The staff at Simpsons were used to seeing all manner of highly distinguished guests from every walk of life, but even they might have given their new visitor a second glance. For in the summer of 1932, 47-year-old Harry St John Philby was something of a celebrity in Britain, a figure of great repute who was the subject of numerous newspaper stories and radio broadcasts. For a time people everywhere seemed to talk about his amazing exploits. It is no exaggeration to say that he was, for this brief period, something of a household name.

It was as an explorer that Philby had made his reputation. He was thought to have been the first person – or at least the first Westerner – to have crossed a vast desert area of the Arabian peninsula that was uninhabited and uninhabitable.[1] To get across Ar Rub al Khali, 'the Empty Quarter', and survive was by any standards an extraordinary feat, one that even local tribesmen had watched with awe, reverence and astonishment. For this was a vast area that was almost entirely barren and where a complete dearth of fresh water would make even camels collapse. If his provisions ran out too soon, as could so easily happen on any expedition, then a traveller faced a long, agonizing death of thirst or hunger.

Philby was, however, a man of astonishing physical stamina and truly remarkable determination. Exploring Ar Rub al Khali had long been one of his ultimate ambitions, and he had pulled out all the stops to arrange it. 'I shall never want anything more from the Arabs', as he wrote to his wife back in London. For more than two years he lobbied the Saudi king for permission to make the journey and eventually, in December 1931, was given the go-ahead. He wanted to move as fast as possible to make his way to his starting-point at Al Hufuf, meeting up along the way with an American geologist by the name of Karl Twitchell and escorting him for part of the journey. He arrived there on Christmas Day and hurriedly hired the camels, guides and provisions that he would have to take with him. Finally, on 7 January, he felt ready to set off, and his caravan – made up of 14 Arabs, 32 camels and three months of supplies – left Al Hufuf in thick fog. For the first few miles the journey would be easy enough, but thereafter, as they faded into the desert sands, he knew that the challenge of crossing over 400 miles of desert would begin in earnest.

If Philby was daunted by the sheer arduousness of the task before him, he did not let it show. 'I was gloriously conscious of physical well-being and spiritual contentment', he later wrote, 'as I marched through the desert in a climate that was as nearly perfect as possible.' Collecting all sorts of fossils, insects and rocks along the way, and carefully charting his course, he felt in his element and gave constant encouragement to the native Arabs at his side, nearly all of whom were soon physically exhausted, demoralized and very frightened by the dire predicament they had willingly put themselves into.

News of Philby's venture had already spread far and wide. It was the talk of the Saudi royal court and the local Arab population but had also proliferated much further, making the columns of British newspapers and the airwaves of its radio broadcasts. But as Philby's caravan disappeared into the deserts – and days became weeks and, eventually, months – many people began to fear the worst. It was only towards the end of March, as the party reached the small town of Bisha, that word broke out that 'Philby had been seen'. The great Englishman had survived his ordeal and appeared to have broken a new record. Within hours, news of his achievement made headlines in the world press.

On his arrival back in London a few weeks later, Philby enjoyed something of a hero's welcome. He was commissioned by *The Times* to write a series of articles and by a number of eminent institutions, notably the Royal Geographical Society, to give lectures about his experiences. A leading publisher of the day signed him up to write a book, while the BBC pressed him for interviews. Philby, it seemed, was a true British hero in the same legendary mould as Lawrence, Burton, Speke and Livingstone. Philby had assumed that he had been invited to Simpsons restaurant on that July day to discuss his travelling experiences. For shortly before he had received a letter from a senior American diplomat in London, Albert Halstead, that suggested introducing him to a particularly important visitor from the USA. 'Please permit me to introduce to you the Honourable Francis B. Loomis, formerly Under Secretary of State of the United States, and a gentleman whom I have known for many years', the letter ran. 'Mr Loomis has been impressed with your work in Arabia, and would like to meet you. I am quite certain that the meeting would be mutually agreeable.' Loomis was in London for a mere three days in the second week of July, and had just enough time to see Philby on the same day as his departure back to the USA.

In the course of their meal, it soon became apparent that the American businessman had rather more on his mind than hearing about Philby's great exploits. His real interest was to win a concession to find Saudi oil, and he wanted to probe the Englishman's interest in working on Socal's behalf. Just a few weeks before, on 31 May, his drillers had struck vast quantities of oil in nearby Bahrain, he told Philby, and the geologists felt sure that Saudi Arabia shared the same geological fault lines. If Philby could help Socal win the contract then he would be amply rewarded. Loomis knew that the discovery of Bahraini oil would put Socal's competitors hot on his heels. Twitchell had toured the office of America's leading oil companies just a few months before and found almost no interest. Now all that was set to change. Saudi Arabia had suddenly become very hot property indeed.

The Standard Oil chief also knew that if any one individual was well placed to help him, then it was surely Harry St John Philby. This was not because he had undertaken such remarkable travels through whole stretches of Saudi, and was also revered by many of the local people as a result; nor was it simply because by this time the Englishman had more or less become one of the Arabs himself. It was essentially because he had the remarkable privilege of having direct access to the king. It was hardly surprising that, compared to Philby, Frank Holmes was yesterday's man, by now a largely forgotten individual who had no influence at all in the closely knit world of Saudi politics.

For any outsiders to have so much influence in the affairs of a notoriously xenophobic country was of course extremely unusual, but Philby was in his own way just as remarkable as the other great Englishman who exerted similar powers, Haji Williamson. Philby's own association with the Middle East had started years before, when at the height of the First World War he had been sent to the region to serve as a British diplomat. A visit to the Arabian Peninsula followed soon after, in 1917, when he formed part of a British legation that was led by Sir Percy Cox, Civil Commissioner of Mesopotamia. One of the mission's chief aims was to meet and win the support of Abdul Aziz Ibn Saud, then the ruler of the Najd and al-Hasa provinces in Arabia. Formidably talented, Philby worked hard to learn the Arabic language, and by the end of the war not only spoke several local dialects but also had acquired a close familiarity with much of the region.

After the war Philby joined the Indian Civil Service, but quickly became disenchanted and eventually began to look for new challenges. His chance came during a stay in London in the summer of 1924, when he happened to meet a city businessman, Remy Fischer, who seemed to have much to offer. Fischer had high ambitions to move into the Middle East and was aware of Philby's close familiarity with the region. Would Philby be interested to work in Arabia on his behalf, he asked? There were a number of business deals in Arabia that he was interested in getting hold of, and he could offer Philby a generous commission if he would help broker them. He was particularly interested, he added, in winning concessions to conduct the flow of pilgrimage traffic to and from Mecca, to open and run a state bank and, finally, to search for minerals.

Philby jumped at the chance, resigning from the civil service and heading straight for Jeddah. Within hours of his arrival, at the end of November 1925, he had renewed his acquaintance with Abdul Aziz, whom he had not seen for eight years. The men talked for hours before Philby raised the issues that had prompted him to make his trip. The Arabian leader mulled over the outline of the concessionary proposals before replying that he would consider them further, in due course, before reaching any firm decision.

Abdul Aziz was keen to establish a good rapport with his English visitor, recognizing how useful he could be. Speaking excellent Arabic, Philby could act on the king's behalf as an intermediary in any dealings with the various Western businesses – not least the giant American car manufacturer Ford – that were trying to establish a foothold in the kingdom; and speaking fluent French, he could also liaise with the Egyptians, with whom the Arabian leader was hoping to open up a new diplomatic dialogue. So Abdul Aziz knew that he would be able to make good use of Philby in this capacity as an intermediary, and wanted him to stay there to work on his behalf.

Philby was anxious to stay. For, like Williamson before him, he 'had fallen in love with Arabia'.[2] He now based himself in Jeddah, buying a house at Bait Baghdadi, a spot close to the town centre that gave him easy access to the king and his officials. His home, he wrote, was 'a huge, ramshackle and rather picturesque building, about a century old and built in piles of land reclaimed from the sea', and one of the largest and finest buildings in Jeddah, built out of local stone and teak coloured wood imported from Java.[3] His many visitors were always particular impressed by the roof garden, where he carefully cultivated flowers that were very rarely seen elsewhere in the Arabian peninsula.

Among the two dozen or so other Westerners in the town, Philby made a powerful impression. This was not always a flattering one since he had always been well known for his irascibility, arrogance and conceit, but his hospitality was always generous and his conversation usually fascinating. The Winchester and Cambridge-educated intellectual also had some wide-ranging interests, including a strong affection for his pet baboons, which lived in some large cages in his home and which were often seen walking through the town at the side of, and usually hand-in-hand with, an eccentric Englishman who seemed to enjoy rebelling against established conventions. 'I was an iconoclast with marked leanings to the left and was generally regarded in Jeddah society as something of a Bolshevik', as he later wrote in his memoirs.[4]

Over the next four years, Philby established a close working relationship with the royal court, gaining the king's trust and good favour. But he was still something of an outsider, not just because he was by birth an Englishman but above all because he was an infidel. In August 1930, however, mainly for career reasons but perhaps also as a gesture of defiance towards his own homeland,

Philby converted to Islam. In his memoirs he presented this in rather more idealistic terms, claiming that 'ever since my early days in India I had been greatly attracted by Islam and its highly simplified emphasis on what seemed to me the eternal verities of life and philosophy. I had long ceased to be a Christian [but] it was not till I went to Arabia that I came into contact with what seemed to me undeniably a pure form of Islam, deriving exclusively from the original sources of its inspiration, the Koran and the Traditions of the Prophet.'[5] But whatever the exact reasons may have been, Philby was now a Muslim and was given the new name of Abdullah, or 'The Slave of God'.

From the moment of his conversion, Philby's professional career in the Middle East took a huge step forward, for now that he was a fellow Muslim the king felt that he could trust him far more closely than ever before. Philby also knew that he at last had a real chance of fulfilling a long-cherished ambition. He had long been pressing the king for permission to cross Ar Rub al Khali, but the king had always flatly turned his request down, reluctant to let any infidel cross his kingdom's holy soil. But Philby's patience was finally rewarded, for within a few months of his conversion the king gave his assent. He also began to give the Englishman – by now a long-standing acquaintance – closer access than ever before to the very heart of his government. By 1931 Philby had in effect become a close and trusted adviser to the Saudi king, nearly always standing at his side or within very close proximity, travelling with a handful of other very senior officials who had also won royal trust. It was hardly surprising that foreign businessmen like Francis Loomis were only too keen to get to know this remarkable man and get him on their side.

In the refined atmosphere of Simpsons restaurant, the world of Saudi politics must have seemed far away when, that summer day of 1932, Philby met with his American visitor. Philby's reaction to Loomis' proposal was mixed. The American, it was true, was offering to pay him generously in return for his support but, on the other hand, he felt sure he would have more to gain if Socal had more competition on its heels: at that time the American giant was the only candidate for a Saudi oil concession, and it could therefore afford to keep its financial offer relatively low.

Keen to keep the Americans on their toes, Philby quickly tipped off a contact, Dr G. Martin Lees, in the Anglo-Persian Oil Company. 'I can pass on for your private ear', he wrote to Lees, 'a piece of information about a territory in which I understood from you that your folk might be interested. I have been approached by an American concern to apply to the Government for a concession of the exploration and exploitation rights in the Hasa province. I am not in any way committed to serve the interests of said company; but I am generally disposed to help anyone practically interested in such matters ... my main object is to get the concession going in the interests of the Government.' Emphasizing that 'financial

stringency is beginning to open the doors of Arabia to industrial exploitation', he asked Lees directly if Anglo-Persian would also be interested to meet the challenge and throw down the gauntlet.[6] He knew that the Red Line Agreement blocked Anglo-Persian's path but thought that the largely British-owned Turkish Petroleum Company – now renamed the Iraq Petroleum Company – would still be able to proceed.[7]

By the time Philby made his way back to Arabia, towards the end of the year, the race for the Saudi oil concession was well and truly under way. At Jeddah representatives of the two contestants had arrived and were getting ready to fight it out. Socal's representatives were Lloyd Hamilton, a 40-year-old New York lawyer who could negotiate his way through the technicalities of the agreement, and Karl Twitchell, whom Socal had hired as a consultant geologist. Pitched against them was the representative of the Iraq Petroleum Company, one Stephen Longrigg. He did not promise to be a pushover, since he was a brilliant speaker of Arabic and also had the full support of the British government's diplomatic representative to the kingdom, Sir Andrew Ryan.

Ryan had only just arrived in the kingdom and was slowly getting used not just to its climate and people but also to the antics of Harry Philby, who seemed to harbour a strong aversion to his former colleagues in the civil service and was always quick to find an excuse to bait them. Ryan had first reached the harbour on board HMS *Clematis* and one night, as he was half-asleep, was surprised to hear someone singing. It was pitch dark but he looked down from the deck onto the water below and, to his astonishment, could make out the figure of a drunken Philby, sitting on board a small rowing boat. The eccentric Englishman, it turned out, had composed a poem of welcome whose every line rhymed with 'Ryan', and had then rowed the boat out from the quay in order to give the bewildered diplomat a special recital.

But the rivalry between the two camps was nonetheless always good spirited, and in such a small expatriate community both were grateful for the others' company. The Americans stayed at the best hotel in town, the Egyptian Hotel – 'not exactly a first-class establishment', as Philby put it, 'but the best we had to offer in those days' – while Longrigg lodged at the British Legation.[8] The handful of Western travellers who passed through the kingdom at this time noted the good rapport between them: 'the rivalry does not appear to spoil the friendly relations existing between all parties, even when Mr Longrigg discovers broken glass in his coffee cup!', wrote one British traveller who dined with them in Jeddah one evening. 'After dinner we played bridge and on breaking up the party at midnight, the moon looked so enticing that several of us went for a drive in the desert to the creek and had a bathe.'[9] This was because there were so few Westerners in town, she continued, that 'everyone seems determined to make the best of life, though entertaining is somewhat difficult, as with the exception of

meat all foodstuff are imported from Egypt and have a heavy duty to pay, while alcoholic drinks of every description are strictly forbidden'.[10]

Philby spoke at length and in detail with the king about how best to proceed. He felt that the discovery of Bahraini oil gave them the clear upper hand in negotiations, and he persuaded the king to insist on a payment of £100,000 in return for the concession. The Americans were awash with cash, he emphasized, and could easily afford such a fee now that their appetites for oil had been whetted. Philby was wrong, however, to suppose that events had been working in his favour. On the contrary, the stringent Saudi demands seemed all the more unreasonable because they contrasted so unfavourably with the very generous terms of the Iraqi oil concession. By early 1933 the Anglo-Persian Oil Company was also too embroiled in disputes with the Persian leader, Shah Reza Pahlavi, to start making active bids anywhere. Philby recognized these pressures, and on 16 January wrote a letter to Loomis saying that 'I quite understand that the speculative nature of the Hasa terrain deters your friends from immediate acceptance of the Government's conditions … the lavish arrangements made with the Iraq Government by the Iraq Petroleum Company have rather queered the pitch for concession hunters in this part of the world, while the action of the Persian Government in respect of the D'Arcy Concession has not been without its effect'. He was adamant, however, that none of this should put the Americans off the Saudi trail. 'But the main point is that Ibn Saud's government owes a good deal of money, and has had to default on its payments to its creditors.'[11]

The negotiating process between the two companies now threatened to drag on for some considerable while, but Abdullah Philby knew that he could capitalize on these long delays if he was hired by one of them and was paid regularly. He knew that Socal had far more money at its disposal than the IPC and in April struck a deal to work on the Americans' behalf in return for generous payment. Under the terms of the deal he would receive $1,000 per month, which would be backdated to January, and a further $10,000 fee if Socal went on to win the concession. This was not all, for there would be a further $25,000 sum if oil were found in commercial quantities plus an additional 50 cents for every ton of exported oil. Even with all of his children at Britain's most expensive boarding schools, Philby could afford to smile.

Philby was ultimately out to line his own pockets, although his fellow British would have needed to offer him considerable sums of extra money to sway him away from their rivals. In his writings he leaves no doubt as to his real loyalties. Although claiming that 'in view of my relationship with King and his Government, I could not decently agree to help any party to the competition in the event of both parties being willing to go all the way', he also admitted that 'in so far as my advice might be of any avail with the Government, I should, for purely political reasons, have been inclined to favour the Americans, whose

record at that time was entirely free of any imperialistic implications'. But in the final analysis he was playing a numbers game: 'otherwise', he concluded, 'I should favour the highest bidder, for the advantage of the government'.[12]

To begin with, he kept secret the news of his deal with Socal, hoping to win the trust and good favour of the British delegation. His acting skills proved effective, prompting Ryan to inform London that he was 'sure Philby was uncommitted'.[13] Eventually, however, word of Philby's new affiliations broke, and Longrigg and Ryan must have realized that they had lost a powerful potential ally to the other side. If the confidence of the British was dented, however, they did not let it show. 'I am sorry that you have decided definitely to throw in your lot with the other camp', wrote Martin Lees to Philby, 'I hope, and expect, that events will prove that you have backed the wrong horse, and that it may be possible for you to change over later.' Ryan, in particular, kept a stiff upper lip, and 'always seemed confident that the outcome of the negotiations would be in accordance with his desires'.[14]

As the negotiations got under way, the American team gained an early clear lead. They had far more financial clout at their disposal and were determined to outbid anything their rivals could offer. As the different contestants sat around an enormous table and put their bids in, the Americans spoke in terms of thousands while Longrigg was authorized only to talk in hundreds. The Saudis also feared that the British bid might come with political strings attached. One Saudi official present, Muhammed al Mana, recalled how 'we all felt that the British were still tainted by colonialism. If they came for our oil, we could never be sure to what extent they would come to influence our government as well. The Americans on the other hand would simply be after the money, a motive which the Arabs as born traders could readily appreciate and approve.'[15]

For a brief moment, towards the end of March, Hamilton and Twitchell did become genuinely afraid of just one individual who suddenly stepped into the Saudi scene. His name was Frank Holmes and, never one to give up easily, he had come bouncing back into the world of oil negotiations. Socal officials were mindful of the remarkable reputation he had acquired throughout the Middle East, and they felt concerned enough to monitor his movements and keep their Saudi representatives fully informed. On 26 March a cable was sent from Socal's office in Bahrain stating that Holmes had left the island bound for Saudi while two weeks later, on 10 April, the great man duly arrived at Jeddah on the steamer SS *Taif*.

Word spread fast about the new arrival. Philby was pleased to introduce himself to the New Zealander, who struck him as 'a man of considerable personal charm, with a bluff, breezy, blustering buccaneering way about him … in the best sense of these epithets'.[16] But despite his remarkable personal qualities, Holmes was not much of a contender for the Saudi concession. Proposing to divide the

kingdom between the three main competitors, he balked at the amount of cash
he would have to fork out for his own share. Not only that but he had very limited
credibility with the Saudi leader, since he had won the al-Hasa oil concession
nearly a decade before but had been unable to find a buyer and then run short
of cash. Philby later wrote that 'the gallant Major undoubtedly had the faculty
of impressing people; and he certainly had achieved some striking successes. But
I never thought that he had a chance of securing the Hasa concession for the
second time, and for a song.'[17] Holmes, not surprisingly, did not last long and
soon after his arrival Lloyd Hamilton wrote to Philby saying that he had been
forced to postpone a meeting 'as I am busy getting the Major off on the *Taif* this
morning'.

What really now clinched the deal for the Americans, however, was not Philby's
own influence so much as the complete reluctance of the British negotiators to
offer the Saudi king what he really wanted: gold. For Abdul Aziz gold was the best
form of hard currency in a part of the world where prices were apt to shoot up
with alarming rapidity, and Longrigg, Ryan and their bosses, completely failing
to grasp just how important it was for the king, offered him only rupees to clinch
the deal. As Longrigg himself later admitted, 'the IPC directors were slow and
cautious in their offers and would speak only of rupees when gold was demanded.
Their negotiator could do little, and agreement was reached without difficulty
between Hamilton and Sheikh Abdullah.'[18]

Now that they were the only runners in the race, Hamilton felt free to cut the
Saudi demands down to size. The king had initially asked for £100,000 but the
Americans offered a relatively meagre £50,000 and refused to budge. The king
may have been disappointed by the huge reduction but Philby advised him to
lower his demands and strike a deal on similar terms. So on 8 May Abdullah
Suleiman and the king nodded their assent to Socal's offer for a concession that
covered al-Hasa province: the Americans would make an initial payment of
£35,000 in gold sovereigns, but subsequent payments would bring this figure up
to £60,000 after two years. If oil was discovered 'in commercial quantities' then
Socal would pay 'the sum of £50,000 gold, with a further sum of £50,000 gold a
year later'.

There were a lot more details for Hamilton and the king's lawyers to work
through, but within two weeks draft contracts had been drawn up, and the
long negotiating process finally culminated at the king's Kazam palace in Nazla,
a suburb of Jeddah, on 29 May. King Abdul Aziz put his own signature to the
concession while Najib Salaha, an official of the Saudi government who was
acting as interpreter, passed the elaborate fountain pen to Lloyd Hamilton and
whispered to tell him where he should sign. Within weeks, Standard Oil had made
special arrangements to ship to the kingdom £30,000-worth of gold sovereigns,
each and every one of which was specially counted out at the Jeddah branch

of the Netherlands Trading Society Ltd, witnessed and watched by handpicked representatives of both sides on 25 August.

For the moment at least, Philby's work as an intermediary was done, and he could afford to take some leave. Just before he set sail for England, however, he made a point of calling on Ryan, ostensibly to inform him of the new deal, struck in secret between the king and Socal, but really just to gloat. 'I suppose you have heard that the Americans have got the concession', he told the British diplomat quietly, feigning a slight sympathy. 'He was thunderstruck', recorded Philby, 'and his face darkened with anger and disappointment. He had made certain that his influence behind the scenes, unobtrusive as it certainly was, would have turned the scales in favour of the British competitor. But it was not to be: even he had not appreciated the fundamental issue at stake, the size of the initial loan, of which Ibn Saud's government stood in urgent need.'[19] Philby also thought that Ryan had made the mistake of overestimating the reputation of the British government among the Arabs, and had wrongly supposed that the king's 'love of Britain would make him oblivious of the charms of others'. But Ryan had failed to realize, in Philby's opinion, that 'true love must be reciprocal' and that the Saudis did not feel that London had always done its best for them.[20]

The way was now open for the newly formed California Arabian Standard Oil Company, or 'Casoc', to begin its search in earnest. On 23 September two of their leading geologists, R.P. 'Bert' Miller and S.B. 'Krug' Henry, landed on the eastern coast of Arabia alongside Karl Twitchell, who had driven across Arabia from Jeddah to meet them. They wasted little time in getting straight to work, hiring a number of camels and lodging overnight with their Saudi agents before moving straight on to Jabal Dhahran, five miles inland from the coastal village of Dammam. After that they made a long journey to the oasis around Al Hufuf, where they began their detailed geological surveillance in earnest. To begin with this work was done on the ground, as they carefully inspected local rocks and searched for signs of oil seepages, but the following spring they also hired a light aircraft, using new aerial reconnaissance techniques to search for the right rock structures.

After several months' work, the Casoc team earmarked a site near to Jabal Dhahran that they deemed suitable for drilling, and in 1934 began to set up a permanent camp where the drilling team could be based. Things had of course changed rather dramatically since the days of Reynolds and Rosenplaenter. The engineers had found a spring under the sea that gave them fresh water and built a road that linked the camp with the coast, making it much easier to move the constant flow of materials and manpower to and from the site. These drillers also had all the same modern amenities as their contemporaries back home – bars, restaurants, air conditioning units, swimming pools, saunas and tennis courts – and could at least withstand the ferocious summer heat in relative luxury.

Drilling work at Well No. 1 got under way on 30 April 1935, and a year later it had reached a depth of 3,200 feet, while a second well had been dug down to a depth of 1,700 feet. By the spring of 1938 a total of six wells had been dug and nearly all of them had borne some fruit. The trouble was that none were yielding oil in anything like the quantities that any of the geologists had hoped for. Well No. 1 produced a mere 100 barrels a day, while No. 2 poured out barely 4,000 before suddenly starting to run dry. The other four yielded far less, even though each had been bored down to a considerable depth of 2,000 feet.

The explorers redoubled their efforts, tantalized by the knowledge that oil was close at hand but still hard to unearth. Desperate to find some clues, they spent days looking inside caves, often crawling on their hands and knees in search of fossils embedded in rocks, molluscs and seashells that would allow them to date the various geological formation they came across. Finally, in early 1938, the Americans pinpointed what seemed to be the most promising location, and decided to deepen the particular well, No. 7, that was closest. On 16 March Well No. 7 started to gush out more than 2,000 barrels a day and showed no signs of running dry. Saudi oil had now started to flow properly.

Ryan, Longrigg and the senior officials in the Iraq Petroleum Company must have watched the Americans strike black gold with the greatest envy, but all the more so as their own bid to find Saudi oil had in the meantime proved doubly disappointing. For, having lost the concessionary rights elsewhere, the IPC had in early 1936 decided to apply for permission to drill in the Hijaz province on the east coast of the Red Sea. This was a largely volcanic region, but it was bordered seawards by a thin strip of sedimentary rock that several geologists felt was worth exploring, and their optimism prompted the IPC to form Petroleum Development (Western Arabia) Ltd in return for initial payment of 35,000 gold sovereigns. Starting in 1937, the company's geologists spent more than two years exploring the region and drilling in carefully selected places, concentrating their work on an area on the Farsan Islands which seemed to offer particular promise. But, despite drilling seventeen wells over eight of the islands, no trace of oil was ever found, and the operation was abandoned.

The IPC did have a bit more luck elsewhere in the region. In the course of the Saudi negotiations, their geologists had also become interested in the flat and arid peninsula of Qatar that lay across shallow seas to the east of Bahrain. This promised to be an even more desolate place to work than Saudi, for its only real settlement was the village capital, Doha, while the land was barely cultivated and had no water supply. It was made up of only a few thousand people, some of whom were desert nomads while others subsisted simply from fishing.

The explorers were undeterred, however, and in June 1930 a British official, acting on behalf of the IPC, visited the Qatar capital of Doha and visited the elderly Sheikh Abdullah al Jasim al Thani to take things a stage further. The

sheikh gave him permission to explore the kingdom over the next two years, and after this initial surveying was finished, in early 1933, the IPC was keen to push for a full concession. In May 1935 the sheikh yielded to British pressure and assigned Anglo-Persian the exclusive rights to drill for oil in return for an initial payment of 400,000 rupees, an annual rental of 150,000 rupees and a share of royalties if oil was discovered. Anglo-Persian immediately transferred its rights to the Iraq Petroleum Company, and work got under way.

The Qatar concession did bear some fruit, although it took some time to do so. Being such a remote and backward region, it took the IPC considerable time to build up the necessary infrastructure and establish a link with the outside world: a jetty at the port Zakrit was built at considerable expense, telephone networks and a water supply established, and while materials and a workforce, made up of Arab and Indian labourers, were specially shipped in. But when drilling began in October 1938 it quickly became apparent that the underground rocks were far more resilient than expected. Eventually, however, after boring down to the very considerable depth of 5,500 feet, oil was discovered in commercial quantities: an initial survey assessed the well's likely output to be around 5,000 barrels per day, and by the outbreak of the Second World War, in September 1939, Qatar's future as an oil producer seemed secure.

The centuries-old rumours, it had turned out, were true after all. The Middle East was awash with oil.

this leading role in the years ahead, even if other regions, notably the African continent, are fast catching up. Over the past century oil discoveries have had vast and far-reaching repercussions both for the Middle East and for the wider world. Kingdoms that were in every respect once backward, largely unknown and insignificant were quickly transformed into global powerhouses awash with staggering sums of petrodollars and harbouring oil supplies that that could potentially be used to hold the rest of the world to ransom – which did indeed happen after the Arab–Israeli war of 1973.[1] This pattern of bloody turbulence looks set to continue for many years to come.

The critics of the oil hunters will highlight this dark side of their legacy, adding that the proceeds of oil have allowed the Gulf rulers to stifle democracy and rule with an iron grip. Others might add that their extraordinary achievements led to the oppression and exploitation of oil-producing kingdoms by foreign governments that became highly dependent on their output as a source of supply. It is certainly true that, almost from the moment that Persian oil was struck, the authorities in Tehran levelled charges of exploitation and demanded the renegotiation of existing concessionary terms. And the 1953 British–American coup against the Iranian prime minister, Mohammed Mossadeq – who sought to nationalize the Anglo-Iranian Oil Company and perhaps provide a gateway for the Soviet Union – is the most glaring example that such critics would point to. But these criticisms are surely more than outweighed by the huge benefits bestowed by the extraordinary achievements of the oil hunters. Above all, their discoveries transformed unknown, backward places into hugely wealthy oil states, dramatically accelerated the pace of economic progress and considerably raised standards of living throughout the world.

Perhaps the explorers' most visible single legacy in the world of oil was their contribution to the development of the big oil companies that continue to dominate the contemporary scene. D'Arcy's own creation, the Anglo-Persian Oil Company, rebranded itself British Petroleum in 1954 and its strong links to the British government, forged in the run-up to the First World War, remained uninterrupted and are alleged still to be strong today.[2] Other Western-owned companies, such as Shell, Standard Oil of California and Gulf Oil, were nurtured by the flow of oil from several parts of the world, but the dramatic discoveries in the Middle East – notably Iraq, Bahrain, Saudi and Kuwait – were instrumental in enabling them to grow into the vast international conglomerates that they have now become.[3]

The story of the explorers has another relevance to the contemporary age, one that in itself makes their story worth telling, for they teach us a lesson that is relevant to the future of oil and a lot more besides. Nearly every one of the key individuals in this book was an outstanding personality, not just because of their resilience and stamina, but also because of their remarkable independence of mind. The contemporary wisdom of the age was that there was no oil to be found in the Middle East, at least not in any real commercial quantities, and the many ruined business ventures seemed to pay ample testimony to the complete dearth of resources in the region. Jacques de Morgan had of course concluded that Persia was 'unquestionably petroliferous territory', but it was far from certain that any such petroleum deposits existed in quantities that were worth exploring for. Yet William Knox D'Arcy was prepared to spend several years under immense financial pressure, risking personal ruin, because of his conviction that Persia harboured large deposits of oil that would justify his venture, even though in narrowly scientific terms he had very little evidence to work on. Ultimately gut feeling and intuition guided both D'Arcy and his great explorer, George Reynolds, rather than any scientific expertise.

When Frank Holmes began his search for Middle Eastern oil concessions in 1922, he had even less evidence to work on than D'Arcy. He had no geological equivalent of de Morgan's report to justify the time and expense of travelling through the region, or with which to convince local leaders to sacrifice their highly prized independence. On the contrary, there was strong scientific consensus of a dearth of oil in Bahrain, Kuwait, Saudi Arabia and their immediate vicinity. Highly respected geologists of the day, such as Guy Pilgrim and S. Lister James had made close studies of these regions and strongly advised companies such as Anglo-Persian to keep well away.[4]

But with hindsight it is clear that Holmes had a much finer instinct for finding oil supplies than nearly all of his contemporaries. This remarkable attribute was also noticed by contemporaries such as Rihani, who recorded that Holmes 'knows what's in the bosom of the land; can see the invisible streams of water that flow from the Persian mountains under the Gulf through the veins of the Hasa soil and can track the bubbling oil and the sparking minerals to their depths and beyond; he has the modern Argus eye of science and finance'.[5] The highly trained and experienced experts of the day, in other words, were utterly confounded by the poorly educated and humble oil hunter who had left school at a young age without any formal qualifications.

This teaches an important lesson for the contemporary world. Today it is often claimed by highly respected experts that the moment of 'peak oil' has either already arrived or is about to do so. Defined as the moment when the world's crude oil production reaches its maximum output before it starts to decline, peak oil is anticipated by some of the more optimistic observers to eventuate in the 2020s or 2030s. According to the more pessimistic viewpoint, however, this moment was reached at the end of 2005, while in July 2007 the International Energy Agency reported that: 'The concept of peak oil production and its timing are emotive subjects which raise intense debate. Much rests on the definition of which segment of global oil production is deemed to be at or approaching peak. Certainly our forecast suggests that the non-OPEC, conventional crude component of global production appears, for now, to have reached an effective plateau, rather than a peak.'[6]

However the concept is defined, and whenever that definitive moment has or will be reached, the implications are of course dire. Such shortages would cause spiralling prices at the pumps and have numerous other repercussions. Private transport, for example, would become something of a luxury, forcing many people either to move closer to their workplaces or rely on public transport, while the price of every item transported by road, rail or ship would also increase dramatically. These and the many other repercussions of 'peak oil' – some certain, others speculative and hypothetical – have already been the subject of many well-publicized books and independent research studies.

But the story of the Middle Eastern oil explorers puts a fitting perspective upon all the fears and insecurities that are borne of the theory of 'peak oil'. The experiences of Holmes and others should remind us that all the predictions of 'experts' are a very long way from revealing any gospel truth about matters so complex. They are instead mere opinions that are only useful in helping us find our way, and not an infallible guide to any final destination. There is, in fact, good reason to be particularly sceptical of predictions about the future of oil. Oil data is, for example, inherently uncertain, because such a gaseous liquid is far harder accurately to measure than most other substances. 'Oil market data is generally a black art like using a set of chicken bones', as one observer has put it; 'if Columbus had thought he'd hit India when in fact he was in the Caribbean, that's about the level of oil market data'. Another adds that 'oil data is like paint thrown across a canvas: you get the broad outline of the situation. But even then it's not just a Jackson Pollock painting, the paint actually moves of its own accord after it has been applied.' This is one reason why previous forecasts about the supply of and demand for oil have often been proved not just slightly but seriously flawed. 'I don't rate IEA data', says an industry analyst; 'they have horrendously underestimated demand in the past. It is one of the reasons we are where we are now. They are little more than a data collection agency, and the data they are given is already tarnished'. In the words of another analyst, 'it is no longer appropriate to accept glib demand forecasts from oil companies, financial institutions and government suggestions that oil consumption will grow up to 120 million barrels per day by 2020 and that automobile and airline traffic will increase at extraordinary rates are futile and damaging'.[7]

Perhaps too the story of the explorers should remind the contemporary age not just to be sceptical about the role of the expert and of contemporary wisdom, particularly in the world of oil, but also of human rationality in general. In the present day we are undoubtedly better educated and more literate than any of our predecessors. We have a vast scientific knowledge of the world around us, and make use of this knowledge in everyday ways that we take for granted. But are we in danger of placing too much faith in this approach? Frank Holmes is the supreme example of an individual who brought enormous benefits to so many, in the Middle East and beyond, but did so only because of his own gut feeling, instinct and intuition. He, without doubt, would have been the first to argue that our age does face this danger, and would perhaps have smiled with amusement at our modern follies.

Notes

Notes to Introduction

1 In September 2007 Alan Greenspan, the former chairman of the US Federal Reserve, publicly declared his personal view that 'the Iraq war is largely about oil'. For a general history of oil and its pivotal role in the twentieth century see Daniel Yergin's book *The Prize*.

2 Constantinople was not officially renamed Istanbul until 1930.

3 The British occupation of the Suez Canal Zone lasted until 1954

Notes to Chapter 1: The Intrepid Frenchman

1 Tiflis is today better known as Tbilisi

2 See Lord Curzon's book *Persia and the Persian Question*, vol. 1 (London: Longmans, 1892), p. 29

3 Morier uses the term 'naptha' liberally instead of 'oil'.

4 James Morier, *Journey through Persia* (London, 1812), p. 78.

5 Jacques de Morgan, *Mission Scientifiques en Perse*, vol. 1 (Paris, 1894–1905), p. xli.

6 Later renamed Khorramshahr.

7 de Morgan, *Mission Scientifiques*, vol. 1, p. lxxi.

8 de Morgan, *Mission Scientifiques*, vol. 2, pp. 80–7.

9 In 1885 oil imports to Bushire were valued at £2,245, and by 1888 this had reached £7,780.

Notes to Chapter 2: The Great Investor

1 Sir Henry Drummond Wolff, *Rambling Recollections*, vol. 2 (London: Macmillan, 1908), p. 329.

2 British Petroleum Archive (BP) H12/35 Kitabgi to Drummond Wolff 25 December 1900

3 Public Records Office (PRO) Foreign Office archive (FO) 60511, Drummond Wolff to Salisbury.

4 *The Statist* (24 March 1900).

5   *The Memoirs of Ali Khan Amin al-Dawlah*, ed. H. Farman Farmayan (Tehran: Amir Kabir Press, 1962), p. 107.
6   Lepel Griffin to Lord Roseberry (6 December 1912), quoted in R.W. Ferrier, *A History of British Petroleum*, vol. 1 (Cambridge: Cambridge University Press, 1982), p. 26.
7   BP H12/ 35 Drummond Wolff to Kitabgi (25 November 1900).
8   BP H17/47.

Notes to Chapter 3: Marriott Plays the Great Game

1   Curzon, *Persia*, vol. 1, pp. 298–9.
2   Samuel Benjamin, *Persia and the Persians* (London: Jonathan Cape, 1928; repr. 2003), p. 26.
3   BP H12/35, p. 73, Kitabgi to Drummond Wolff, November 1901.
4   BP H 12/35 (12 September 1901).
5   BP H 12/35 (12 September 1901).
6   Sir Arthur Hardinge, *A Diplomatist in the East* (London: Jonathan Cape, 1928), p. 272.
7   Hardinge, *A Diplomatist*, p. 271.
8   Hardinge, *A Diplomatist*, p. 268.
9   Hardinge, *A Diplomatist*, p. 275.
10 See generally, Drummond Wolff, *Rambling Recollections*, vol. 2.
11 William Dalrymple, *The Last Mughal* (Bloomsbury, 2006), p. 332.
12 Firuz Kazemzadeh, *Russia and Britain in Persia 1864–1914* (New Haven: Yale University Press, 1968), p. 10.
13 Memorandum on British policy in Persia 31 October 1906; FO 881/8526.
14 Curzon's memo of 21 September 1899 FO 60/615.
15 Hardinge, *A Diplomatist*, p. 285.
16 Drummond Wolff, *Rambling Recollections*, p. 329.
17 Hardinge, *A Diplomatist*, p. 281.
18 Hardinge, *A Diplomatist*, p. 269.
19 Hardinge, *A Diplomatist*, p. 281.
20 FO 60/630.
21 Hardinge, *A Diplomatist*, pp. 283–4.
22 Sir Martin Gosselin to Hardinge 12 March 1901. Quoted in Ferrier, *History of BP*, p. 33.
23 FO 60/731 Hardinge to Lansdowne 26 April 1901.
24 FO 60/731 Hardinge to Lansdowne 12 April 1901.
25 FO 60/731 Hardinge to Lansdowne 30 May 1901. The Atabeg-i Azam was another term for the grand vizier.
26 FO 60/660 Hardinge to Lansdowne 30 May 1901.
27 Curzon, *Persia*, vol. 1, p. 441.

Notes to Chapter 4: The Spies Fight Over D'Arcy

1   Kazemzadeh, *Russia and Britain*, p. 356.
2   Political resident in the Persian Gulf to Arthur Hardinge, Telegram no. 79, Bushire 5 June 1899, no. 692.
3   By 1900 the US accounted for 43 per cent, and Russia 51 per cent, of the total global output of oil.
4   FO 60/505, 'Report on Persian Oil' by Consul General Ross.
5   Kazemzadeh, *Russia and Britain*, p. 359.
6   Memorandum of the XVIth Congress of the Baku Oil Producers, 18 July 1902.
7   Kazemzadeh, *Russia and Britain*, p. 356.
8   Kazemzadeh, *Russia and Britain*, p. 356.
9   FO 60/660 Hardinge to Lansdowne no. 32 Tehran 14 March 1902.
10 Drummond Wolff, *Rambling Recollections*, pp. 372–3.
11 Mentioned in a letter of Hardinge to Lansdowne no. 17 Tehran 4 February 1902.
12 Hardinge to Lansdowne no. 23 Tehran 14 February 1902.
13 This is the cloth worn by pilgrims travelling to the holy city of Mecca.
14 This is mentioned in Hardinge's letter to Lansdowne no.32 Tehran 27 February 1902. See Kazemzadeh, *Russia and Britain*, p. 392.
15 Kazemzadeh, *Russia and Britain*, p. 382.
16 FO 371/102 Hardinge to Sir Edward Grey London 23 December 1905.
17 FO 60/660. Mentioned in Hardinge's despatch to Lansdowne 1 February 1902.

Notes to Chapter 5: The Great Explorer

1   Sir Arnold Wilson, *SW Persia: A Political Officer's Diary 1907–14* (London: Oxford University Press, 1941), p. 27.
2   BP H12/ 35 p. 60 10 September 1901
3   FO 60/73.
4   S. Benjamin, *Persia and the Persians* (London: John Murray, 1887).
5   Benjamin, *Persia*, p. 48.
6   Benjamin, *Persia*, p. 49.
7   See Ferrier, *History of BP*, p. 79.
8   Ferrier, *History of BP*, p. 65.
9   Quoted in Ferrier, *History of BP*, p. 58.

Notes to Chapter 6: The Oil Hunters Take On the Tribes

1   *Asiatic Annual Register: Or a View of the History of Hindustan*, ed. Lawrence Dundas Campbell (London: J. Debrett, 1812), p. 51.
2   Baron C.A. de Bode, *Travels in Luristan and Arabistan* (London: J. Madden & Co, 1845), vol. 2, p. 93.
3   De Bode, *Travels*, vol. 2, p. 3.

4   De Bode, *Travels*, vol. 2, p. 89.

5   De Bode, *Travels*, vol. 2, p. 89.

6   BP H16/90 D'Arcy to Preece 1 January 1907E

7   Letter from D'Arcy to his assistant David Jenkin 24 March 1903.

8   No. 772 Spring Rice to Grey, 16 December 1905, IO Political Dept X (3653/05).

9   H.R. Sykes, 'Our Recent Progress in Southern Persia and its Possibilities', Central Asia Society, London (1905), 18–19, 1 March 1905.

10   Kazemzadeh, *Russia and Britain*, p. 406.

11   ADM 116/3807, Cargill to Redwood 6 October 1904.

12   BP H17/898 Reynolds to the Concession Syndicates Ltd (CSL) 4 December 1905.

13   BP 77/49/13 to CSL 5 January 1905.

14   BP H16/90 D'Arcy to Preece 1 January 1907.

15   FO 416/26 Hardinge to Grey 23 December 1905.

Notes to Chapter 7: Lieutenant Wilson to the Rescue

1   Sir Arnold Wilson, *SW Persia: A Political Officer's Diary 1907–14* (London: Oxford University Press, 1941), p. 19.

2   Wilson, *SW Persia*, pp. 45.

3   Wilson, *SW Persia*, p. 20.

4   Wilson, *SW Persia*, pp. 21–2.

5   Wilson, *SW Persia*, p. 27.

6   Wilson, *SW Persia*, p. 28.

7   Wilson, *SW Persia*, p. 32.

8   Wilson, *SW Persia*, p. 25.

9   Wilson, *SW Persia*, p. 34.

10   Wilson, *SW Persia*, p. 31.

11   Wilson, *SW Persia*, p. 34.

12   Wilson, *SW Persia*, p. 37.

13   Wilson, *SW Persia*, p. 39.

Notes to Chapter 8: Admiral Chester Eyes Mesopotamia

1   Maras is today known as Kahramanmaras.

2   Alexandretta (now known as Iskanderun) is today located in northern Syria.

3   This is the same region that Iraq now covers.

4   Paul Rohrbach, *Die Bagdadbahn* (Berlin, 1903), pp. 26–8.

5   Rohrbach, *Die Bagdadbahn*, p. 16.

6   Rohrbach, *Die Bagdadbahn*, p. 16.

7   FO 371/345. Letter to Sir Edward Grey 6 February 1907.

8   US Dept of State: papers relating to FA, 1908, p. 750.

9   US Dept of State: papers relating to FA, 1911, p. xx.

Notes to Chapter 9: The Great Gulbenkian

1   Marian Kent, *Oil and Empire* (London: Macmillan 1976), p. 75.
2   See generally Daniel Yergin's history, *The Prize: The Epic Quest for Oil, Money and Power*, (London: Simon & Schuster, 1991), ch. 8.
3   Quoted in Yergin, *The Prize*, p. 159.
4   FO 371/1486. Minutes by Grey, Nicholson and Mallet 6–11 November 1912.
5   Letter to the Foreign Office 2 April 1907.
6   Quoted in Ralph Hewins, *Mr Five Per Cent* (London: Hutchinson, 1957), p. 84.
7   Hewins, *Five Per Cent*, p. 84.

Notes to Chapter 10: The Irrepressible Admiral

1   Walter Teagle was the president of Standard Oil New Jersey.
2   See Charles E. Hughes 'Recent Concessions and Negotiations', Address to the Council of Foreign Relations, Washington DC 23 January 1924.
3   *Public Ledger* 20 May 1923.
4   *Philadephia Evening Ledger* 14 April 1923.
5   Embassy Archives correspondence 1923.
6   Address to the House of Lords 13 February 1923

Notes to Chapter 11: Frank Holmes Strides into the Middle East

1   Abyssinia is modern-day Ethiopia.
2   Quoted in Angela Clarke, *Bahrain Oil and Development* (London: Immel, 1991), p. 34.
3   Ameen Rihani, *Ibn Saud of Arabia: Its People and Its Land* (1928; repr. London: Kegan Paul 2005), p. 81.
4   H.R.P. Dickson, *Kuwait and Her Neighbours* (London: George Allen & Unwin, 1956), p. 269.
5   Dickson, *Kuwait*, p. 270.
6   Rihani, *Ibn Saud*, pp. 80–2.
7   Dickson, *Kuwait*, p. 270.
8   Letter of Pat Davies and James Taylor to GC Chester and W. McLaughlin 17 May 1930. Quoted in Clarke, *Bahrain Oil*, p. 115.
9   Rihani, *Ibn Saud*, p. 82.
10 Rihani, *Ibn Saud*, p. 83.
11 Dickson, *Kuwait*, p. 272.
12 Rihani, *Ibn Saud*, p. 79.
13 Rihani, *Ibn Saud*, p. 83.
14 Dickson, *Kuwait*, p. 277.
15 Dickson, *Kuwait*, p. 278.
16 Dickson, *Kuwait*, p. 278.

17 Dickson, *Kuwait*, p. 272.
18 Minutes of APOC Management Committee 8 May 1923.
19 Minutes of APOC Management Committee 9 September 1924.
20 Dickson, *Kuwait*, p. 270.

Notes to Chapter 12: Holmes Bids for Kuwait and Bahrain

1 Dickson, *Kuwait*, p. 258.
2 R/15/1/317, IOR. Report of 9 June 1905.
3 Minutes of APOC's board of directors, 22 September 1924.
4 Letter of 23 April 1904, quoted in Angela Clarke, *Bahrain Oil and Development 1929–89* (Immel, 1991), p. 44.
5 Frederick Lee Moore Jr, quoted in Clarke, *Bahrain*, p. 14.
6 Taylor, Davies letter of 24 May 1928.

Notes to Chapter 13: The Incredible Haji

1 See above, pp. 125–6.
2 Thomas E. Ward, *Negotiations for Oil Concessions in Bahrain, El Hasa (Saudi Arabia), The Neutral Zone, Qatar and Kuwait* (private publication, New York, 1965), pp. 29–32.
3 Letter to Eastern and General Syndicate 9 April 1927.
4 Quoted in Thomas Ward, *Negotiations for Oil*, p. 46.
5 See A.T.H. Chisholm, *Kuwait Oil Concession* (London: Frank Cass & Co, 1975), p. 20.

Notes to Chapter 14: The Great Philanthropist

1 Letter from John O. Crane to Walter S. Rogers 22 January 1929.
2 David Hapgood, *Charles R. Crane: The Man Who Bet on People* (Philadelphia: Xlibris Books, 2000), p. 78.
3 Harry St John Philby, *Arabian Oil Ventures* (Washington, DC: Middle East Institute, 1964), p. 75.
4 Lady Evelyn Cobbold, *Visit to Arabia* (London: John Murray, 1934), p. 8.
5 Harry St John Philby, *Arabian Days: An Autobiography* (London: Robert Hale, 1948), p. 150.
6 Robert Lacey, *The Kingdom* (London: Fontana, 1981), p. 230.
7 Lacey, *The Kingdom*, p. 230.
8 See generally Karl Twitchell, *Saudi Arabia* (Princeton: Princeton University Press, 1958) which has an account of the development of its natural resources.

Notes to Chapter 15: The Battle for Kuwait

1   Chisholm, *Kuwait Oil*, p. 20.
2   Quoted in Clarke, *Bahrain Oil*, pp. 112–13.
3   Clarke, *Bahrain Oil*, p. 115.
4   Supplementary Report pp. 10–11, 23–4.
5   See Clarke, *Bahrain Oil*, pp. 130–2.
6   Chisholm, *Kuwait Oil*, p. 26.
7   Chisholm, *Kuwait Oil*, p. 28.
8   Chisholm, *Kuwait Oil*, p. 59.

Notes to Chapter 16: Philby of Arabia

1   Philby claimed to have been the first person to do this, although he was in fact wrong: Bertram Thomas had beaten him to it by a few months.
2   Philby, *Arabian Days*, p. 279.
3   Philby, *Arabian Days*, p. 274.
4   Philby, *Arabian Days*, p. 276.
5   Philby, *Arabian Days*, p. 278.
6   Philby, *Arabian Oil Ventures*, p. 81.
7   The Red Line Agreement is described above, pp. 164–5.
8   Philby, *Arabian Oil Ventures*, p. 87.
9   Cobbold, *Visit to Arabia*, p. 16.
10   Cobbold, *Visit to Arabia*, p. 19.
11   Philby, *Arabian Oil Ventures*, p. 83.
12   Philby, *Arabian Oil Ventures*, p. 86.
13   FO/371/1680.E1498/487/25 28 February 1933.
14   Philby, *Arabian Oil Ventures*, p. 88.
15   Lacey, *The Kingdom*, p. 236.
16   Philby, *Arabian Oil Ventures*, p. 98.
17   Philby, *Arabian Oil Ventures*, p. 99.
18   Stephen Lonrigg, *Oil in the Middle East* (London: Oxford University Press, 1968), p. 107.
19   Philby, *Arabian Oil Ventures*, p. 125.
20   Philby, *Arabian Oil Ventures*, p. 126.

Notes to Chapter 17: The Legacy of the Oil Hunters

1   For a general history of Middle Eastern oil see Daniel Yergin's epic history *The Prize: The Epic Quest for Oil, Money and Power* (London: Simon & Schuster, 1991).
2   A British Member of Parliament, Norman Baker, has spearheaded a drive to expose what he claims are very strong links between BP and the UK government.
3   Socal became Chevron, which merged with Gulf Oil in 1984.

4   See Chapter 12.
5   Rihani, *Ibn Saud of Arabia*, p. 83.
6   *IEA Medium-Term Oil Market Report*, July 2007
7   All quotes in this paragraph are from the article 'How much oil do we really have?', BBC News 15 July 2005.

Index